MznLnx

Missing Links Exam Preps

Exam Prep for

Macroeconomics

Samuelson, Nordhaus, 18th Edition

The MznLnx Exam Prep is your link from the texbook and lecture to your exams.
The MznLnx Exam Preps are unauthorized and comprehensive reviews of your textbooks.

All material provided by MznLnx and Rico Publications (c) 2010
Textbook publishers and textbook authors do not particpate in or contribute to these reviews.

MznLnx

Rico Publications

Exam Prep for Macroeconomics
18th Edition
Samuelson, Nordhaus

Publisher: Raymond Houge
Assistant Editor: Michael Rouger
Text and Cover Designer: Lisa Buckner
Marketing Manager: Sara Swagger
Project Manager, Editorial Production: Jerry Emerson
Art Director: Vernon Lowerui

Product Manager: Dave Mason
Editorial Assitant: Rachel Guzmanji
Pedagogy: Debra Long
Cover Image: Jim Reed/Getty Images
Text and Cover Printer: City Printing, Inc.
Compositor: Media Mix, Inc.

(c) 2010 Rico Publications

ALL RIGHTS RESERVED. No part of this work covered by the copyright may be reproduced or used in any form or by an means--graphic, electronic, or mechanical, including photocopying, recording, taping, Web distribution, information storage, and retrieval systems, or in any other manner--without the written permission of the publisher.

For more information about our products, contact us at:

Dave.Mason@RicoPublications.com

For permission to use material from this text or product, submit a request online to:

Dave.Mason@RicoPublications.com

Printed in the United States
ISBN:

Contents

CHAPTER 1
The Fundamentals of Economics — 1

CHAPTER 2
Markets and Government in a Modern Economy — 11

CHAPTER 3
Basic Elements of Supply and Demand — 33

CHAPTER 4
Overview of Macroeconomics — 39

CHAPTER 5
Measuring Economic Activity — 53

CHAPTER 6
Consumption and Investment — 67

CHAPTER 7
Business Fluctuations and the Theory of Aggregate Demand — 78

CHAPTER 8
The Multiplier Model — 89

CHAPTER 9
Financial Markets and the Special Case of Money — 100

CHAPTER 10
Central Banking and Monetary Policy — 117

CHAPTER 11
The Process of Economic Growth — 133

CHAPTER 12
The Challenge of Economic Development — 145

CHAPTER 13
Exchange Rates and the International Financial System — 162

CHAPTER 14
Open-Economy Macroeconomics — 178

CHAPTER 15
Unemployment and the Foundations of Aggregate Supply — 192

CHAPTER 16
Ensuring Price Stability — 201

CHAPTER 17
The Warring Schools of Macroeconomics — 213

CHAPTER 18
Policies for Growth and Stability — 227

ANSWER KEY — 242

TO THE STUDENT

COMPREHENSIVE

The *MznLnx* Exam Prep series is designed to help you pass your exams. Editors at MznLnx review your textbooks and then prepare these practice exams to help you master the textbook material. Unlike study guides, workbooks, and practice tests provided by the texbook publisher and textbook authors, *MznLnx* gives you **all** of the material in each chapter in exam form, not just samples, so you can be sure to nail your exam.

MECHANICAL

The MznLnx Exam Prep series creates exams that will help you learn the subject matter as well as test you on your understanding. Each question is designed to help you master the concept. Just working through the exams, you gain an understanding of the subject--its a simple mechanical process that produces success.

INTEGRATED STUDY GUIDE AND REVIEW

MznLnx is not just a set of exams designed to test you, its also a comprehensive review of the subject content. Each exam question is also a review of the concept, making sure that you will get the answer correct without having to go to other sources of material. You learn as you go! Its the easiest way to pass an exam.

HUMOR

Studying can be tedious and dry. MznLnx's instructional design includes moderate humor within the exam questions on occassion, to break the tedium and revitalize the brain

Chapter 1. The Fundamentals of Economics

1. _____s is the social science that studies the production, distribution, and consumption of goods and services. The term _____s comes from the Ancient Greek oá¼°κονομῖα from oá¼¶κος (oikos, 'house') + vïŒμος (nomos, 'custom' or 'law'), hence 'rules of the house(hold)'. Current _____ models developed out of the broader field of political economy in the late 19th century, owing to a desire to use an empirical approach more akin to the physical sciences.
    a. Economic
    b. Inflation
    c. Energy economics
    d. Opportunity cost

2. A _____ is an object whose consumption increases the utility of the consumer, for which the quantity demanded exceeds the quantity supplied at zero price. _____s are usually modeled as having diminishing marginal utility. The first individual purchase has high utility; the second has less.
    a. Merit good
    b. Composite good
    c. Pie method
    d. Good

3. _____ was a survey conducted by the U.S. Department of Justice to gauge the prevalence of alcohol and illegal drug use among prior arrestees. It was a reformulation of the prior Drug Use Forecasting (DUF) program, focused on five drugs in particular: cocaine, marijuana, methamphetamine, opiates, and PCP.

    Participants were randomly selected from arrest records in major metropolitan areas; because no personally identifying information is taken from each record chosen, the resulting data can be correlated to arrest rates, but not to the total population of persons charged.

    a. ACCRA Cost of Living Index
    b. AD-IA Model
    c. Arrestee Drug Abuse Monitoring
    d. ACEA agreement

4. _____ was a Scottish moral philosopher and a pioneer of political economy. One of the key figures of the Scottish Enlightenment, Smith is the author of The Theory of Moral Sentiments and An Inquiry into the Nature and Causes of the Wealth of Nations. The latter, usually abbreviated as The Wealth of Nations, is considered his magnum opus and the first modern work of economics.
    a. Alan Greenspan
    b. Adam Smith
    c. Adolf Hitler
    d. Adolph Fischer

5. _____s is concerned with the tasks of developing and applying quantitative or statistical methods to the study and elucidation of economic principles. _____s combines economic theory with statistics to analyze and test economic relationships. Theoretical _____s considers questions about the statistical properties of estimators and tests, while applied _____s is concerned with the application of _____ methods to assess economic theories.
    a. Econometric
    b. Economic
    c. Experimental economics
    d. Evolutionary economics

6. The _____ was written by the English economist John Maynard Keynes. The book, generally considered to be his magnum opus, is largely credited with creating the terminology and shape of modern macroeconomics. Published in February 1936 it sought to bring about a revolution, commonly referred to as the 'Keynesian Revolution', in the way economists thought - especially in relation to the proposition that a market economy tends naturally to restore itself to full employment after temporary shocks.
    a. Human Action
    b. The General Theory of Employment, Interest and Money
    c. Black Book of Communism
    d. General Theory of Employment, Interest and Money

Chapter 1. The Fundamentals of Economics

7. The _____ was a worldwide economic downturn starting in most places in 1929 and ending at different times in the 1930s or early 1940s for different countries. It was the largest and most important economic depression in the 20th century, and is used in the 21st century as an example of how far the world's economy can fall. The _____ originated in the United States; historians most often use as a starting date the stock market crash on October 29, 1929, known as Black Tuesday.
   a. Wall Street Crash of 1929
   b. Jarrow March
   c. British Empire Economic Conference
   d. Great Depression

8. _____ is a fee paid on borrowed assets. It is the price paid for the use of borrowed money, or, money earned by deposited funds. Assets that are sometimes lent with _____ include money, shares, consumer goods through hire purchase, major assets such as aircraft, and even entire factories in finance lease arrangements.
   a. Asset protection
   b. Insolvency
   c. Interest
   d. Internal debt

9. _____, 1st Baron Keynes was a renowned economist from Britain whose many ideas on economic and political theories as well as on many governments' monetary policies influenced America. He advocated a government that played an active role in the lives of people regarding business, economy, etc. In this role, the government would use fiscal measures to reduce the consequences of recessions, economic depressions and booms.
   a. John Maynard Keynes
   b. Adam Smith
   c. Adolph Fischer
   d. Adolf Hitler

10. _____ is a branch of economics that deals with the performance, structure, and behavior of a national or regional economy as a whole. Along with microeconomics, _____ is one of the two most general fields in economics. It is the study of the behavior and decision-making of entire economies.
    a. New Trade Theory
    b. Macroeconomics
    c. Tobit model
    d. Nominal value

11. A _____ is an economy based on the division of labor in which the prices of goods and services are determined in a free price system set by supply and demand. This is often contrasted with a planned economy, in which a central government determines the price of goods and services using a fixed price system. Market economies are contrasted with mixed economy where the price system is not entirely free but under some government control that is not extensive enough to constitute a planned economy.
    a. Network Economy
    b. Commons-based peer production
    c. Market economy
    d. Nutritional Economics

12. _____ is a branch of economics that studies how individuals, households and firms and some states make decisions to allocate limited resources, typically in markets where goods or services are being bought and sold. _____ examines how these decisions and behaviours affect the supply and demand for goods and services, which determines prices; and how prices, in turn, determine the supply and demand of goods and services.

Whereas macroeconomics involves the 'sum total of economic activity, dealing with the issues of growth, inflation and unemployment, and with national economic policies relating to these issues' and the effects of government actions on them.

a. Countercyclical
b. Microeconomics
c. Recession
d. New Keynesian economics

13. An Inquiry into the Nature and Causes of the _____ is the magnum opus of the Scottish economist Adam Smith. It is a clearly written account of economics at the dawn of the Industrial Revolution, as well as a rhetorical piece written for the generally educated individual of the 18th century - advocating a free market economy as more productive and more beneficial to society.

The work is credited as a watershed in history and economics due to its comprehensive, largely accurate characterization of economic mechanisms that survive in modern economics; and also for its effective use of rhetorical technique, including structuring the work to contrast real world examples of free and fettered markets.

a. The Bell Curve
b. Black Book of Communism
c. Wealth of Nations
d. The Rise and Fall of the Great Powers

14. A _____ arises when one infers that something is true of the whole from the fact that it is true of some part of the whole (or even of every proper part.) For example: 'This fragment of metal cannot be broken with a hammer, therefore the machine of which it is a part cannot be broken with a hammer.' This is clearly fallacious, because many machines can be broken into their constituent parts without any of those parts being breakable.

This fallacy is often confused with the fallacy of hasty generalization, in which an unwarranted inference is made from a statement about a sample to a statement about the population from which it is drawn.

a. 130-30 fund
b. 100-year flood
c. 1921 recession
d. Fallacy of composition

15. _____ is a socioeconomic structure and political ideology that promotes the establishment of an egalitarian, classless, stateless society based on common ownership and control of the means of production and property in general. In political science, the term '_____' is sometimes used to refer to communist states, a form of government in which the state operates under a one-party system and declares allegiance to Marxism-Leninism or a derivative thereof, even if the party does not actually claim that it has already reached _____.

Forerunners of communist ideas existed in antiquity and particularly in the 18th and early 19th century France, with thinkers such as Jean-Jacques Rousseau and the more radical Gracchus Babeuf.

a. Democratic centralism
b. New Communist Movement
c. Social fascism
d. Communism

16. To _____ is to impose a financial charge or other levy upon a taxpayer by a state or the functional equivalent of a state.

_____es are also imposed by many subnational entities. _____es consist of direct _____ or indirect _____, and may be paid in money or as its labour equivalent (often but not always unpaid.)

a. Tax
b. 100-year flood
c. 1921 recession
d. 130-30 fund

17. A _____ is a reduction in taxes. Economic stimulus via _____s, along with interest rate intervention and deficit spending, are one of the central tenets of Keynesian economics.

The immediate effects of a _____ are, generally, a decrease in the real income of the government and an increase in the real income of those whose tax rate has been lowered.

a. Tax cut
b. Popiwek
c. Direct taxes
d. Withholding tax

18. The _____, sometimes called the fundamental _____, is one of the fundamental economic theories in the operation of any economy. It asserts that there is scarcity, that the finite resources available are insufficient to satisfy all human wants. The problem then becomes how to determine what is to be produced and how the factors of production (such as capital and labour) are to be allocated.

a. Economic nationalism
b. Eclectic paradigm
c. Endogenous growth theory
d. Economic problem

19. In economics, _____ is how a natione;s total economy is distributed among its population. . _____ has always been a central concern of economic theory and economic policy. Classical economists such as Adam Smith, Thomas Malthus and David Ricardo were mainly concerned with factor _____, that is, the distribution of income between the main factors of production, land, labour and capital.

a. Equipment trust certificate
b. Income distribution
c. Authorised capital
d. Eco commerce

20. _____ is the branch of economics that incorporates value judgments (that is, normative judgements) about what the economy ought to be like or what particular policy actions ought to be recommended to achieve a desirable goal. _____ looks at the desirability of certain aspects of the economy. It underlies expressions of support for particular economic policies.

a. Broad money
b. Double bottom line
c. Nanoeconomics
d. Normative economics

21. _____ is the branch of economics that concerns the description and explanation of economic phenomena (Wong, 1987, p. 920.) It focuses on facts and cause-and-effect relationships and includes the development and testing of economics theories.

a. 100-year flood
b. Positive economics
c. Regulatory economics
d. 130-30 fund

22. In economics, the term _____ of income or _____ refers to a simple economic model which describes the reciprocal circulation of income between producers and consumers. In the _____ model, the inter-dependent entities of producer and consumer are referred to as 'firms' and 'households' respectively and provide each other with factors in order to facilitate the flow of income. Firms provide consumers with goods and services in exchange for consumer expenditure and 'factors of production' from households.

Chapter 1. The Fundamentals of Economics

a. Circular flow
c. 100-year flood
b. 1921 recession
d. 130-30 fund

23. A _____ or directed economy is an economic system in which the government or workers' councils manages the economy. It is an economic system in which the central government makes all decisions on the production and consumption of goods and services. Its most extensive form is referred to as a _____, centrally planned economy, or command and control economy.

a. Nutritional Economics
c. Transition economy
b. Command economy
d. Subsistence economy

24. An _____ or Å"conomic system is a system that involves the production, distribution and consumption of goods and services between the entities in a particular society. It is the method used by society to produce and distribute goods and services. The _____ is composed of people and institutions, including their relationships to productive resources, such as through the convention of property.

a. Intention economy
c. Information economy
b. Indicative planning
d. Economic system

25. _____ is a term used to describe a policy of allowing events to take their own course. The term is a French phrase literally meaning 'let do'. It is a doctrine that states that government generally should not intervene in the marketplace.

a. Communization
c. Theory of Productive Forces
b. Heroic capitalism
d. Laissez-faire

26. _____ is used to assign the available resources in an economic way. It is part of resource management.

In strategic planning, is a plan for using available resources, for example human resources, especially in the near term, to achieve goals for the future.

a. 100-year flood
c. 1921 recession
b. 130-30 fund
d. Resource allocation

27. A _____ is any systematic process enabling many market players to bid and ask: helping bidders and sellers interact and make deals. It is not just the price mechanism but the entire system of regulation, qualification, credentials, reputations and clearing that surrounds that mechanism and makes it operate in a social context.

Because a _____ relies on the assumption that players are constantly involved and unequally enabled, a _____ is distinguished specifically from a voting system where candidates seek the support of voters on a less regular basis.

a. Price mechanism
c. Market system
b. Competitive equilibrium
d. Contestable market

28. A _____ is an economic system that incorporates a mixture of private and government ownership or control, or a mixture of capitalism and socialism.

There is not one single definition for a _____, but relevant aspects include: a degree of private economic freedom (including privately owned industry) intermingled with centralized economic planning and government regulation (which may include regulation of the market for environmental concerns and social welfare, or state ownership and management of some of the means of production for national or social objectives.)

For some states, there is not a consensus on whether they are capitalist, socialist, or mixed economies.

- a. Hunter-gatherer
- b. Mixed economy
- c. Planned liberalism
- d. Dual economy

29. In economics, _____ are the resources employed to produce goods and services. They facilitate production but do not become part of the product (as with raw materials) or significantly transformed by the production process (as with fuel used to power machinery.) To 19th century economists, the _____ were land (natural resources, gifts from nature), labor (the ability to work), and capital goods (human-made tools and equipment.)
- a. Product Pipeline
- b. Long-run
- c. Factors of production
- d. Hicks-neutral technical change

30. _____ is the term denoting either an entrance or changes which are inserted into a system and which activate/modify a process. It is an abstract concept, used in the modeling, system(s) design and system(s) exploitation. It is usually connected with other terms, e.g., _____ field, _____ variable, _____ parameter, _____ value, _____ signal, _____ device and _____ file.
- a. ACCRA Cost of Living Index
- b. AD-IA Model
- c. ACEA agreement
- d. Input

31. In microeconomics, _____ is quite simply the conversion of inputs into outputs. It is an economic process that uses resources to create a good or service that is suitable for exchange. This can include manufacturing, storing, shipping, and packaging.
- a. Red Guards
- b. MET
- c. Solved
- d. Production

32. In economics, a _____ is a function that specifies the output of a firm, an industry, or an entire economy for all combinations of inputs. A meta-_____ compares the practice of the existing entities converting inputs X into output y to determine the most efficient practice _____ of the existing entities, whether the most efficient feasible practice production or the most efficient actual practice production. In either case, the maximum output of a technologically-determined production process is a mathematical function of input factors of production.
- a. Production function
- b. Constant elasticity of substitution
- c. Post-Fordism
- d. Short-run

33. A _____ is an expression that compares quantities relative to each other. The most common examples involve two quantities, but any number of quantities can be compared. _____s are represented mathematically by separating each quantity with a colon, for example the _____ 2:3, which is read as the _____ 'two to three'.
- a. Y-intercept
- b. Ratio
- c. 100-year flood
- d. 130-30 fund

Chapter 1. The Fundamentals of Economics

34. _____ is the increase in the amount of the goods and services produced by an economy over time. It is conventionally measured as the percent rate of increase in real gross domestic product, or real GDP. Growth is usually calculated in real terms, i.e. inflation-adjusted terms, in order to net out the effect of inflation on the price of the goods and services produced.
    a. AD-IA Model
    b. ACEA agreement
    c. ACCRA Cost of Living Index
    d. Economic growth

35. In economics, a _____ is a good that is non-rivaled and non-excludable. This means, respectively, that consumption of the good by one individual does not reduce availability of the good for consumption by others; and that no one can be effectively excluded from using the good. In the real world, there may be no such thing as an absolutely non-rivaled and non-excludable good; but economists think that some goods approximate the concept closely enough for the analysis to be economically useful.
    a. Neoclassical synthesis
    b. Public good
    c. Demand-pull theory
    d. Happiness economics

36. _____ is a common concept in economics, and gives rise to derived concepts such as consumer debt. Generally _____ is defined by opposition to production. But the precise definition can vary because different schools of economists define production quite differently.
    a. Cash or share options
    b. Federal Reserve Bank Notes
    c. Consumption
    d. Foreclosure data providers

37. In economics, economic output is divided into physical goods and intangible services. Consumption of _____ is assumed to produce utility. It is often used when referring to a _____ Tax.
    a. Composite good
    b. Manufactured goods
    c. Private good
    d. Goods and services

38. A _____ is defined in economics as a good that exhibits these properties:

    - Excludable - it is reasonably possible to prevent a class of consumers (e.g. those who have not paid for it) from consuming the good.
    - Rivalrous - consumptions by one consumer prevents simultaneous consumption by other consumers. _____s satisfies an individual want while public good satisfies a collective want of the society.

    A _____ is the opposite of a public good, as they are almost exclusively made for profit.

    An example of the _____ is bread: bread eaten by a given person cannot be consumed by another (rivalry), and it is easy for a baker to refuse to trade a loaf (excludable

    a. Pie method
    b. Private good
    c. Demerit good
    d. Positional goods

39. _____ is that which is owed; usually referencing assets owed, but the term can also cover moral obligations and other interactions not requiring money. In the case of assets, _____ is a means of using future purchasing power in the present before a summation has been earned. Some companies and corporations use _____ as a part of their overall corporate finance strategy.

a. Debt
b. Collateral Management
c. Hard money loan
d. Debenture

40. _____ in economics refers to metrics and measures of output from production processes, per unit of input. Labor _____, for example, is typically measured as a ratio of output per labor-hour, an input. _____ may be conceived of as a metrics of the technical or engineering efficiency of production.
a. Productivity
b. Piece work
c. Fordism
d. Production-possibility frontier

41. _____ or economic opportunity loss is the value of the next best alternative foregone as the result of making a decision. _____ analysis is an important part of a company's decision-making processes but is not treated as an actual cost in any financial statement. The next best thing that a person can engage in is referred to as the _____ of doing the best thing and ignoring the next best thing to be done.
a. Opportunity cost
b. Economic ideology
c. Economic
d. Industrial organization

42. _____ occurs when the economy is operating at its production possibility frontier (PPF.) This takes place when production of one good is achieved at the lowest cost possible, given the production of the other good(s.) Equivalently, it is when the highest possible output of one good is produced, given the production level of the other good(s.)
a. Productive efficiency
b. Free contract
c. Discretionary spending
d. Preclusive purchasing

43. A _____ is a situation that involves losing one quality or aspect of something in return for gaining another quality or aspect. It implies a decision to be made with full comprehension of both the upside and downside of a particular choice.

In economics the term is expressed as opportunity cost, referring the most preferred alternative given up.

a. Whitemail
b. Trade-off
c. Friedman-Savage utility function
d. Nonmarket

44. The term _____ refers to economy-wide fluctuations in production or economic activity over several months or years. These fluctuations occur around a long-term growth trend, and typically involve shifts over time between periods of relatively rapid economic growth (expansion or boom), and periods of relative stagnation or decline (contraction or recession.)

These fluctuations are often measured using the growth rate of real gross domestic product.

a. Consumer theory
b. Nominal value
c. Tobit model
d. Business cycle

45. _____ Theory (or _____ Theory) is a class of macroeconomic models in which business cycle fluctuations to a large extent can be accounted for by real (in contrast to nominal) shocks. (The four primary economic fluctuations are secular (trend), business cycle, seasonal, and random.) Unlike other leading theories of the business cycle, it sees recessions and periods of economic growth as the efficient response to exogenous changes in the real economic environment.

Chapter 1. The Fundamentals of Economics

a. Monetary policy reaction function
b. SIMIC
c. Balanced-growth equilibrium
d. Real business cycle

46. In economics, a _____ is a general slowdown in economic activity over a sustained period of time, or a business cycle contraction. During _____s, many macroeconomic indicators vary in a similar way. Production as measured by Gross Domestic Product (GDP), employment, investment spending, capacity utilization, household incomes and business profits all fall during _____s.
   a. Treasury View
   b. Monetary economics
   c. Leading indicators
   d. Recession

47. In economics, the _____ measures the payments that flow between any individual country and all other countries. It is used to summarize all international economic transactions for that country during a specific time period, usually a year. The _____ is determined by the country's exports and imports of goods, services, and financial capital, as well as financial transfers.
   a. Balance of payments
   b. Gross world product
   c. Gross domestic product per barrel
   d. Skyscraper Index

48. A _____ is the transfer of wealth from one party (such as a person or company) to another. A _____ is usually made in exchange for the provision of goods, services or both, or to fulfill a legal obligation.

The simplest and oldest form of _____ is barter, the exchange of one good or service for another.

   a. Social gravity
   b. Soft count
   c. Going concern
   d. Payment

49. _____ in political thought refers to economic theories of social organization advocating collective ownership and administration of the means of production and distribution of goods, and a society characterized by equality for all individuals, with an egalitarian method of compensation. Modern _____ originated in the late 19th-century intellectual and working class political movement that criticized the effects of industrialization and private ownership on society. Karl Marx posited that _____ would be achieved via class struggle and a proletarian revolution after a transitional stage from capitalism called the dictatorship of the proletariat.
   a. Adolph Fischer
   b. Adolf Hitler
   c. Adam Smith
   d. Socialism

50. An inverse or negative relationship is a mathematical relationship in which one variable, say y, decreases as another, say x, increases. For a linear (straight-line) relation, this can be expressed as y = a-bx, where -b is a constant value less than zero and a is a constant. For example, there is an _____ between education and unemployment -- that is, as education increases, the rate of unemployment decreases.
   a. Inverse relationship
   b. ACEA agreement
   c. ACCRA Cost of Living Index
   d. AD-IA Model

Chapter 1. The Fundamentals of Economics

51. In mathematics, a _____ system is a system which is not linear, that is, a system which does not satisfy the superposition principle, or whose output is not proportional to its input. Less technically, a _____ system is any problem where the variable(s) to be solved for cannot be written as a linear combination of independent components. A nonhomogeneous system, which is linear apart from the presence of a function of the independent variables, is _____ according to a strict definition, but such systems are usually studied alongside linear systems, because they can be transformed to a linear system of multiple variables.

   a. 130-30 fund
   b. Nonlinear system
   c. 100-year flood
   d. Nonlinear

52. In economics, the _____ is a single mathematical function used to express consumer spending. It was developed by John Maynard Keynes and detailed most famously in his book The General Theory of Employment, Interest, and Money. The function is used to calculate the amount of total consumption in an economy.

   a. DAD-SAS model
   b. Liquidity preference
   c. Procyclical
   d. Consumption function

53. The _____ or gross domestic income (GDI), a basic measure of an economy's economic performance, is the market value of all final goods and services produced within the borders of a nation in a year. _____ can be defined in three ways, all of which are conceptually identical. First, it is equal to the total expenditures for all final goods and services produced within the country in a stipulated period of time (usually a 365-day year.)

   a. Market structure
   b. Monopolistic competition
   c. Gross Domestic Product
   d. Countercyclical

54. _____ is an economic model based on price, utility and quantity in a market. It predicts that in a competitive market, price will function to equalize the quantity demanded by consumers, and the quantity supplied by producers, resulting in an economic equilibrium of price and quantity. The model incorporates other factors changing equilibrium as a shift of demand and/or supply.

   a. Joint demand
   b. Supply and demand
   c. Rational addiction
   d. Deferred gratification

55. Economics:

   - _____, the desire to own something and the ability to pay for it
   - _____ curve, a graphic representation of a _____ schedule
   - _____ deposit, the money in checking accounts
   - _____ pull theory, the theory that inflation occurs when _____ for goods and services exceeds existing supplies
   - _____ schedule, a table that lists the quantity of a good a person will buy it each different price
   - _____ side economics, the school of economics at believes government spending and tax cuts open economy by raising _____

   a. Demand
   b. Production
   c. McKesson ' Robbins scandal
   d. Variability

Chapter 2. Markets and Government in a Modern Economy 11

1. _____ was a survey conducted by the U.S. Department of Justice to gauge the prevalence of alcohol and illegal drug use among prior arrestees. It was a reformulation of the prior Drug Use Forecasting (DUF) program, focused on five drugs in particular: cocaine, marijuana, methamphetamine, opiates, and PCP.

Participants were randomly selected from arrest records in major metropolitan areas; because no personally identifying information is taken from each record chosen, the resulting data can be correlated to arrest rates, but not to the total population of persons charged.

   a. ACCRA Cost of Living Index
   b. ACEA agreement
   c. Arrestee Drug Abuse Monitoring
   d. AD-IA Model

2. _____ is an economic system in which wealth, and the means of producing wealth, are privately owned. Through _____, the land, labor, and capital are owned, operated, and traded for the purpose of generating profits, without force or fraud, by private individuals either singly or jointly, and investments, distribution, income, production, pricing and supply of goods, commodities and services are determined by voluntary private decision in a market economy. A distinguishing feature of _____ is that each person owns his or her own labor and therefore is allowed to sell the use of it to employers.

   a. Late capitalism
   b. Capitalism
   c. Creative capitalism
   d. Socialism for the rich and capitalism for the poor

3. A _____ or directed economy is an economic system in which the government or workers' councils manages the economy. It is an economic system in which the central government makes all decisions on the production and consumption of goods and services. Its most extensive form is referred to as a _____, centrally planned economy, or command and control economy.

   a. Command economy
   b. Nutritional Economics
   c. Subsistence economy
   d. Transition economy

4. _____s is the social science that studies the production, distribution, and consumption of goods and services. The term _____s comes from the Ancient Greek οἰκονομῖα from οἶκος (oikos, 'house') + νόμος (nomos, 'custom' or 'law'), hence 'rules of the house(hold)'. Current _____ models developed out of the broader field of political economy in the late 19th century, owing to a desire to use an empirical approach more akin to the physical sciences.

   a. Economic
   b. Opportunity cost
   c. Inflation
   d. Energy economics

5. An _____ or Ä"conomic system is a system that involves the production, distribution and consumption of goods and services between the entities in a particular society. It is the method used by society to produce and distribute goods and services. The _____ is composed of people and institutions, including their relationships to productive resources, such as through the convention of property.

   a. Intention economy
   b. Indicative planning
   c. Economic system
   d. Information economy

6. _____ is a term used to describe a policy of allowing events to take their own course. The term is a French phrase literally meaning 'let do'. It is a doctrine that states that government generally should not intervene in the marketplace.

   a. Heroic capitalism
   b. Communization
   c. Theory of Productive Forces
   d. Laissez-faire

Chapter 2. Markets and Government in a Modern Economy

7. A _____ is an economy based on the division of labor in which the prices of goods and services are determined in a free price system set by supply and demand. This is often contrasted with a planned economy, in which a central government determines the price of goods and services using a fixed price system. Market economies are contrasted with mixed economy where the price system is not entirely free but under some government control that is not extensive enough to constitute a planned economy.

- a. Nutritional Economics
- b. Market economy
- c. Network Economy
- d. Commons-based peer production

8. _____ is a term from economics referring to the use of money exchanged by buyers and sellers with an open and understood system of value and time trade offs to produce the best distribution of goods and services. The use of the _____ does not imply a free market: there can be captive or controlled markets which seek to use supply and demand, or some other form of charging for scarcity, both in social situations and in engineering.

The _____ assumes perfect competition and is regulated by demand and supply.

- a. Partial equilibrium
- b. Market mechanism
- c. Two-sided markets
- d. Product-Market Growth Matrix

9. _____ is the incidence or process of transferring ownership of a business, enterprise, agency or public service from the public sector (government) to the private sector (business.) In a broader sense, _____ refers to transfer of any government function to the private sector including governmental functions like revenue collection and law enforcement.

The term '_____' also has been used to describe two unrelated transactions.

- a. Performance reports
- b. Compound empowerment
- c. Ricardian equivalence
- d. Privatization

10. _____ was a Scottish moral philosopher and a pioneer of political economy. One of the key figures of the Scottish Enlightenment, Smith is the author of The Theory of Moral Sentiments and An Inquiry into the Nature and Causes of the Wealth of Nations. The latter, usually abbreviated as The Wealth of Nations, is considered his magnum opus and the first modern work of economics.

- a. Alan Greenspan
- b. Adolph Fischer
- c. Adolf Hitler
- d. Adam Smith

11. An Inquiry into the Nature and Causes of the _____ is the magnum opus of the Scottish economist Adam Smith. It is a clearly written account of economics at the dawn of the Industrial Revolution, as well as a rhetorical piece written for the generally educated individual of the 18th century - advocating a free market economy as more productive and more beneficial to society.

The work is credited as a watershed in history and economics due to its comprehensive, largely accurate characterization of economic mechanisms that survive in modern economics; and also for its effective use of rhetorical technique, including structuring the work to contrast real world examples of free and fettered markets.

- a. The Bell Curve
- b. Wealth of Nations
- c. The Rise and Fall of the Great Powers
- d. Black Book of Communism

Chapter 2. Markets and Government in a Modern Economy

12. There are two main interpretations of the idea of a _____:

    - A model in which the state assumes primary responsibility for the welfare of its citizens. This responsibility in theory ought to be comprehensive, because all aspects of welfare are considered and universally applied to citizens as a 'right'. _____ can also mean the creation of a 'social safety net' of minimum standards of varying forms of welfare. Here is found some confusion between a '_____' and a 'welfare society' in common debate about the definition of the term.
    - The provision of welfare in society. In many '_____s', especially in continental Europe, welfare is not actually provided by the state, but by a combination of independent, voluntary, mutualist and government services. The functional provider of benefits and services may be a central or state government, a state-sponsored company or agency, a private corporation, a charity or another form of non-profit organization. However, this phenomenon has been more appropriately termed a 'welfare society,' and the term 'welfare system' has been used to describe the range of _____ and welfare society mixes that are found.

The English term '_____' is believed by Asa Briggs to have been coined by Archbishop William Temple during the Second World War, contrasting wartime Britain with the 'warfare state' of Nazi Germany. Friedrich Hayek contends that the term derived from the older German word Wohlfahrtsstaat, which itself was used by nineteenth century historians to describe a variant of the ideal of Polizeistaat . It was fully developed by the German academic Sozialpolitiker--'socialists of the chair'--from 1870 and first implemented through Bismarck's 'state socialism'. Bismarck's policies have also been seen as the creation of a _____.

a. 100-year flood
b. 1921 recession
c. 130-30 fund
d. Welfare state

13. _____ has several particular meanings:

    - in mathematics
        - _____ function
        - Euler _____
        - _____
        - _____ subgroup
        - method of _____s (partial differential equations)
    - in physics and engineering
        - any _____ curve that shows the relationship between certain input- and output parameters, e.g.
        - an I-V or current-voltage _____ is the current in a circuit as a function of the applied voltage
        - Receiver-Operator _____
    - in fiction
        - in Dungeons ' Dragons, _____ is another name for ability score

a. Demand
b. Russian financial crisis
c. Characteristic
d. Technocracy

14. A _____ is an economic system that incorporates a mixture of private and government ownership or control, or a mixture of capitalism and socialism.

Chapter 2. Markets and Government in a Modern Economy

There is not one single definition for a _____, but relevant aspects include: a degree of private economic freedom (including privately owned industry) intermingled with centralized economic planning and government regulation (which may include regulation of the market for environmental concerns and social welfare, or state ownership and management of some of the means of production for national or social objectives.)

For some states, there is not a consensus on whether they are capitalist, socialist, or mixed economies.

    a. Dual economy
    c. Hunter-gatherer
    b. Mixed economy
    d. Planned liberalism

15. The _____ , established in 1848, is the world's oldest futures and options exchange. More than 50 different options and futures contracts are traded by over 3,600 _____ members through open outcry and eTrading. Volumes at the exchange in 2003 were a record breaking 454 million contracts.
    a. 100-year flood
    c. 130-30 fund
    b. New York Mercantile Exchange
    d. Chicago Board of Trade

16. _____s are a type of administrative division, in some countries managed by a local government. They vary greatly in size, spanning entire regions or counties, several municipalities, or subdivisions of municipalities.

In Austria, a _____ or Bezirk is an administrative division normally encompassing several municipalities, roughly equivalent to the Landkreis in Germany.

    a. 100-year flood
    c. 130-30 fund
    b. District
    d. 1921 recession

17. A _____ is the space, actual or metaphorical, in which a market operates. The term is also used in a trademark law context to denote the actual consumer environment, ie. the 'real world' in which products and services are provided and consumed.
    a. Marketplace
    c. 1921 recession
    b. 100-year flood
    d. 130-30 fund

18. The _____ is the world's largest physical commodity futures exchange, located in New York City. Its two principal divisions are the _____ and Commodity Exchange, Inc (COMEX) which were once separate but are now merged. The parent company of the _____, Inc., New York Mercantile ExchangeX Holdings, Inc.
    a. 130-30 fund
    c. Commodity Exchange
    b. 100-year flood
    d. New York Mercantile Exchange

19. A _____ is any systematic process enabling many market players to bid and ask: helping bidders and sellers interact and make deals. It is not just the price mechanism but the entire system of regulation, qualification, credentials, reputations and clearing that surrounds that mechanism and makes it operate in a social context.

Because a _____ relies on the assumption that players are constantly involved and unequally enabled, a _____ is distinguished specifically from a voting system where candidates seek the support of voters on a less regular basis.

a. Price mechanism
b. Contestable market
c. Market system
d. Competitive equilibrium

20. _____ is a broad label that refers to any individuals or households that use goods and services generated within the economy. The concept of a _____ is used in different contexts, so that the usage and significance of the term may vary.

Typically when business people and economists talk of _____s they are talking about person as _____, an aggregated commodity item with little individuality other than that expressed in the buy/not-buy decision.

a. 1921 recession
b. 100-year flood
c. Consumer
d. 130-30 fund

21. _____ are final goods specifically intended for the mass market. For instance, _____ do not include investment assets, like precious antiques, even though these antiques are final goods.

Manufactured goods are goods that have been processed by way of machinery.

a. Bulgarian-American trade
b. Fiscal stimulus plans
c. G-20 Leaders Summit on Financial Markets and the World Economy
d. Consumer goods

22. The _____, sometimes called the fundamental _____, is one of the fundamental economic theories in the operation of any economy. It asserts that there is scarcity, that the finite resources available are insufficient to satisfy all human wants. The problem then becomes how to determine what is to be produced and how the factors of production (such as capital and labour) are to be allocated.

a. Endogenous growth theory
b. Eclectic paradigm
c. Economic nationalism
d. Economic problem

23. In economics, _____ are the resources employed to produce goods and services. They facilitate production but do not become part of the product (as with raw materials) or significantly transformed by the production process (as with fuel used to power machinery.) To 19th century economists, the _____ were land (natural resources, gifts from nature), labor (the ability to work), and capital goods (human-made tools and equipment.)

a. Hicks-neutral technical change
b. Factors of production
c. Product Pipeline
d. Long-run

24. In economics, economic equilibrium is simply a state of the world where economic forces are balanced and in the absence of external influences the (equilibrium) values of economic variables will not change. It is the point at which quantity demanded and quantity supplied are equal. _____, for example, refers to a condition where a market price is established through competition such that the amount of goods or services sought by buyers is equal to the amount of goods or services produced by sellers.

a. Product-Market Growth Matrix
b. Market equilibrium
c. Marketization
d. Regulated market

Chapter 2. Markets and Government in a Modern Economy

25. _____ is an economic concept with commonplace familiarity. It is the price that a good or service is offered at, or will fetch, in the marketplace. It is of interest mainly in the study of microeconomics.
   a. Paper trading
   b. Market price
   c. Noisy market hypothesis
   d. Market anomaly

26. _____ in economics and business is the result of an exchange and from that trade we assign a numerical monetary value to a good, service or asset. If Alice trades Bob 4 apples for an orange, the _____ of an orange is 4 apples. Inversely, the _____ of an apple is 1/4 oranges.
   a. Price book
   b. Premium pricing
   c. Price war
   d. Price

27. A _____ is message sent to consumers and producers in the form of a price charged for a commodity; this is seen as indicating a signal for producers to increase supplies and/or consumers to reduce demand.

   For example, in a free price system, rising prices may indicate a shortage of supply, increase in demand, or a rise in input costs. Regardless of the underlying reason--and without the consumer needing to know the cause--the price increase communicates the notion that consumer demand (at this new, higher price) should recede or that supplies should increase.

   a. Market demand schedule
   b. Mohring effect
   c. Threshold population
   d. Price signal

28. In economics, _____ is the process by which a firm determines the price and output level that returns the greatest profit. There are several approaches to this problem. The total revenue--total cost method relies on the fact that profit equals revenue minus cost, and the marginal revenue--marginal cost method is based on the fact that total profit in a perfectly competitive market reaches its maximum point where marginal revenue equals marginal cost.
   a. Profit margin
   b. Normal profit
   c. Profit maximization
   d. 100-year flood

29. _____ is an economic model based on price, utility and quantity in a market. It predicts that in a competitive market, price will function to equalize the quantity demanded by consumers, and the quantity supplied by producers, resulting in an economic equilibrium of price and quantity. The model incorporates other factors changing equilibrium as a shift of demand and/or supply.
   a. Deferred gratification
   b. Rational addiction
   c. Supply and demand
   d. Joint demand

30. In economics, the term _____ of income or _____ refers to a simple economic model which describes the reciprocal circulation of income between producers and consumers. In the _____ model, the inter-dependent entities of producer and consumer are referred to as 'firms' and 'households' respectively and provide each other with factors in order to facilitate the flow of income. Firms provide consumers with goods and services in exchange for consumer expenditure and 'factors of production' from households.
   a. 130-30 fund
   b. 100-year flood
   c. 1921 recession
   d. Circular flow

Chapter 2. Markets and Government in a Modern Economy

31. Economics:

    - _____, the desire to own something and the ability to pay for it
    - _____ curve, a graphic representation of a _____ schedule
    - _____ deposit, the money in checking accounts
    - _____ pull theory, the theory that inflation occurs when _____ for goods and services exceeds existing supplies
    - _____ schedule, a table that lists the quantity of a good a person will buy it each different price
    - _____ side economics, the school of economics at believes government spending and tax cuts open economy by raising _____

    a. Production
    b. Demand
    c. McKesson ' Robbins scandal
    d. Variability

32. A _____ is an object whose consumption increases the utility of the consumer, for which the quantity demanded exceeds the quantity supplied at zero price. _____s are usually modeled as having diminishing marginal utility. The first individual purchase has high utility; the second has less.

    a. Good
    b. Merit good
    c. Pie method
    d. Composite good

33. _____ describes a deliberate attempt to interfere with the free and fair operation of the market and create artificial, false or misleading appearances with respect to the price of a security, commodity or currency. _____ is prohibited under Section 9(a)(2) of the Securities Exchange Act of 1934, and in Australia under Section s 1041A of the Corporations Act 2001. The Act defines _____ as transactions which create an artificial price or maintain an artificial price for a tradable security.

    a. Market manipulation
    b. Managerial economics
    c. Legal monopoly
    d. Net domestic product

34. In microeconomics, _____ is quite simply the conversion of inputs into outputs. It is an economic process that uses resources to create a good or service that is suitable for exchange. This can include manufacturing, storing, shipping, and packaging.

    a. MET
    b. Solved
    c. Red Guards
    d. Production

35. The _____ consists of a number of economic theories which describe the nature of the firm, company including its existence, its behaviour, and its relationship with the market.

    In simplified terms, the _____ aims to answer these questions:

    1. Existence - why do firms emerge, why are not all transactions in the economy mediated over the market?
    2. Boundaries - why the boundary between firms and the market is located exactly there? Which transactions are performed internally and which are negotiated on the market?
    3. Organization - why are firms structured in such specific way? What is the interplay of formal and informal relationships?

Despite looking simple, these questions are not answered by the established economic theory, which usually views firms as given, and treats them as black boxes without any internal structure.

The First World War period saw a change of emphasis in economic theory away from industry-level analysis which mainly included analysing markets to analysis at the level of the firm, as it became increasingly clear that perfect competition was no longer an adequate model of how firms behaved. Economic theory till then had focussed on trying to understand markets alone and there had been little study on understanding why firms or organisations exist.

- a. Khazzoom-Brookes postulate
- b. Policy Ineffectiveness Proposition
- c. Technology gap
- d. Theory of the firm

36. _____ are the prices that the factors of production of a finished item attract.

There has been some economic debate as to what determines these prices. Classical and Marxist economists argued that the _____ decided the value of a product and so value was intrinsic within the product.

- a. Marginal product
- b. Productivity model
- c. Marginal product of labor
- d. Factor prices

37. In economics, _____ is how a natione;s total economy is distributed among its population. ._____ has always been a central concern of economic theory and economic policy. Classical economists such as Adam Smith, Thomas Malthus and David Ricardo were mainly concerned with factor _____, that is, the distribution of income between the main factors of production, land, labour and capital.
- a. Equipment trust certificate
- b. Income distribution
- c. Authorised capital
- d. Eco commerce

38. In economics, a _____ is a function that specifies the output of a firm, an industry, or an entire economy for all combinations of inputs. A meta-_____ compares the practice of the existing entities converting inputs X into output y to determine the most efficient practice _____ of the existing entities, whether the most efficient feasible practice production or the most efficient actual practice production. In either case, the maximum output of a technologically-determined production process is a mathematical function of input factors of production.
- a. Post-Fordism
- b. Short-run
- c. Production function
- d. Constant elasticity of substitution

39. _____ is a common concept in economics, and gives rise to derived concepts such as consumer debt. Generally _____ is defined by opposition to production. But the precise definition can vary because different schools of economists define production quite differently.
- a. Cash or share options
- b. Consumption
- c. Foreclosure data providers
- d. Federal Reserve Bank Notes

40. In economics, the _____ is the term economists use to describe the self-regulating nature of the marketplace. The _____ is a metaphor coined by the economist Adam Smith in The Wealth of Nations.

Chapter 2. Markets and Government in a Modern Economy

Adam Smith mentions the metaphor in Book IV of The Wealth of Nations, arguing that people in any society will certainly employ their capital in foreign trading only if the profits available by that method far exceed those available locally, and that in such a case it is better for society as a whole if they so did.

a. ACEA agreement
b. ACCRA Cost of Living Index
c. AD-IA Model
d. Invisible hand

41. _____ is a mechanism that allows people easily to buy and sell products. Services are often included in the scope of the term. _____ regulation is an economic term that describes restrictions in the market.
a. Fixed exchange rate system
b. Market dominance
c. Financialization
d. Product market

42. _____ is the increase in the amount of the goods and services produced by an economy over time. It is conventionally measured as the percent rate of increase in real gross domestic product, or real GDP. Growth is usually calculated in real terms, i.e. inflation-adjusted terms, in order to net out the effect of inflation on the price of the goods and services produced.
a. AD-IA Model
b. ACEA agreement
c. ACCRA Cost of Living Index
d. Economic growth

43. The _____ was a period in the late 18th and early 19th centuries when major changes in agriculture, manufacturing, mining, and transportation had a profound effect on the socioeconomic and cultural conditions in Britain. The changes subsequently spread throughout Europe, North America, and eventually the world. The onset of the _____ marked a major turning point in human society; almost every aspect of daily life was eventually influenced in some way.
a. Adolph Fischer
b. Adolf Hitler
c. Adam Smith
d. Industrial Revolution

44. In economics, a _____ exists when the production or use of goods and services by the market is not efficient. That is, there exists another outcome where all involved can be made better off. _____s can be viewed as scenarios where individuals' pursuit of pure self-interest leads to results that are not efficient - that can be improved upon from the societal point-of-view.
a. Financial economics
b. Fixed exchange rate
c. General equilibrium
d. Market failure

45. In economics, a _____ exists when a specific individual or enterprise has sufficient control over a particular product or service to determine significantly the terms on which other individuals shall have access to it. Monopolies are thus characterized by a lack of economic competition for the good or service that they provide and a lack of viable substitute goods. The verb 'monopolize' refers to the process by which a firm gains persistently greater market share than what is expected under perfect competition.
a. 100-year flood
b. 1921 recession
c. 130-30 fund
d. Monopoly

Chapter 2. Markets and Government in a Modern Economy

46. In neoclassical economics and microeconomics, _____ describes the perfect being a market in which there are many small firms, all producing homogeneous goods. In the short term, such markets are productively inefficient as output will not occur where mc is equal to ac, but allocatively efficient, as output under _____ will always occur where mc is equal to mr, and therefore where mc equals ar. However, in the long term, such markets are both allocatively and productively efficient.
   a. Co-operative economics
   b. Perfect competition
   c. General equilibrium
   d. Law of supply

47. _____ is exchange of capital, goods, and services across international borders or territories. In most countries, it represents a significant share of gross domestic product (GDP.) While _____ has been present throughout much of history, its economic, social, and political importance has been on the rise in recent centuries.
   a. Incoterms
   b. Import license
   c. International trade
   d. Intra-industry trade

48. _____ is a term used to describe how different aspects between economies are integrated. The basics of this theory were written by the Hungarian Economist Béla Balassa in the 1960s. As _____ increases, the barriers of trade between markets diminishes.
   a. Import license
   b. Import
   c. Inward investment
   d. Economic integration

49. In economics, a _____ is a mechanism that allows people to easily buy and sell (trade) financial securities (such as stocks and bonds), commodities (such as precious metals or agricultural goods), and other fungible items of value at low transaction costs and at prices that reflect the efficient-market hypothesis.

   _____s have evolved significantly over several hundred years and are undergoing constant innovation to improve liquidity.

   Both general markets (where many commodities are traded) and specialized markets (where only one commodity is traded) exist.

   a. Convertible arbitrage
   b. Noise trader
   c. Market anomaly
   d. Financial market

50. _____ in its literal sense is the process of transformation of local or regional phenomena into global ones. It can be described as a process by which the people of the world are unified into a single society and function together.

   This process is a combination of economic, technological, sociocultural and political forces.

   a. Globally Integrated Enterprise
   b. Helsinki Process on Globalisation and Democracy
   c. Global Cosmopolitanism
   d. Globalization

51. In economics, economic output is divided into physical goods and intangible services. Consumption of _____ is assumed to produce utility. It is often used when referring to a _____ Tax.
   a. Composite good
   b. Goods and services
   c. Manufactured goods
   d. Private good

52. _____ is subcontracting a process, such as product design or manufacturing, to a third-party company. The decision to outsource is often made in the interest of lowering cost or making better use of time and energy costs, redirecting or conserving energy directed at the competencies of a particular business, or to make more efficient use of land, labor, capital, (information) technology and resources. _____ became part of the business lexicon during the 1980s.
  a. Outsourcing
  b. Electronic business
  c. Averch-Johnson effect
  d. Additional Funds Needed

53. _____ is the economic policy of restraining trade between states, through methods such as tariffs on imported goods, restrictive quotas, and a variety of other restrictive government regulations designed to discourage imports, and prevent foreign take-over of local markets and companies. This policy is closely aligned with anti-globalization, and contrasts with free trade, where government barriers to trade are kept to a minimum. The term is mostly used in the context of economics, where _____ refers to policies or doctrines which 'protect' businesses and workers within a country by restricting or regulating trade with foreign nations.
  a. Knowledge economy
  b. Google economy
  c. Protectionism
  d. Digital economy

54. _____ is a term used in economics to describe how an economic quantity is related to economic fluctuations. It is the opposite of procyclical. However, it has more than one meaning.
  a. Countercyclical
  b. Mathematical economics
  c. Price revolution
  d. Law of comparative advantage

55. _____ is that which is owed; usually referencing assets owed, but the term can also cover moral obligations and other interactions not requiring money. In the case of assets, _____ is a means of using future purchasing power in the present before a summation has been earned. Some companies and corporations use _____ as a part of their overall corporate finance strategy.
  a. Hard money loan
  b. Collateral Management
  c. Debenture
  d. Debt

56. In economics a _____ is an entity that owes a debt to someone else. The entity may be an individual, a firm, a government, a company or other legal person. The counterparty is called a creditor.
  a. Duration gap
  b. Senior stretch loan
  c. Decision process tool
  d. Debtor

57. _____ is that part of the total debt in a country that is owed to creditors outside the country. The debtors can be the government, corporations or private households. The debt includes money owed to private commercial banks, other governments, or international financial institutions such as the IMF and World Bank.
  a. Internal debt
  b. External debt
  c. International debt collection
  d. Asset protection

58. A _____ is the transfer of wealth from one party (such as a person or company) to another. A _____ is usually made in exchange for the provision of goods, services or both, or to fulfill a legal obligation.

The simplest and oldest form of _____ is barter, the exchange of one good or service for another.

Chapter 2. Markets and Government in a Modern Economy

a. Social gravity
b. Going concern
c. Payment
d. Soft count

59. _____ in economics refers to metrics and measures of output from production processes, per unit of input. Labor _____, for example, is typically measured as a ratio of output per labor-hour, an input. _____ may be conceived of as a metrics of the technical or engineering efficiency of production.
    a. Productivity
    b. Fordism
    c. Piece work
    d. Production-possibility frontier

60. The _____ is the central banking system of the United States. Created in 1913 by the enactment of the Federal Reserve Act (signed by Woodrow Wilson), it is a quasi-public and quasi-private (government entity with private components) banking system that comprises (1) the presidentially appointed Board of Governors of the _____ in Washington, D.C.; (2) the Federal Open Market Committee; (3) twelve regional Federal Reserve Banks located in major cities throughout the nation acting as fiscal agents for the U.S. Treasury, each with its own nine-member board of directors; (4) numerous other private U.S. member banks, which subscribe to required amounts of non-transferable stock in their regional Federal Reserve Banks; and (5) various advisory councils. Since February 2006, Ben Bernanke has served as the Chairman of the Board of Governors of the _____.
    a. Federal Reserve System Open Market Account
    b. Term auction facility
    c. Federal Reserve System
    d. Monetary Policy Report to the Congress

61. The term financial crisis is applied broadly to a variety of situations in which some financial institutions or assets suddenly lose a large part of their value. In the 19th and early 20th centuries, many _____ were associated with banking panics, and many recessions coincided with these panics. Other situations that are often called _____ include stock market crashes and the bursting of other financial bubbles, currency crises, and sovereign defaults.
    a. General equilibrium
    b. Microeconomics
    c. Georgism
    d. Financial crises

62. In economics, _____ is inflation that is very high or 'out of control', a condition in which prices increase rapidly as a currency loses its value. Definitions used by the media vary from a cumulative inflation rate over three years approaching 100% to 'inflation exceeding 50% a month.' In informal usage the term is often applied to much lower rates. As a rule of thumb, normal inflation is reported per year, but _____ is often reported for much shorter intervals, often per month.
    a. 100-year flood
    b. 130-30 fund
    c. 1921 recession
    d. Hyperinflation

63. In economics, _____ is the total amount of money available in an economy at a particular point in time. There are several ways to define 'money', but standard measures usually include currency in circulation and demand deposits.

    _____ data are recorded and published, usually by the government or the central bank of the country.

    a. Money supply
    b. Velocity of money
    c. Veil of money
    d. Neutrality of money

64. The _____ is the market for securities, where companies and governments can raise longterm funds. It is a market in which money is lent for periods longer than a year. The _____ includes the stock market and the bond market.

Chapter 2. Markets and Government in a Modern Economy

a. Capital Market
c. Financial instrument
b. Performance attribution
d. Multi-family office

65. _____ is money accepted for exchange of goods in an economy. The prevalence of one money over another arises, usually, when a government designates through decrees that the government shall accept only particular notes and coins in payment for taxes. Typically, money of _____ consists of stamped coins and minted paper bills.
a. Totnes pound
c. Local currency
b. Security thread
d. Currency

66. A _____ is a monetary authority which is required to maintain a fixed exchange rate with a foreign currency. This policy objective requires the conventional objectives of a central bank to be subordinated to the exchange rate target.

The main qualities of an orthodox _____ are:

- A _____'s foreign currency reserves must be sufficient to ensure that all holders of its notes and coins (and all banks creditor of a Reserve Account at the _____) can convert them into the reserve currency (usually 110-115% of the monetary base M0.)
- A _____ maintains absolute, unlimited convertibility between its notes and coins and the currency against which they are pegged (the anchor currency), at a fixed rate of exchange, with no restrictions on current-account or capital-account transactions.
- A _____ only earns profit from interests on foreign reserves (less the expense of note-issuing), and does not engage in forward-exchange transactions. These foreign reserves exist (1) because local notes have been issued in exchange, or (2) because commercial banks must by regulation deposit a minimum reserve at the _____. (1) generates a seignorage revenue. (2) is the revenue on minimum reserves (revenue of investment activities less cost of minimum reserves remuneration)
- A _____ has no discretionary powers to effect monetary policy and does not lend to the government. Governments cannot print money, and can only tax or borrow to meet their spending commitments.
- A _____ does not act as a lender of last resort to commercial banks, and does not regulate reserve requirements.
- A _____ does not attempt to manipulate interest rates by establishing a discount rate like a central bank. The peg with the foreign currency tends to keep interest rates and inflation very closely aligned to those in the country against whose currency the peg is fixed.

The _____ in question will no longer issue fiat money but instead will only issue one unit of local currency for each unit (or decided amount) of foreign currency it has in its vault (often a hard currency such as the U.S. dollar or the euro.) The surplus on the balance of payments of that country is reflected by higher deposits local banks hold at the central bank as well as (initially) higher deposits of the (net) exporting firms at their local banks.

a. Currency competition
c. Petrodollar
b. Reserve currency
d. Currency board

67. The term _____ is applied broadly to a variety of situations in which some financial institutions or assets suddenly lose a large part of their value. In the 19th and early 20th centuries, many financial crises were associated with banking panics, and many recessions coincided with these panics. Other situations that are often called financial crises include stock market crashes and the bursting of other financial bubbles, currency crises, and sovereign defaults.

Chapter 2. Markets and Government in a Modern Economy

a. Co-operative economics
c. Macroeconomics
b. Financial crisis
d. Market failure

68. In economics, _____ is a rise in the general level of prices of goods and services in an economy over a period of time. When the general price level rises, each unit of currency buys fewer goods and services; consequently, _____ is also a decline in the real value of money--a loss of purchasing power in the medium of exchange which is also the monetary unit of account in the economy. A chief measure of general price-level _____ is the general _____ rate, which is the percentage change in a general price index (normally the Consumer Price Index) over time.
   a. Inflation
   c. Energy economics
   b. Economic
   d. Opportunity cost

69. A _____ is an expression that compares quantities relative to each other. The most common examples involve two quantities, but any number of quantities can be compared. _____s are represented mathematically by separating each quantity with a colon, for example the _____ 2:3, which is read as the _____ 'two to three'.
   a. Ratio
   c. 130-30 fund
   b. Y-intercept
   d. 100-year flood

70. A _____ is the exclusive authority to determine how a resource is used, whether that resource is owned by government or by individuals. All economic goods have a _____s attribute. This attribute has three broad components

   1. The right to use the good
   2. The right to earn income from the good
   3. The right to transfer the good to others

The concept of _____s as used by economists and legal scholars are related but distinct. The distinction is largely seen in the economists' focus on the ability of an individual or collective to control the use of the good.

   a. High-reeve
   c. Property right
   b. Post-sale restraint
   d. Holder in due course

71. _____ is used to assign the available resources in an economic way. It is part of resource management.

In strategic planning,is a plan for using available resources, for example human resources, especially in the near term, to achieve goals for the future.

   a. 1921 recession
   c. 130-30 fund
   b. 100-year flood
   d. Resource allocation

72. _____ is the concept or idea of fairness in economics, particularly as to taxation or welfare economics.

In welfare economics, _____ may be distinguished from economic efficiency in overall evaluation of social welfare. Although '_____' has broader uses, it may be posed as a counterpart to economic inequality in yielding a 'good' distribution of welfare.

a. Equity
b. ACEA agreement
c. ACCRA Cost of Living Index
d. AD-IA Model

73. In calculus, a function f defined on a subset of the real numbers with real values is called _____, if for all x and y such that x >≤ y one has f(x) >≤ f(y), so f preserves the order. In layman's terms, the sign of the slope is always positive (the curve tending upwards) or zero (i.e., non-decreasing, or asymptotic, or depicted as a horizontal, flat line) Likewise, a function is called monotonically decreasing (non-increasing) if, whenever x >≤ y, then f(x) >≥ f(y), so it reverses the order.
    a. 130-30 fund
    b. 100-year flood
    c. Monotonic
    d. 1921 recession

74. Competition law, known in the United States as _____ law, has three main elements:

- prohibiting agreements or practices that restrict free trading and competition between business entities. This includes in particular the repression of cartels.
- banning abusive behaviour by a firm dominating a market, or anti-competitive practices that tend to lead to such a dominant position. Practices controlled in this way may include predatory pricing, tying, price gouging, refusal to deal, and many others.
- supervising the mergers and acquisitions of large corporations, including some joint ventures. Transactions that are considered to threaten the competitive process can be prohibited altogether, or approved subject to 'remedies' such as an obligation to divest part of the merged business or to offer licences or access to facilities to enable other businesses to continue competing.

The substance and practice of competition law varies from jurisdiction to jurisdiction. Protecting the interests of consumers (consumer welfare) and ensuring that entrepreneurs have an opportunity to compete in the market economy are often treated as important objectives. Competition law is closely connected with law on deregulation of access to markets, state aids and subsidies, the privatisation of state owned assets and the establishment of independent sector regulators. In recent decades, competition law has been viewed as a way to provide better public services.

a. Antitrust
b. Intellectual property law
c. Anti-Inflation Act
d. United Kingdom competition law

75. _____, known in the United States as antitrust law, has three main elements:

- prohibiting agreements or practices that restrict free trading and competition between business entities. This includes in particular the repression of cartels.
- banning abusive behaviour by a firm dominating a market, or anti-competitive practices that tend to lead to such a dominant position. Practices controlled in this way may include predatory pricing, tying, price gouging, refusal to deal, and many others.
- supervising the mergers and acquisitions of large corporations, including some joint ventures. Transactions that are considered to threaten the competitive process can be prohibited altogether, or approved subject to 'remedies' such as an obligation to divest part of the merged business or to offer licences or access to facilities to enable other businesses to continue competing.

The substance and practice of _____ varies from jurisdiction to jurisdiction. Protecting the interests of consumers (consumer welfare) and ensuring that entrepreneurs have an opportunity to compete in the market economy are often treated as important objectives. _____ is closely connected with law on deregulation of access to markets, state aids and subsidies, the privatisation of state owned assets and the establishment of independent sector regulators. In recent decades, _____ has been viewed as a way to provide better public services.

a. Due diligence
b. Competition law
c. Fee simple
d. Hostile work environment

76. In economic theory, _____ is the competitive situation in any market where the conditions necessary for perfect competition are not satisfied. It is a market structure that does not meet the conditions of perfect competition.

Forms of _____ include:

- Monopoly, in which there is only one seller of a good.
- Oligopoly, in which there is a small number of sellers.
- Monopolistic competition, in which there are many sellers producing highly differentiated goods.
- Monopsony, in which there is only one buyer of a good.
- Oligopsony, in which there is a small number of buyers.

There may also be _____ in markets due to buyers or sellers lacking information about prices and the goods being traded.

There may also be _____ due to a time lag in a market.

a. Imperfect competition
b. ACCRA Cost of Living Index
c. AD-IA Model
d. ACEA agreement

77. Many _____ are related to the environmental consequences of production and use

- Systemic risk describes the risks to the overall economy arising from the risks which the banking system takes. That the private costs of banking failure may be smaller than the social costs justifies banking regulations, although regulations could create a moral hazard.

- Anthropogenic climate change is attributed to greenhouse gas emissions from burning oil, gas, and coal. Global warming has been ranked as the #1 externality of all economic activity, in the magnitude of potential harms and yet remains unmitigated.

a. White certificates
b. Green certificate
c. Negative externalities
d. Total Economic Value

78. Examples of _____ include:

- A beekeeper keeps the bees for their honey. A side effect or externality associated with his activity is the pollination of surrounding crops by the bees. The value generated by the pollination may be more important than the value of the harvested honey.

- An individual planting an attractive garden in front of his house may provide benefits to others living in the area, and even financial benefits in the form of increased property values for all property owners.

- An individual buying a product that is interconnected in a network (e.g., a video cellphone) will increase the usefulness of such phones to other people who have a video cellphone. When each new user of a product increases the value of the same product owned by others, the phenomenon is called a network externality or a network effect. Network externalities often have 'tipping points' where, suddenly, the product reaches general acceptance and near-universal usage, a phenomenon which can be seen in the near universal take-up of cellphones in some Scandinavian countries.

- Knowledge spillover of inventions and information - once an invention (or most other forms of practical information) is discovered or made more easily accessible, others benefit by exploiting the invention or information. Copyright and intellectual property law are mechanisms to allow the inventor or creator to benefit from a temporary, state-protected monopoly in return for 'sharing' the information through publication or other means.

a. Weighted average cost of carbon
b. Negative externalities
c. Total Economic Value
d. Positive externalities

79. _____s are externalities of economic activity or processes upon those who are not directly involved in it. Odours from a rendering plant are negative _____s upon its neighbours; the beauty of a homeowner's flower garden is a positive _____ upon neighbours.

In the same way, the economic benefits of increased trade are the _____s anticipated in the formation of multilateral alliances of many of the regional nation states: e.g. SARC (South Asian Regional Cooperation), ASpillover effectAN (Association of South East Asian Nations)

In reference to psychology, the _____ is when other people's emotions affect the emotions of those around them.

a. Public good
b. Cobb-Douglas
c. Business sector
d. Spillover effect

80. In economics, a _____ is a good that is non-rivaled and non-excludable. This means, respectively, that consumption of the good by one individual does not reduce availability of the good for consumption by others; and that no one can be effectively excluded from using the good. In the real world, there may be no such thing as an absolutely non-rivaled and non-excludable good; but economists think that some goods approximate the concept closely enough for the analysis to be economically useful.

a. Neoclassical synthesis
b. Happiness economics
c. Demand-pull theory
d. Public good

Chapter 2. Markets and Government in a Modern Economy

81. In mathematics, an _____ is a statement about the relative size or order of two objects, or about whether they are the same or not

- The notation a < b means that a is less than b.
- The notation a > b means that a is greater than b.
- The notation a ≠ b means that a is not equal to b, but does not say that one is greater than the other or even that they can be compared in size.

In each statement above, a is not equal to b. These relations are known as strict inequalities. The notation a < b may also be read as 'a is strictly less than b'.

a. ACEA agreement
b. AD-IA Model
c. ACCRA Cost of Living Index
d. Inequality

82. _____ is the prospect that a party insulated from risk may behave differently from the way it would behave if it were fully exposed to the risk. In insurance, _____ that occurs without conscious or malicious action is called morale hazard.

_____ is related to information asymmetry, a situation in which one party in a transaction has more information than another.

a. Moral hazard
b. 130-30 fund
c. 1921 recession
d. 100-year flood

83. In finance, the _____s between two currencies specifies how much one currency is worth in terms of the other. It is the value of a foreign natione;s currency in terms of the home natione;s currency. For example an _____ of 102 Japanese yen to the United States dollar means that JPY 102 is worth the same as USD 1.

a. ACEA agreement
b. ACCRA Cost of Living Index
c. Interbank market
d. Exchange rate

84. To _____ is to impose a financial charge or other levy upon a taxpayer by a state or the functional equivalent of a state.

_____es are also imposed by many subnational entities. _____es consist of direct _____ or indirect _____, and may be paid in money or as its labour equivalent (often but not always unpaid.)

a. 1921 recession
b. 130-30 fund
c. 100-year flood
d. Tax

85. To tax is to impose a financial charge or other levy upon a taxpayer by a state or the functional equivalent of a state.

_____ are also imposed by many subnational entities. _____ consist of direct tax or indirect tax, and may be paid in money or as its labour equivalent (often but not always unpaid.)

a. 130-30 fund
b. 100-year flood
c. 1921 recession
d. Taxes

Chapter 2. Markets and Government in a Modern Economy

86. The term _____ refers to economy-wide fluctuations in production or economic activity over several months or years. These fluctuations occur around a long-term growth trend, and typically involve shifts over time between periods of relatively rapid economic growth (expansion or boom), and periods of relative stagnation or decline (contraction or recession.)

These fluctuations are often measured using the growth rate of real gross domestic product.

- a. Consumer theory
- b. Tobit model
- c. Nominal value
- d. Business cycle

87. A _____, reserve bank, or monetary authority is the entity responsible for the monetary policy of a country or of a group of member states. It is a bank that can lend money to other banks in times of need. Its primary responsibility is to maintain the stability of the national currency and money supply, but more active duties include controlling subsidized-loan interest rates, and acting as a lender of last resort to the banking sector during times of financial crisis (private banks often being integral to the national financial system.)

- a. 130-30 fund
- b. 1921 recession
- c. Central bank
- d. 100-year flood

88. _____ is a term that refers both to:

- a formal discipline used to help appraise, or assess, the case for a project or proposal, which itself is a process known as project appraisal; and
- an informal approach to making decisions of any kind.

Under both definitions the process involves, whether explicitly or implicitly, weighing the total expected costs against the total expected benefits of one or more actions in order to choose the best or most profitable option. The formal process is often referred to as either CBA (_____) or BCost-benefit analysis

A hallmark of CBA is that all benefits and all costs are expressed in money terms, and are adjusted for the time value of money, so that all flows of benefits and flows of project costs over time (which tend to occur at different points in time) are expressed on a common basis in terms of their e;present value.e; Closely related, but slightly different, formal techniques include Cost-effectiveness analysis, Economic impact analysis, Fiscal impact analysis and Social Return on Investment(SROI) analysis. The latter builds upon the logic of _____, but differs in that it is explicitly designed to inform the practical decision-making of enterprise managers and investors focused on optimising their social and environmental impacts.

- a. 130-30 fund
- b. Decision theory
- c. 100-year flood
- d. Cost-benefit analysis

89. _____ refers to an absence of excessive fluctuations in the macroeconomy. An economy with fairly constant output growth and low and stable inflation would be considered economically stable. An economy with frequent large recessions, a pronounced business cycle, very high or variable inflation, or frequent financial crises would be considered economically unstable.

- a. Export subsidy
- b. Export-led growth
- c. Income effect
- d. Economic stability

90. The term _____ refers to government debt, expenditures and revenues, or to finance (particularly financial revenue) in general.

- _____ deficit is the budget deficit of federal or local government
- _____ policy is the discretionary spending of governments. Contrasts with monetary policy.
- _____ year and _____ quarter are reporting periods for firms and other agencies.

a. Bucket shop
b. Procter ' Gamble
c. Drawdown
d. Fiscal

91. In economics, _____ is the use of government spending and revenue collection to influence the economy.

_____ can be contrasted with the other main type of economic policy, monetary policy, which attempts to stabilize the economy by controlling interest rates and the supply of money. The two main instruments of _____ are government spending and taxation.

a. Fiscal policy
b. 100-year flood
c. Sustainable investment rule
d. Fiscalism

92. In economics, _____ is the transfer of income, wealth or property from some individuals to others.

One premise of _____ is that money should be distributed to benefit the poorer members of society, and that the rich have an obligation to assist the poor, thus creating a more financially egalitarian society. Another argument is that the rich exploit the poor or otherwise gain unfair benefits.

a. Redistribution
b. 1921 recession
c. 130-30 fund
d. 100-year flood

93. _____, 1st Baron Keynes was a renowned economist from Britain whose many ideas on economic and political theories as well as on many governments' monetary policies influenced America. He advocated a government that played an active role in the lives of people regarding business, economy, etc. In this role, the government would use fiscal measures to reduce the consequences of recessions, economic depressions and booms.

a. Adolph Fischer
b. Adam Smith
c. John Maynard Keynes
d. Adolf Hitler

94. _____ and Keynesian Theory) is a macroeconomic theory based on the ideas of 20th-century British economist John Maynard Keynes. _____ argues that private sector decisions sometimes lead to inefficient macroeconomic outcomes and therefore advocates active policy responses by the public sector, including monetary policy actions by the central bank and fiscal policy actions by the government to stabilize output over the business cycle.

The theories forming the basis of _____ were first presented in The General Theory of Employment, Interest and Money, published in 1936.

a. Market failure
b. Deflation
c. Keynesian economics
d. Rational choice theory

95. The _____ was a fundamental reworking of economic theory concerning the factors determining employment levels in the overall economy. The revolution was set against the orthodox classical economic framework, which based on Say's Law argued that unless special conditions prevailed the free market would naturally establish full employment equilibrium with no need for government intervention. Employers will be able to make a profit by employing all available workers as long as workers drop their wages below the value of the total output they are able to produce - and classical economics assumed that in a free market workers would be willing to lower their wage demands accordingly , because they are rational agents who would rather work for less than face unemployment.
a. Speculative demand
b. Neo-Keynesian economics
c. Military Keynesianism
d. Keynesian revolution

96. In economics, a _____ is a general slowdown in economic activity over a sustained period of time, or a business cycle contraction. During _____ s, many macroeconomic indicators vary in a similar way. Production as measured by Gross Domestic Product (GDP), employment, investment spending, capacity utilization, household incomes and business profits all fall during _____ s.
a. Recession
b. Monetary economics
c. Leading indicators
d. Treasury View

97. In economics, a _____ is a redistribution of income in the market system. These payments are considered to be nonexhaustive because they do not directly absorb resources or create output. Examples of certain _____ s include welfare (financial aid), social security, and government subsidies for certain businesses (firms.)
a. Transfer payment
b. 100-year flood
c. 130-30 fund
d. 1921 recession

98. In economics, _____ is the total demand for final goods and services in the economy (Y) at a given time and price level. It is the amount of goods and services in the economy that will be purchased at all possible price levels. This is the demand for the gross domestic product of a country when inventory levels are static.
a. Aggregate expenditure
b. Aggregate demand
c. Aggregation problem
d. Aggregate supply

99. _____ was an American economist, statistician and public intellectual, and a recipient of the Nobel Memorial Prize in Economic Sciences. He is best known among scholars for his theoretical and empirical research, especially consumption analysis, monetary history and theory, and for his demonstration of the complexity of stabilization policy. A global public followed his restatement of a political philosophy that insisted on minimizing the role of government in favor of the private sector.
a. Adolf Hitler
b. Adam Smith
c. Adolph Fischer
d. Milton Friedman

100. _____ is the public sector analogy to market failure and occurs when a government intervention causes a more inefficient allocation of goods and resources than would occur without that intervention. Likewise, the government's failure to intervene in a market failure that would result in a socially preferable mix of output is referred to as passive _____ (Weimer and Vining, 2004.) Just as with market failures, there are many different kinds of _____ s that describe corresponding distortions.

a. Natural monopoly
b. Privatizing profits and socializing losses
c. Government-granted monopoly
d. Government failure

101. _____ is the socio-economic status of unfree peasants under feudalism, and specifically relates to Manorialism. It was a condition of bondage or modified slavery which developed primarily during the High Middle Ages in Europe. _____ was the enforced labour of serfs on the fields of landowners, in return for protection and the right to work on their leased fields.
   a. Metayage
   b. Landwirtschaftliche Produktionsgenossenschaft
   c. Rural tenancy
   d. Serfdom

102. _____ in political thought refers to economic theories of social organization advocating collective ownership and administration of the means of production and distribution of goods, and a society characterized by equality for all individuals, with an egalitarian method of compensation. Modern _____ originated in the late 19th-century intellectual and working class political movement that criticized the effects of industrialization and private ownership on society. Karl Marx posited that _____ would be achieved via class struggle and a proletarian revolution after a transitional stage from capitalism called the dictatorship of the proletariat.
   a. Socialism
   b. Adolph Fischer
   c. Adam Smith
   d. Adolf Hitler

Chapter 3. Basic Elements of Supply and Demand

1. In economics, _____ is the total demand for final goods and services in the economy (Y) at a given time and price level. It is the amount of goods and services in the economy that will be purchased at all possible price levels. This is the demand for the gross domestic product of a country when inventory levels are static.
   a. Aggregate expenditure
   b. Aggregate supply
   c. Aggregation problem
   d. Aggregate demand

2. In economics, _____ is the total supply of goods and services produced by a national economy during a specific time period. It is the total amount of goods and services in the economy available at all possible price levels.
   a. Aggregate expenditure
   b. Aggregate demand
   c. Aggregation problem
   d. Aggregate supply

3. _____ is a broad label that refers to any individuals or households that use goods and services generated within the economy. The concept of a _____ is used in different contexts, so that the usage and significance of the term may vary.

   Typically when business people and economists talk of _____s they are talking about person as _____, an aggregated commodity item with little individuality other than that expressed in the buy/not-buy decision.

   a. 100-year flood
   b. 1921 recession
   c. Consumer
   d. 130-30 fund

4. _____ is an economic concept with commonplace familiarity. It is the price that a good or service is offered at, or will fetch, in the marketplace. It is of interest mainly in the study of microeconomics.
   a. Market price
   b. Market anomaly
   c. Paper trading
   d. Noisy market hypothesis

5. _____ in economics and business is the result of an exchange and from that trade we assign a numerical monetary value to a good, service or asset. If Alice trades Bob 4 apples for an orange, the _____ of an orange is 4 apples. Inversely, the _____ of an apple is 1/4 oranges.
   a. Price
   b. Premium pricing
   c. Price book
   d. Price war

6. A _____ or market-based mechanism is any of a wide variety of ways to match up buyers and sellers.

   An example of a _____ uses announced bid and ask prices. Generally speaking, when two parties wish to engage in a trade, the purchaser will announce a price he is willing to pay (the bid price) and seller will announce a price he is willing to accept (the ask price.)

   a. Horizontal market
   b. Marketization
   c. Market equilibrium
   d. Price mechanism

7. _____ is an economic model based on price, utility and quantity in a market. It predicts that in a competitive market, price will function to equalize the quantity demanded by consumers, and the quantity supplied by producers, resulting in an economic equilibrium of price and quantity. The model incorporates other factors changing equilibrium as a shift of demand and/or supply.

a. Supply and demand
c. Joint demand
b. Rational addiction
d. Deferred gratification

8. Economics:

- _____, the desire to own something and the ability to pay for it
- _____ curve, a graphic representation of a _____ schedule
- _____ deposit, the money in checking accounts
- _____ pull theory, the theory that inflation occurs when _____ for goods and services exceeds existing supplies
- _____ schedule, a table that lists the quantity of a good a person will buy it each different price
- _____ side economics, the school of economics at believes government spending and tax cuts open economy by raising _____

a. Demand
c. McKesson ' Robbins scandal
b. Production
d. Variability

9. In microeconomics, _____ is quite simply the conversion of inputs into outputs. It is an economic process that uses resources to create a good or service that is suitable for exchange. This can include manufacturing, storing, shipping, and packaging.
   a. Solved
   c. MET
   b. Red Guards
   d. Production

10. _____ is a concept with somewhat disparate meanings in several fields. It also has a common meaning which has a loose connection with some of those more definite meanings.

Casually, it is typically used to denote a lack of order, or purpose, or cause.

   a. 130-30 fund
   c. 100-year flood
   b. 1921 recession
   d. Randomness

11. In economics, the _____ can be defined as the graph depicting the relationship between the price of a certain commodity, and the amount of it that consumers are willing and able to purchase at that given price. It is a graphic representation of a demand schedule. The _____ for all consumers together follows from the _____ of every individual consumer: the individual demands at each price are added together.
   a. Kuznets curve
   c. Wage curve
   b. Cost curve
   d. Demand curve

12. In economics, a _____ is a table that lists the quantity of a good a person will buy it each different price See Demand curve.
   a. Federal Reserve districts
   c. Rational irrationality
   b. Free contract
   d. Demand schedule

Chapter 3. Basic Elements of Supply and Demand   35

13. The _____ or gross domestic income (GDI), a basic measure of an economy's economic performance, is the market value of all final goods and services produced within the borders of a nation in a year. _____ can be defined in three ways, all of which are conceptually identical. First, it is equal to the total expenditures for all final goods and services produced within the country in a stipulated period of time (usually a 365-day year.)
 a. Countercyclical   b. Market structure
 c. Monopolistic competition   d. Gross Domestic Product

14. Necessary _____ s:

If x is a necessary _____ of y, then the presence of y necessarily implies the presence of x. The presence of x, however, does not imply that y will occur.

Sufficient _____ s:

If x is a sufficient _____ of y, then the presence of x necessarily implies the presence of y.

 a. Political philosophy   b. Philosophy of economics
 c. Cause   d. Materialism

15. A _____ is an object whose consumption increases the utility of the consumer, for which the quantity demanded exceeds the quantity supplied at zero price. _____s are usually modeled as having diminishing marginal utility. The first individual purchase has high utility; the second has less.
 a. Composite good   b. Pie method
 c. Merit good   d. Good

16. In economics, economic output is divided into physical goods and intangible services. Consumption of _____ is assumed to produce utility. It is often used when referring to a _____ Tax.
 a. Composite good   b. Manufactured goods
 c. Private good   d. Goods and services

17. In economics, the _____ is the change in consumption resulting from a change in real income.

Another important item that can change is the money income of the consumer. The _____ is the phenomenon observed through changes in purchasing power.

 a. Export subsidy   b. Equilibrium wage
 c. Inflation hedge   d. Income effect

18. _____ in economics refers to metrics and measures of output from production processes, per unit of input. Labor _____, for example, is typically measured as a ratio of output per labor-hour, an input. _____ may be conceived of as a metrics of the technical or engineering efficiency of production.
 a. Fordism   b. Production-possibility frontier
 c. Piece work   d. Productivity

Chapter 3. Basic Elements of Supply and Demand

19. In economics, the _____ measures the payments that flow between any individual country and all other countries. It is used to summarize all international economic transactions for that country during a specific time period, usually a year. The _____ is determined by the country's exports and imports of goods, services, and financial capital, as well as financial transfers.
    - a. Balance of payments
    - b. Gross world product
    - c. Gross domestic product per barrel
    - d. Skyscraper Index

20. A _____ is the transfer of wealth from one party (such as a person or company) to another. A _____ is usually made in exchange for the provision of goods, services or both, or to fulfill a legal obligation.

    The simplest and oldest form of _____ is barter, the exchange of one good or service for another.
    - a. Social gravity
    - b. Soft count
    - c. Going concern
    - d. Payment

21. In economics, _____ is the total amount of money available in an economy at a particular point in time. There are several ways to define 'money', but standard measures usually include currency in circulation and demand deposits.

    _____ data are recorded and published, usually by the government or the central bank of the country.
    - a. Neutrality of money
    - b. Money supply
    - c. Velocity of money
    - d. Veil of money

22. In economics, _____ refers to how the marginal contribution of a factor of production usually decreases as more of the factor is used. According to this relationship, in a production system with fixed and variable inputs, beyond some point, each additional unit of the variable input yields smaller and smaller increases in output. Conversely, producing one more unit of output costs more and more in variable inputs.
    - a. Derivatives law
    - b. Community property
    - c. Patent troll
    - d. Diminishing returns

23. _____ is the term denoting either an entrance or changes which are inserted into a system and which activate/modify a process. It is an abstract concept, used in the modeling, system(s) design and system(s) exploitation. It is usually connected with other terms, e.g., _____ field, _____ variable, _____ parameter, _____ value, _____ signal, _____ device and _____ file.
    - a. AD-IA Model
    - b. ACEA agreement
    - c. ACCRA Cost of Living Index
    - d. Input

24. _____ is a term that is used to describe the overall process of invention, innovation and diffusion of technology or processes. The term is redundant with technological development, technological achievement, and technological progress. In essence _____ is the invention of a technology (or a process), the continuous process of improving a technology (in which it often becomes cheaper) and its diffusion throughout industry or society.
    - a. 1921 recession
    - b. 130-30 fund
    - c. 100-year flood
    - d. Technological change

Chapter 3. Basic Elements of Supply and Demand

25. In algebra, a _____ is a function depending on n that associates a scalar, det(A), to an n×n square matrix A. The fundamental geometric meaning of a _____ is a scale factor for measure when A is regarded as a linear transformation. _____s are important both in calculus, where they enter the substitution rule for several variables, and in multilinear algebra.

For a fixed nonnegative integer n, there is a unique _____ function for the n×n matrices over any commutative ring R. In particular, this function exists when R is the field of real or complex numbers.

a. 100-year flood
b. 130-30 fund
c. 1921 recession
d. Determinant

26. In economics, economic equilibrium is simply a state of the world where economic forces are balanced and in the absence of external influences the (equilibrium) values of economic variables will not change. It is the point at which quantity demanded and quantity supplied are equal. _____, for example, refers to a condition where a market price is established through competition such that the amount of goods or services sought by buyers is equal to the amount of goods or services produced by sellers.

a. Product-Market Growth Matrix
b. Marketization
c. Market equilibrium
d. Regulated market

27. _____s is the social science that studies the production, distribution, and consumption of goods and services. The term _____s comes from the Ancient Greek oá¼°κονομῖα from oá¼¶κος (oikos, 'house') + vÏŒμος (nomos, 'custom' or 'law'), hence 'rules of the house(hold)'. Current _____ models developed out of the broader field of political economy in the late 19th century, owing to a desire to use an empirical approach more akin to the physical sciences.

a. Opportunity cost
b. Energy economics
c. Inflation
d. Economic

28. In economics, the term _____ of income or _____ refers to a simple economic model which describes the reciprocal circulation of income between producers and consumers. In the _____ model, the inter-dependent entities of producer and consumer are referred to as 'firms' and 'households' respectively and provide each other with factors in order to facilitate the flow of income. Firms provide consumers with goods and services in exchange for consumer expenditure and 'factors of production' from households.

a. 1921 recession
b. 100-year flood
c. Circular flow
d. 130-30 fund

29. _____ to the arrival of new individuals into a habitat or population. It is a biological concept and is important in population ecology, differentiated from emigration and migration.

_____ is a modern phenomenon.

a. ACEA agreement
b. AD-IA Model
c. ACCRA Cost of Living Index
d. Immigration

30. _____ is the increase in the amount of the goods and services produced by an economy over time. It is conventionally measured as the percent rate of increase in real gross domestic product, or real GDP. Growth is usually calculated in real terms, i.e. inflation-adjusted terms, in order to net out the effect of inflation on the price of the goods and services produced.

a. AD-IA Model
b. Economic growth
c. ACCRA Cost of Living Index
d. ACEA agreement

31. _____ is a term from economics referring to the use of money exchanged by buyers and sellers with an open and understood system of value and time trade offs to produce the best distribution of goods and services. The use of the _____ does not imply a free market: there can be captive or controlled markets which seek to use supply and demand, or some other form of charging for scarcity, both in social situations and in engineering.

The _____ assumes perfect competition and is regulated by demand and supply.

a. Market mechanism
b. Product-Market Growth Matrix
c. Two-sided markets
d. Partial equilibrium

32. _____ is the controlled distribution of resources and scarce goods or services. _____ controls the size of the ration, one's allotted portion of the resources being distributed on a particular day or at a particular time.

In economics, it is often common to use the word '_____' to refer to one of the roles that prices play in markets, while _____ is called 'non-price _____.' Using prices to ration means that those with the most money (or other assets) and who want a product the most are first to receive it.

a. Rationing
b. 130-30 fund
c. 1921 recession
d. 100-year flood

33. A _____ or directed economy is an economic system in which the government or workers' councils manages the economy. It is an economic system in which the central government makes all decisions on the production and consumption of goods and services. Its most extensive form is referred to as a _____, centrally planned economy, or command and control economy.

a. Command economy
b. Nutritional Economics
c. Transition economy
d. Subsistence economy

34. The _____, sometimes called the fundamental _____, is one of the fundamental economic theories in the operation of any economy. It asserts that there is scarcity, that the finite resources available are insufficient to satisfy all human wants. The problem then becomes how to determine what is to be produced and how the factors of production (such as capital and labour) are to be allocated.

a. Endogenous growth theory
b. Eclectic paradigm
c. Economic nationalism
d. Economic problem

Chapter 4. Overview of Macroeconomics

1. The term _____ refers to economy-wide fluctuations in production or economic activity over several months or years. These fluctuations occur around a long-term growth trend, and typically involve shifts over time between periods of relatively rapid economic growth (expansion or boom), and periods of relative stagnation or decline (contraction or recession.)

These fluctuations are often measured using the growth rate of real gross domestic product.

   a. Consumer theory
   b. Nominal value
   c. Business cycle
   d. Tobit model

2. The _____ was a worldwide economic downturn starting in most places in 1929 and ending at different times in the 1930s or early 1940s for different countries. It was the largest and most important economic depression in the 20th century, and is used in the 21st century as an example of how far the world's economy can fall. The _____ originated in the United States; historians most often use as a starting date the stock market crash on October 29, 1929, known as Black Tuesday.
   a. Great Depression
   b. British Empire Economic Conference
   c. Jarrow March
   d. Wall Street Crash of 1929

3. _____, 1st Baron Keynes was a renowned economist from Britain whose many ideas on economic and political theories as well as on many governments' monetary policies influenced America. He advocated a government that played an active role in the lives of people regarding business, economy, etc. In this role, the government would use fiscal measures to reduce the consequences of recessions, economic depressions and booms.
   a. Adam Smith
   b. Adolph Fischer
   c. Adolf Hitler
   d. John Maynard Keynes

4. _____ is a branch of economics that deals with the performance, structure, and behavior of a national or regional economy as a whole. Along with microeconomics, _____ is one of the two most general fields in economics. It is the study of the behavior and decision-making of entire economies.
   a. Tobit model
   b. Nominal value
   c. New Trade Theory
   d. Macroeconomics

5. _____ is a branch of economics that studies how individuals, households and firms and some states make decisions to allocate limited resources, typically in markets where goods or services are being bought and sold. _____ examines how these decisions and behaviours affect the supply and demand for goods and services, which determines prices; and how prices, in turn, determine the supply and demand of goods and services.

Whereas macroeconomics involves the 'sum total of economic activity, dealing with the issues of growth, inflation and unemployment, and with national economic policies relating to these issues' and the effects of government actions on them.

   a. Countercyclical
   b. New Keynesian economics
   c. Recession
   d. Microeconomics

Chapter 4. Overview of Macroeconomics

6. _____ is an economic situation in which inflation and economic stagnation occur simultaneously and remain unchecked for a period of time. The portmanteau _____ is generally attributed to British politician Iain Macleod, who coined the term in a speech to Parliament in 1965. The concept is notable partly because, in postwar macroeconomic theory, inflation and recession were regarded as mutually exclusive, and also because _____ has generally proven to be difficult and costly to eradicate once it gets started.
   a. Real interest rate
   b. Stagflation
   c. Price/wage spiral
   d. Chronic inflation

7. _____ are the inflation-indexed bonds issued by the U.S. Treasury. The principal is adjusted to the Consumer Price Index, the commonly used measure of inflation. The coupon rate is constant, but generates a different amount of interest when multiplied by the inflation-adjusted principal, thus protecting the holder against inflation.
   a. 100-year flood
   b. 130-30 fund
   c. 1921 recession
   d. Treasury Inflation-Protected Securities

8. The _____ is an economic and political union of 27 member states, located primarily in Europe. It was established by the Treaty of Maastricht on 1 November 1993, upon the foundations of the pre-existing European Economic Community. With a population of almost 500 million, the _____ generates an estimated 30% share (US$18.4 trillion in 2008) of the nominal gross world product.
   a. European Union
   b. ACEA agreement
   c. ACCRA Cost of Living Index
   d. European Court of Justice

9. The _____ or gross domestic income (GDI), a basic measure of an economy's economic performance, is the market value of all final goods and services produced within the borders of a nation in a year. _____ can be defined in three ways, all of which are conceptually identical. First, it is equal to the total expenditures for all final goods and services produced within the country in a stipulated period of time (usually a 365-day year.)
   a. Monopolistic competition
   b. Countercyclical
   c. Market structure
   d. Gross domestic product

10. _____ in economics and business is the result of an exchange and from that trade we assign a numerical monetary value to a good, service or asset. If Alice trades Bob 4 apples for an orange, the _____ of an orange is 4 apples. Inversely, the _____ of an apple is 1/4 oranges.
    a. Premium pricing
    b. Price
    c. Price book
    d. Price war

11. In economics, _____ is a rise in the general level of prices of goods and services in an economy over a period of time. When the general price level rises, each unit of currency buys fewer goods and services; consequently, _____ is also a decline in the real value of money--a loss of purchasing power in the medium of exchange which is also the monetary unit of account in the economy. A chief measure of general price-level _____ is the general _____ rate, which is the percentage change in a general price index (normally the Consumer Price Index) over time.
    a. Energy economics
    b. Inflation
    c. Opportunity cost
    d. Economic

12. _____ refers to a business or organization attempting to acquire goods or services to accomplish the goals of the enterprise. Though there are several organizations that attempt to set standards in the _____ process, processes can vary greatly between organizations. Typically the word '_____' is not used interchangeably with the word 'procurement', since procurement typically includes Expediting, Supplier Quality, and Traffic and Logistics (T'L) in addition to _____.

a. 100-year flood
b. 130-30 fund
c. Free port
d. Purchasing

13. Unemployment occurs when a person is available to work and seeking work but currently without work. The prevalence of unemployment is usually measured using the _____, which is defined as the percentage of those in the labor force who are unemployed. The _____ is also used in economic studies and economic indexes such as the United States' Conference Board's Index of Leading Indicators as a measure of the state of the macroeconomics.
   a. ACCRA Cost of Living Index
   b. AD-IA Model
   c. Unemployment rate
   d. ACEA agreement

14. The _____ is the central banking system of the United States. Created in 1913 by the enactment of the Federal Reserve Act (signed by Woodrow Wilson), it is a quasi-public and quasi-private (government entity with private components) banking system that comprises (1) the presidentially appointed Board of Governors of the _____ in Washington, D.C.; (2) the Federal Open Market Committee; (3) twelve regional Federal Reserve Banks located in major cities throughout the nation acting as fiscal agents for the U.S. Treasury, each with its own nine-member board of directors; (4) numerous other private U.S. member banks, which subscribe to required amounts of non-transferable stock in their regional Federal Reserve Banks; and (5) various advisory councils. Since February 2006, Ben Bernanke has served as the Chairman of the Board of Governors of the _____.
   a. Monetary Policy Report to the Congress
   b. Term auction facility
   c. Federal Reserve System Open Market Account
   d. Federal Reserve System

15. The _____ was written by the English economist John Maynard Keynes. The book, generally considered to be his magnum opus, is largely credited with creating the terminology and shape of modern macroeconomics. Published in February 1936 it sought to bring about a revolution, commonly referred to as the 'Keynesian Revolution', in the way economists thought - especially in relation to the proposition that a market economy tends naturally to restore itself to full employment after temporary shocks.
   a. Black Book of Communism
   b. The General Theory of Employment, Interest and Money
   c. General Theory of Employment, Interest and Money
   d. Human Action

16. _____ is a fee paid on borrowed assets. It is the price paid for the use of borrowed money, or, money earned by deposited funds. Assets that are sometimes lent with _____ include money, shares, consumer goods through hire purchase, major assets such as aircraft, and even entire factories in finance lease arrangements.
   a. Insolvency
   b. Asset protection
   c. Interest
   d. Internal debt

17. _____ and Keynesian Theory) is a macroeconomic theory based on the ideas of 20th-century British economist John Maynard Keynes. _____ argues that private sector decisions sometimes lead to inefficient macroeconomic outcomes and therefore advocates active policy responses by the public sector, including monetary policy actions by the central bank and fiscal policy actions by the government to stabilize output over the business cycle.

The theories forming the basis of _____ were first presented in The General Theory of Employment, Interest and Money, published in 1936.

a. Keynesian economics
b. Market failure
c. Deflation
d. Rational choice theory

18. A _____ is a situation that involves losing one quality or aspect of something in return for gaining another quality or aspect. It implies a decision to be made with full comprehension of both the upside and downside of a particular choice.

In economics the term is expressed as opportunity cost, referring the most preferred alternative given up.

a. Trade-off
b. Friedman-Savage utility function
c. Nonmarket
d. Whitemail

19. _____s is the social science that studies the production, distribution, and consumption of goods and services. The term _____s comes from the Ancient Greek οἰκονομία from οἶκος (oikos, 'house') + νόμος (nomos, 'custom' or 'law'), hence 'rules of the house(hold)'. Current _____ models developed out of the broader field of political economy in the late 19th century, owing to a desire to use an empirical approach more akin to the physical sciences.

a. Energy economics
b. Inflation
c. Economic
d. Opportunity cost

20. _____ is the increase in the amount of the goods and services produced by an economy over time. It is conventionally measured as the percent rate of increase in real gross domestic product, or real GDP. Growth is usually calculated in real terms, i.e. inflation-adjusted terms, in order to net out the effect of inflation on the price of the goods and services produced.

a. AD-IA Model
b. ACCRA Cost of Living Index
c. ACEA agreement
d. Economic growth

21. An _____, in economics, is the amount by which the real Gross domestic product exceeds potential GDP. The real GDP is also known as GDP 'adjusted for inflation', 'constant prices' GDP or 'constant dollar' GDP, because it measures the aggregate output in a country's income accounts in a given year, expressed in base-year prices. On the other hand, the potential GDP is the quantity of real GDP when a country's economy is at full-employment.

a. AD-IA Model
b. ACCRA Cost of Living Index
c. Inflationary gap
d. ACEA agreement

22. In economics, the people in the _____ are the suppliers of labor. The _____ is all the nonmilitary people who are employed or unemployed. In 2005, the worldwide _____ was over 3 billion people.

a. Distributed workforce
b. Departmentalization
c. Grenelle agreements
d. Labor force

23. _____ is a misspelled phrase from Latin 'pro capite' phrase meaning per head with pro meaning 'per' or 'for each' and capite meaning 'head.' Both words together equate to the phrase 'for each head.'

It is usually used in the field of statistics to indicate the average per person for any given concern, such as income, crime rate, etc.

It is also used in wills to indicate that each of the named beneficiaries should receive, by devise or bequest, equal shares of the estate. This is in contrast to a per stirpes division, in which each branch of the inheriting family inherits an equal share of the estate.

Chapter 4. Overview of Macroeconomics

a. Sargan test
b. Population statistics
c. Per capita
d. False positive rate

24. In economics, a _____ is a general slowdown in economic activity over a sustained period of time, or a business cycle contraction. During _____s, many macroeconomic indicators vary in a similar way. Production as measured by Gross Domestic Product (GDP), employment, investment spending, capacity utilization, household incomes and business profits all fall during _____s.
a. Recession
b. Leading indicators
c. Monetary economics
d. Treasury View

25. In economics, the _____ is a measure of inflation, the rate of increase of a price index (for example, a consumer price index.)It is the percentage rate of change in price level over time. The rate of decrease in the purchasing power of money is approximately equal.

It's used to calculate the real interest rate, as well as real increases in wages, and official measurements of this rate act as input variables to COLA adjustments and Inflation derivatives prices.

a. Equity value
b. Interest rate option
c. Inflation rate
d. Edgeworth paradox

26. _____ is a broad label that refers to any individuals or households that use goods and services generated within the economy. The concept of a _____ is used in different contexts, so that the usage and significance of the term may vary.

Typically when business people and economists talk of _____s they are talking about person as _____, an aggregated commodity item with little individuality other than that expressed in the buy/not-buy decision.

a. 1921 recession
b. 100-year flood
c. 130-30 fund
d. Consumer

27. A _____ is a measure of the average price of consumer goods and services purchased by households. A _____ measures a price change for a constant market basket of goods and services from one period to the next within the same area (city, region, or nation.) It is a price index determined by measuring the price of a standard group of goods meant to represent the typical market basket of a typical urban consumer.
a. Lipstick index
b. CPI
c. Cost-of-living index
d. Consumer price index

28. A _____ is a normalized average (typically a weighted average) of prices for a given class of goods or services in a given region, during a given interval of time. It is a statistic designed to help to compare how these prices, taken as a whole, differ between time periods or geographical locations.

Price indices have several potential uses.

a. Transactional Net Margin Method
c. Product sabotage
b. Two-part tariff
d. Price index

29. In economics, the _____ measures the payments that flow between any individual country and all other countries. It is used to summarize all international economic transactions for that country during a specific time period, usually a year. The _____ is determined by the country's exports and imports of goods, services, and financial capital, as well as financial transfers.
   a. Balance of payments
   c. Gross world product
   b. Gross domestic product per barrel
   d. Skyscraper Index

30. A _____ is the transfer of wealth from one party (such as a person or company) to another. A _____ is usually made in exchange for the provision of goods, services or both, or to fulfill a legal obligation.

The simplest and oldest form of _____ is barter, the exchange of one good or service for another.

   a. Going concern
   c. Social gravity
   b. Soft count
   d. Payment

31. In economics, _____ is a sustained decrease in the general price level of goods and services. _____ occurs when the annual inflation rate falls below zero percent, resulting in an increase in the real value of money -- a negative inflation rate. This should not be confused with disinflation, a slow-down in the inflation rate (i.e. when the inflation decreases, but still remains positive.)
   a. Deflation
   c. Price revolution
   b. Tobit model
   d. Literacy rate

32. In economics, _____ is inflation that is very high or 'out of control', a condition in which prices increase rapidly as a currency loses its value. Definitions used by the media vary from a cumulative inflation rate over three years approaching 100% to 'inflation exceeding 50% a month.' In informal usage the term is often applied to much lower rates. As a rule of thumb, normal inflation is reported per year, but _____ is often reported for much shorter intervals, often per month.
   a. Hyperinflation
   c. 1921 recession
   b. 100-year flood
   d. 130-30 fund

33. A _____ is an economy based on the division of labor in which the prices of goods and services are determined in a free price system set by supply and demand. This is often contrasted with a planned economy, in which a central government determines the price of goods and services using a fixed price system. Market economies are contrasted with mixed economy where the price system is not entirely free but under some government control that is not extensive enough to constitute a planned economy.
   a. Commons-based peer production
   c. Network Economy
   b. Nutritional Economics
   d. Market economy

34. A _____, reserve bank, or monetary authority is the entity responsible for the monetary policy of a country or of a group of member states. It is a bank that can lend money to other banks in times of need. Its primary responsibility is to maintain the stability of the national currency and money supply, but more active duties include controlling subsidized-loan interest rates, and acting as a lender of last resort to the banking sector during times of financial crisis (private banks often being integral to the national financial system.)

Chapter 4. Overview of Macroeconomics

a. 100-year flood
b. 130-30 fund
c. 1921 recession
d. Central bank

35. The term _____ is applied broadly to a variety of situations in which some financial institutions or assets suddenly lose a large part of their value. In the 19th and early 20th centuries, many financial crises were associated with banking panics, and many recessions coincided with these panics. Other situations that are often called financial crises include stock market crashes and the bursting of other financial bubbles, currency crises, and sovereign defaults.

a. Macroeconomics
b. Co-operative economics
c. Market failure
d. Financial crisis

36. The term _____ refers to government debt, expenditures and revenues, or to finance (particularly financial revenue) in general.

- _____ deficit is the budget deficit of federal or local government
- _____ policy is the discretionary spending of governments. Contrasts with monetary policy.
- _____ year and _____ quarter are reporting periods for firms and other agencies.

a. Procter ' Gamble
b. Bucket shop
c. Drawdown
d. Fiscal

37. In economics, _____ is the use of government spending and revenue collection to influence the economy.

_____ can be contrasted with the other main type of economic policy, monetary policy, which attempts to stabilize the economy by controlling interest rates and the supply of money. The two main instruments of _____ are government spending and taxation.

a. Fiscalism
b. Sustainable investment rule
c. Fiscal policy
d. 100-year flood

38. In economics, a _____ is a redistribution of income in the market system. These payments are considered to be nonexhaustive because they do not directly absorb resources or create output. Examples of certain _____ s include welfare (financial aid), social security, and government subsidies for certain businesses (firms.)

a. Transfer payment
b. 1921 recession
c. 130-30 fund
d. 100-year flood

46 *Chapter 4. Overview of Macroeconomics*

39. A _____ is:

- Rewrite _____, in generative grammar and computer science
- Standardization, a formal and widely-accepted statement, fact, definition, or qualification
- Operation, a determinate _____ for performing a mathematical operation and obtaining a certain result (Mathematics, Logic)
    - Unary operation
    - Binary operation
- _____ of inference, a function from sets of formulae to formulae (Mathematics, Logic)
- _____ of thumb, principle with broad application that is not intended to be strictly accurate or reliable for every situation. Also often simply referred to as a _____
- Moral, an atomic element of a moral code for guiding choices in human behavior
- Heuristic, a quantized '_____' which shows a tendency or probability for successful function
- A regulation, as in sports
- A Production _____, as in computer science
- Procedural law, a _____ set governing the application of laws to cases
    - A law, which may informally be called a '_____'
    - A court ruling, a decision by a court
- In the U.S. Government, a regulation mandated by Congress, but written or expanded upon by the Executive Branch.
- Norm (sociology), an informal but widely accepted _____, concept, truth, definition, or qualification (social norms, legal norms, coding norms)
- Norm (philosophy), a kind of sentence or a reason to act, feel or believe
- 'Rulership' is the concept of governance by a government:
    - Military _____, governance by a military body
    - Monastic _____, a collection of precepts that guides the life of monks or nuns in a religious order where the superior holds the place of Christ
- Slide _____

- '_____,' a song by Ayumi Hamasaki
- '_____,' a song by rapper Nas
- '_____s,' an album by the band The Whitest Boy Alive
- _____s: Pyaar Ka Superhit Formula, a 2003 Bollywood film
- ruler, an instrument for measuring lengths
- _____, a component of an astrolabe, circumferator or similar instrument
- The _____s, a bestselling self-help book
- _____ Project (Run Up-to-date Linux Everywhere), a project that aims to use up-to-date Linux software on old PCs
- _____ engine, a software system that helps managing business _____s
- Ja _____, a hip hop artist
    - R.U.L.E., a 2005 greatest hits album by rapper Ja _____
- '_____s,' a KMFDM song

a. Technocracy
c. Demand

b. Procter ' Gamble
d. Rule

Chapter 4. Overview of Macroeconomics

40. _____ is the process by which the government, central bank (ii) availability of money, and (iii) cost of money or rate of interest, in order to attain a set of objectives oriented towards the growth and stability of the economy. Monetary theory provides insight into how to craft optimal _____.

_____ is referred to as either being an expansionary policy where an expansionary policy increases the total supply of money in the economy, and a contractionary policy decreases the total money supply.

a. 1921 recession
b. 130-30 fund
c. Monetary policy
d. 100-year flood

41. In economics, _____ is the total amount of money available in an economy at a particular point in time. There are several ways to define 'money', but standard measures usually include currency in circulation and demand deposits.

_____ data are recorded and published, usually by the government or the central bank of the country.

a. Money supply
b. Veil of money
c. Velocity of money
d. Neutrality of money

42. A _____ refers to any type debt instrument, such as a loan, bond, mortgage that does not have a fixed rate of interest over the life of the instrument. Such debt typically uses an index or other base rate for establishing the interest rate for each relevant period. One of the most common rates to use as the basis for applying interest rates is the London Inter-bank Offered Rate, or LIBOR

a. Disposal tax effect
b. Floating interest rate
c. Moneylender
d. Money market

43. _____ in economics are wage and price controls, most commonly instituted as a response to inflation, and usually below market level.

This type of policy dates to the Old Testament, in which Israelites were instructed not to charge interest to other Israelites. It was tried during the Roman Empire.

a. Inflation swap
b. Inflationary Spikes
c. Incomes policies
d. Employment Cost Index

44. To _____ is to impose a financial charge or other levy upon a taxpayer by a state or the functional equivalent of a state.

_____es are also imposed by many subnational entities. _____es consist of direct _____ or indirect _____, and may be paid in money or as its labour equivalent (often but not always unpaid.)

a. 130-30 fund
b. 100-year flood
c. 1921 recession
d. Tax

45. The term _____ describes two different concepts:

- The first is a recognition of partial payment already made towards taxes due.
- The second is a state benefit paid to workers through the tax system, which has the effect of increasing (rather than reducing) net income.

Within the Australian, Canadian, United Kingdom, and United States tax systems, a _____ is a recognition of partial payment already made towards taxes due. A similar concept exists (fr:Avoir fiscal) in the French tax system. This situation arises, for example, when standard rate tax has been deducted at source , but the tax-payer is subject to further taxation at a higher rate. It also applies in dividend imputation systems.

a. 130-30 fund
b. 100-year flood
c. 1921 recession
d. Tax credit

46. The _____ is where currency trading takes place. It is where banks and other official institutions facilitate the buying and selling of foreign currencies. FX transactions typically involve one party purchasing a quantity of one currency in exchange for paying a quantity of another.

a. Currency swap
b. Covered interest arbitrage
c. Foreign exchange market
d. Floating currency

47. _____ in its literal sense is the process of transformation of local or regional phenomena into global ones. It can be described as a process by which the people of the world are unified into a single society and function together.

This process is a combination of economic, technological, sociocultural and political forces.

a. Globally Integrated Enterprise
b. Global Cosmopolitanism
c. Globalization
d. Helsinki Process on Globalisation and Democracy

48. The balance of trade (or net exports, sometimes symbolized as NX) is the difference between the monetary value of exports and imports in an economy over a certain period of time. It is the relationship between a nation's imports and exports. A favorable balance of trade is known as a trade surplus and consists of exporting more than is imported; an unfavorable balance of trade is known as a _____ or, informally, a trade gap.

a. Computational economic
b. Demographics of India
c. Complementary asset
d. Trade deficit

49. _____ is widely regarded as the first modern school of economic thought. It is the idea that free markets can regulate themselves.Its major developers include Adam Smith, David Ricardo, Thomas Malthus and John Stuart Mill. Sometimes the definition of _____ is expanded to include William Petty, Johann Heinrich von Thünen.

a. Schools of economic thought
b. Classical economics
c. Marginalism
d. Tendency of the rate of profit to fall

50. _____ is a term used in economics to describe how an economic quantity is related to economic fluctuations. It is the opposite of procyclical. However, it has more than one meaning.

a. Price revolution
b. Countercyclical
c. Law of comparative advantage
d. Mathematical economics

Chapter 4. Overview of Macroeconomics

51. _____ is that which is owed; usually referencing assets owed, but the term can also cover moral obligations and other interactions not requiring money. In the case of assets, _____ is a means of using future purchasing power in the present before a summation has been earned. Some companies and corporations use _____ as a part of their overall corporate finance strategy.
   a. Debenture
   b. Hard money loan
   c. Collateral Management
   d. Debt

52. _____ refers to the actions that governments take in the economic field. It covers the systems for setting interest rates and government deficit as well as the labour market, national ownership, and many other areas of government.

Such policies are often influenced by international institutions like the International Monetary Fund or World Bank as well as political beliefs and the consequent policies of parties.

   a. ACEA agreement
   b. ACCRA Cost of Living Index
   c. AD-IA Model
   d. Economic policy

53. In economics, an _____ is any good or commodity, transported from one country to another country in a legitimate fashion, typically for use in trade. _____ goods or services are provided to foreign consumers by domestic producers. _____ is an important part of international trade.
   a. ACEA agreement
   b. ACCRA Cost of Living Index
   c. AD-IA Model
   d. Export

54. _____ is that part of the total debt in a country that is owed to creditors outside the country. The debtors can be the government, corporations or private households. The debt includes money owed to private commercial banks, other governments, or international financial institutions such as the IMF and World Bank.
   a. International debt collection
   b. Asset protection
   c. Internal debt
   d. External debt

55. In economics, _____ is the total demand for final goods and services in the economy (Y) at a given time and price level. It is the amount of goods and services in the economy that will be purchased at all possible price levels. This is the demand for the gross domestic product of a country when inventory levels are static.
   a. Aggregate demand
   b. Aggregation problem
   c. Aggregate expenditure
   d. Aggregate supply

56. In economics, _____ is the total supply of goods and services produced by a national economy during a specific time period. It is the total amount of goods and services in the economy available at all possible price levels.
   a. Aggregate demand
   b. Aggregate expenditure
   c. Aggregation problem
   d. Aggregate supply

57. Economics:

- _____, the desire to own something and the ability to pay for it
- _____ curve, a graphic representation of a _____ schedule
- _____ deposit, the money in checking accounts
- _____ pull theory, the theory that inflation occurs when _____ for goods and services exceeds existing supplies
- _____ schedule, a table that lists the quantity of a good a person will buy it each different price
- _____ side economics, the school of economics at believes government spending and tax cuts open economy by raising _____

a. Demand
b. McKesson ' Robbins scandal
c. Production
d. Variability

58. In economics, _____ refers to the highest level of real Gross Domestic Product output that can be sustained over the long term. The existence of a limit is due to natural and institutional constraints. If actual GDP rises and stays above _____, then (in the absence of wage and price controls) inflation tends to increase as demand exceeds supply.

a. Potential output
b. Fundamental psychological law
c. Monetary policy reaction function
d. Monetary conditions index

59. A _____ is a hypothetical measure of overall prices for some set of goods and services, in a given region during a given interval, normalized relative to some base set. Typically, a _____ is approximated with a price index.

The classical dichotomy is the assumption that there is a relatively clean distinction between overall increases or decreases in prices and underlying, e;reale; economic variables.

a. Price level
b. Discretionary spending
c. Discouraged worker
d. Price elasticity of supply

60. In economics, the _____ can be defined as the graph depicting the relationship between the price of a certain commodity, and the amount of it that consumers are willing and able to purchase at that given price. It is a graphic representation of a demand schedule. The _____ for all consumers together follows from the _____ of every individual consumer: the individual demands at each price are added together.

a. Cost curve
b. Wage curve
c. Demand curve
d. Kuznets curve

61. In economics, a _____ is a table that lists the quantity of a good a person will buy it each different price See Demand curve.

a. Rational irrationality
b. Federal Reserve districts
c. Free contract
d. Demand schedule

Chapter 4. Overview of Macroeconomics

62. In economics, economic equilibrium is simply a state of the world where economic forces are balanced and in the absence of external influences the (equilibrium) values of economic variables will not change. It is the point at which quantity demanded and quantity supplied are equal. _____, for example, refers to a condition where a market price is established through competition such that the amount of goods or services sought by buyers is equal to the amount of goods or services produced by sellers.
   a. Regulated market
   b. Market equilibrium
   c. Product-Market Growth Matrix
   d. Marketization

63. _____ is an economic concept with commonplace familiarity. It is the price that a good or service is offered at, or will fetch, in the marketplace. It is of interest mainly in the study of microeconomics.
   a. Noisy market hypothesis
   b. Market anomaly
   c. Paper trading
   d. Market price

64. _____ is an economic model based on price, utility and quantity in a market. It predicts that in a competitive market, price will function to equalize the quantity demanded by consumers, and the quantity supplied by producers, resulting in an economic equilibrium of price and quantity. The model incorporates other factors changing equilibrium as a shift of demand and/or supply.
   a. Deferred gratification
   b. Rational addiction
   c. Supply and demand
   d. Joint demand

65. _____ is the a method of technical and economic research of the systems for purpose to optimize a parity between system's consumer functions or properties and expenses to achieve those functions or properties.

This methodology for continuous perfection of production, industrial technologies, organizational structures was developed by Juryj Sobolev in 1948 at the 'Perm telephone factory'

- 1948 Juryj Sobolev - the first success in application of a method analysis at the 'Perm telephone factory' .
- 1949 - the first application for the invention as result of use of the new method.

Today in economically developed countries practically each enterprise or the company use methodology of the kind of functional-cost analysis as a practice of the quality management, most full satisfying to principles of standards of series ISO 9000.

- Interest of consumer not in products itself, but the advantage which it will receive from its usage.
- The consumer aspires to reduce his expenses
- Functions needed by consumer can be executed in the various ways, and, hence, with various efficiency and expenses. Among possible alternatives of realization of functions exist such in which the parity of quality and the price is the optimal for the consumer.

The goal of _____ is achievement of the highest consumer satisfaction of production at simultaneous decrease in all kinds of industrial expenses Classical _____ has three English synonyms - Value Engineering, Value Management, Value Analysis.

a. Willingness to pay
b. Monopoly wage
c. Function cost analysis
d. Staple financing

66. An _____ is the price a borrower pays for the use of money they do not own, for instance a small company might borrow from a bank to kick start their business, and the return a lender receives for deferring the use of funds, by lending it to the borrower. _____s are normally expressed as a percentage rate over the period of one year.

_____s targets are also a vital tool of monetary policy and are used to control variables like investment, inflation, and unemployment.

a. ACCRA Cost of Living Index
b. Enterprise value
c. Arrow-Debreu model
d. Interest rate

67. _____ is a common concept in economics, and gives rise to derived concepts such as consumer debt. Generally _____ is defined by opposition to production. But the precise definition can vary because different schools of economists define production quite differently.
a. Federal Reserve Bank Notes
b. Foreclosure data providers
c. Cash or share options
d. Consumption

68. In microeconomics, _____ is quite simply the conversion of inputs into outputs. It is an economic process that uses resources to create a good or service that is suitable for exchange. This can include manufacturing, storing, shipping, and packaging.
a. MET
b. Solved
c. Red Guards
d. Production

69. A _____ occurs when an entity spends more money than it takes in. The opposite of a _____ is a budget surplus. Debt is essentially an accumulated flow of deficits.
a. Lump-sum tax
b. Funding body
c. Public Financial Management
d. Budget deficit

70. A _____ is a situation in which the government takes in more than it spends.
a. 130-30 fund
b. Budget set
c. Budget surplus
d. 100-year flood

71. _____, or a _____ is the concept of a resulting effect (cf. cause and effect, arising from another action. In general terms, it is used to indicate that all human actions, particularly crime and sin, have profound effects.
a. Consequence
b. Rule
c. Solved
d. Variability

Chapter 5. Measuring Economic Activity

1. The _____ or gross domestic income (GDI), a basic measure of an economy's economic performance, is the market value of all final goods and services produced within the borders of a nation in a year. _____ can be defined in three ways, all of which are conceptually identical. First, it is equal to the total expenditures for all final goods and services produced within the country in a stipulated period of time (usually a 365-day year.)
   a. Countercyclical
   b. Market structure
   c. Monopolistic competition
   d. Gross domestic product

2. The _____ was a worldwide economic downturn starting in most places in 1929 and ending at different times in the 1930s or early 1940s for different countries. It was the largest and most important economic depression in the 20th century, and is used in the 21st century as an example of how far the world's economy can fall. The _____ originated in the United States; historians most often use as a starting date the stock market crash on October 29, 1929, known as Black Tuesday.
   a. Wall Street Crash of 1929
   b. British Empire Economic Conference
   c. Jarrow March
   d. Great Depression

3. A variety of measures of _____ and output are used in economics to estimate total economic activity in a country or region, including gross domestic product (GDP), gross national product (GNP), and net _____

   There are three main ways of calculating these numbers; the output approach, the income approach and the expenditure approach. In theory, the three must yield the same, because total expenditures on goods and services must equal the total income paid to the producers (Gnational income), and that must also equal the total value of the output of goods and services (GNP.)

   a. Volume index
   b. National income
   c. Gross world product
   d. GNI per capita

4. _____ use double-entry accounting to report the monetary value and sources of output produced in a country and the distribution of incomes that production generates. Data are available at the national and industry levels.

   The NIPA summarizes national income on the left (debit, revenue) side and national product on the right (credit, expense) side of a two-column accounting report.

   a. Gross private domestic investment
   b. Current account
   c. Net national product
   d. National income and product accounts

5. _____ is a misspelled phrase from Latin 'pro capite' phrase meaning per head with pro meaning 'per' or 'for each' and capite meaning 'head.' Both words together equate to the phrase 'for each head.'

   It is usually used in the field of statistics to indicate the average per person for any given concern, such as income, crime rate, etc.

   It is also used in wills to indicate that each of the named beneficiaries should receive, by devise or bequest, equal shares of the estate. This is in contrast to a per stirpes division, in which each branch of the inheriting family inherits an equal share of the estate.

Chapter 5. Measuring Economic Activity

a. Sargan test
b. Population statistics
c. False positive rate
d. Per capita

6. An _____, in economics, is the amount by which the real Gross domestic product exceeds potential GDP. The real GDP is also known as GDP 'adjusted for inflation', 'constant prices' GDP or 'constant dollar' GDP, because it measures the aggregate output in a country's income accounts in a given year, expressed in base-year prices. On the other hand, the potential GDP is the quantity of real GDP when a country's economy is at full-employment.
   a. ACCRA Cost of Living Index
   b. ACEA agreement
   c. AD-IA Model
   d. Inflationary gap

7. _____ is a branch of economics that deals with the performance, structure, and behavior of a national or regional economy as a whole. Along with microeconomics, _____ is one of the two most general fields in economics. It is the study of the behavior and decision-making of entire economies.
   a. New Trade Theory
   b. Macroeconomics
   c. Tobit model
   d. Nominal value

8. In economics, the term _____ of income or _____ refers to a simple economic model which describes the reciprocal circulation of income between producers and consumers. In the _____ model, the inter-dependent entities of producer and consumer are referred to as 'firms' and 'households' respectively and provide each other with factors in order to facilitate the flow of income. Firms provide consumers with goods and services in exchange for consumer expenditure and 'factors of production' from households.
   a. 1921 recession
   b. Circular flow
   c. 100-year flood
   d. 130-30 fund

9. _____ is a specific term used in companies' financial reporting from the company-whole point of view. Because that use excludes the effects of changing ownership interest, an economic measure of _____ is necessary for financial analysis from the shareholders' point of view

_____ is defined by the Financial Accounting Standards Board, or FASB, as e;the change in equity [net assets] of a business enterprise during a period from transactions and other events and circumstances from nonowner sources. It includes all changes in equity during a period except those resulting from investments by owners and distributions to owners.e;

_____ is the sum of net income and other items that must bypass the income statement because they have not been realized, including items like an unrealized holding gain or loss from available for sale securities and foreign currency translation gains or losses.

   a. Net national income
   b. Real income
   c. Windfall gain
   d. Comprehensive income

10. A _____ is an object whose consumption increases the utility of the consumer, for which the quantity demanded exceeds the quantity supplied at zero price. _____s are usually modeled as having diminishing marginal utility. The first individual purchase has high utility; the second has less.
    a. Merit good
    b. Pie method
    c. Composite good
    d. Good

Chapter 5. Measuring Economic Activity

11. _____ is a common concept in economics, and gives rise to derived concepts such as consumer debt. Generally _____ is defined by opposition to production. But the precise definition can vary because different schools of economists define production quite differently.

   a. Consumption
   b. Foreclosure data providers
   c. Federal Reserve Bank Notes
   d. Cash or share options

12. _____ are the prices that the factors of production of a finished item attract.

   There has been some economic debate as to what determines these prices. Classical and Marxist economists argued that the _____ decided the value of a product and so value was intrinsic within the product.

   a. Marginal product of labor
   b. Marginal product
   c. Productivity model
   d. Factor prices

13. In economics _____s are goods that are ultimately consumed rather than used in the production of another good. For example, a car sold to a consumer is a _____; the components such as tires sold to the car manufacturer are not; they are intermediate goods used to make the _____.

   When used in measures of national income and output the term _____s only includes new goods.

   a. Luxury good
   b. Substitute good
   c. Goods and services
   d. Final good

14. In economics, economic output is divided into physical goods and intangible services. Consumption of _____ is assumed to produce utility. It is often used when referring to a _____ Tax.

   a. Goods and services
   b. Private good
   c. Manufactured goods
   d. Composite good

15. _____ is a theory of aesthetics based on the theories of Karl Marx. It involves a dialectical approach to the application of Marxism to the cultural sphere, specifically areas related to taste such as art, beauty, etc. Marxists believe that economic and social conditions affect every aspect of an individual's life, from religious beliefs to legal systems to cultural frameworks.

   a. 1921 recession
   b. Marxist aesthetics
   c. 130-30 fund
   d. 100-year flood

16. _____ in economics and business is the result of an exchange and from that trade we assign a numerical monetary value to a good, service or asset. If Alice trades Bob 4 apples for an orange, the _____ of an orange is 4 apples. Inversely, the _____ of an apple is 1/4 oranges.

   a. Premium pricing
   b. Price book
   c. Price
   d. Price war

17. In microeconomics, _____ is quite simply the conversion of inputs into outputs. It is an economic process that uses resources to create a good or service that is suitable for exchange. This can include manufacturing, storing, shipping, and packaging.

a. MET
b. Solved
c. Red Guards
d. Production

18. _____ in economics refers to metrics and measures of output from production processes, per unit of input. Labor _____, for example, is typically measured as a ratio of output per labor-hour, an input. _____ may be conceived of as a metrics of the technical or engineering efficiency of production.
   a. Production-possibility frontier
   b. Fordism
   c. Piece work
   d. Productivity

19. _____ is the a method of technical and economic research of the systems for purpose to optimize a parity between system's consumer functions or properties and expenses to achieve those functions or properties.

This methodology for continuous perfection of production, industrial technologies, organizational structures was developed by Juryj Sobolev in 1948 at the 'Perm telephone factory'

- 1948 Juryj Sobolev - the first success in application of a method analysis at the 'Perm telephone factory'.
- 1949 - the first application for the invention as result of use of the new method.

Today in economically developed countries practically each enterprise or the company use methodology of the kind of functional-cost analysis as a practice of the quality management, most full satisfying to principles of standards of series ISO 9000.

- Interest of consumer not in products itself, but the advantage which it will receive from its usage.
- The consumer aspires to reduce his expenses
- Functions needed by consumer can be executed in the various ways, and, hence, with various efficiency and expenses. Among possible alternatives of realization of functions exist such in which the parity of quality and the price is the optimal for the consumer.

The goal of _____ is achievement of the highest consumer satisfaction of production at simultaneous decrease in all kinds of industrial expenses Classical _____ has three English synonyms - Value Engineering, Value Management, Value Analysis.

   a. Willingness to pay
   b. Monopoly wage
   c. Staple financing
   d. Function cost analysis

20. _____ or producer goods are goods used as inputs in the production of other goods, such as partly finished goods. They are goods used in production of final goods. A firm may make then use _____, or make then sell, or buy then use them.
   a. Economic forecasting
   b. Income distribution
   c. Intermediate goods
   d. Inflation adjustment

21. _____ refers to the additional value of a commodity over the cost of commodities used to produce it from the previous stage of production. An example is the price of gasoline at the pump over the price of the oil in it. In national accounts used in macroeconomics, it refers to the contribution of the factors of production, i.e., land, labor, and capital goods, to raising the value of a product and corresponds to the incomes received by the owners of these factors.

a. Hodrick-Prescott filter
b. Full employment
c. Solow residual
d. Value added

22. A _____ is a normalized average (typically a weighted average) of prices for a given class of goods or services in a given region, during a given interval of time. It is a statistic designed to help to compare how these prices, taken as a whole, differ between time periods or geographical locations.

Price indices have several potential uses.

a. Product sabotage
b. Two-part tariff
c. Price index
d. Transactional Net Margin Method

23. In statistics, a _____ is a value that allows data to be measured over time in terms of some base period ussually through a price index in order to distinguish between changes in the money value of GNP which result from a change in prices and those which result from a change in physical output. It is the measure of the price level for some quantity. A _____ serves as a price index in which the effects of inflation are nulled.

a. Contingent employment
b. Blanket order
c. Deflator
d. Market microstructure

24. _____ is a term used in national accounts statistics and macroeconomics. It basically refers to the net additions to the (physical) capital stock in an accounting period, or, to the value of the increase of the capital stock; though it may occasionally also refer to the (growth of the) total stock of capital formed.

Thus, in UNSNA, _____ equals fixed capital investment, the increase in the value of inventories held, plus (net) lending to foreign countries, during an accounting period.

a. Capital intensity
b. Capital flight
c. Consumption of fixed capital
d. Capital formation

25. _____ is a term used in accounting, economics and finance to spread the cost of an asset over the span of several years.

In simple words we can say that _____ is the reduction in the value of an asset due to usage, passage of time, wear and tear, technological outdating or obsolescence, depletion, inadequacy, rot, rust, decay or other such factors.

In accounting, _____ is a term used to describe any method of attributing the historical or purchase cost of an asset across its useful life, roughly corresponding to normal wear and tear.

a. Salvage value
b. Depreciation
c. Net income per employee
d. Historical cost

26. In economics, _____ refers to an activity of spending which increases the availability of fixed capital goods or means of production. It is the total spending on new fixed investment minus replacement investment, which simply replaces depreciated capital goods.

a. Tangible investments
c. Net investment
b. Greenfield investment
d. Lehman Formula

27. A _____ occurs when an entity spends more money than it takes in. The opposite of a _____ is a budget surplus. Debt is essentially an accumulated flow of deficits.
   a. Budget deficit
   c. Funding body
   b. Public Financial Management
   d. Lump-sum tax

28. The term _____ has more than one meaning.

In the colloquial sense, an _____, or goods and services tax (GST)) is a tax collected by an intermediary (such as a retail store) from the person who bears the ultimate economic burden of the tax (such as the customer.) The intermediary later files a tax return and forwards the tax proceeds to government with the return.

   a. User charge
   c. Olivera-Tanzi effect
   b. Indirect tax
   d. Optimal tax

29. _____ is a fee paid on borrowed assets. It is the price paid for the use of borrowed money, or, money earned by deposited funds. Assets that are sometimes lent with _____ include money, shares, consumer goods through hire purchase, major assets such as aircraft, and even entire factories in finance lease arrangements.
   a. Interest
   c. Insolvency
   b. Asset protection
   d. Internal debt

30. A _____ is a consumption tax charged at the point of purchase for certain goods and services. The tax is usually set as a percentage by the government charging the tax. There is usually a list of exemptions.
   a. 100-year flood
   c. 1921 recession
   b. Sales tax
   d. 130-30 fund

31. In economics, a _____ is a redistribution of income in the market system. These payments are considered to be nonexhaustive because they do not directly absorb resources or create output. Examples of certain _____s include welfare (financial aid), social security, and government subsidies for certain businesses (firms.)
   a. 100-year flood
   c. 1921 recession
   b. Transfer payment
   d. 130-30 fund

32. _____ is that which is owed; usually referencing assets owed, but the term can also cover moral obligations and other interactions not requiring money. In the case of assets, _____ is a means of using future purchasing power in the present before a summation has been earned. Some companies and corporations use _____ as a part of their overall corporate finance strategy.
   a. Hard money loan
   c. Debt
   b. Debenture
   d. Collateral Management

33. A _____ is the transfer of wealth from one party (such as a person or company) to another. A _____ is usually made in exchange for the provision of goods, services or both, or to fulfill a legal obligation.

The simplest and oldest form of _____ is barter, the exchange of one good or service for another.

a. Going concern
b. Payment
c. Social gravity
d. Soft count

34. _____ refers to a business or organization attempting to acquire goods or services to accomplish the goals of the enterprise. Though there are several organizations that attempt to set standards in the _____ process, processes can vary greatly between organizations. Typically the word '_____' is not used interchangeably with the word 'procurement', since procurement typically includes Expediting, Supplier Quality, and Traffic and Logistics (T'L) in addition to _____.
a. Free port
b. 100-year flood
c. 130-30 fund
d. Purchasing

Chapter 5. Measuring Economic Activity

35. A _____ is:

- Rewrite _____, in generative grammar and computer science
- Standardization, a formal and widely-accepted statement, fact, definition, or qualification
- Operation, a determinate _____ for performing a mathematical operation and obtaining a certain result (Mathematics, Logic)
    - Unary operation
    - Binary operation
- _____ of inference, a function from sets of formulae to formulae (Mathematics, Logic)
- _____ of thumb, principle with broad application that is not intended to be strictly accurate or reliable for every situation. Also often simply referred to as a _____
- Moral, an atomic element of a moral code for guiding choices in human behavior
- Heuristic, a quantized '_____' which shows a tendency or probability for successful function
- A regulation, as in sports
- A Production _____, as in computer science
- Procedural law, a _____ set governing the application of laws to cases
    - A law, which may informally be called a '_____'
    - A court ruling, a decision by a court
- In the U.S. Government, a regulation mandated by Congress, but written or expanded upon by the Executive Branch.
- Norm (sociology), an informal but widely accepted _____, concept, truth, definition, or qualification (social norms, legal norms, coding norms)
- Norm (philosophy), a kind of sentence or a reason to act, feel or believe
- 'Rulership' is the concept of governance by a government:
    - Military _____, governance by a military body
    - Monastic _____, a collection of precepts that guides the life of monks or nuns in a religious order where the superior holds the place of Christ
- Slide _____

- '_____,' a song by Ayumi Hamasaki
- '_____,' a song by rapper Nas
- '_____s,' an album by the band The Whitest Boy Alive
- _____s: Pyaar Ka Superhit Formula, a 2003 Bollywood film
- ruler, an instrument for measuring lengths
- _____, a component of an astrolabe, circumferator or similar instrument
- The _____s, a bestselling self-help book
- _____ Project (Run Up-to-date Linux Everywhere), a project that aims to use up-to-date Linux software on old PCs
- _____ engine, a software system that helps managing business _____s
- Ja _____, a hip hop artist
    - R.U.L.E., a 2005 greatest hits album by rapper Ja _____
- '_____s,' a KMFDM song

a. Demand
b. Technocracy
c. Procter ' Gamble
d. Rule

Chapter 5. Measuring Economic Activity 61

36. To _____ is to impose a financial charge or other levy upon a taxpayer by a state or the functional equivalent of a state.

_____es are also imposed by many subnational entities. _____es consist of direct _____ or indirect _____, and may be paid in money or as its labour equivalent (often but not always unpaid.)

a. 100-year flood
c. 130-30 fund
b. 1921 recession
d. Tax

37. To tax is to impose a financial charge or other levy upon a taxpayer by a state or the functional equivalent of a state.

_____ are also imposed by many subnational entities. _____ consist of direct tax or indirect tax, and may be paid in money or as its labour equivalent (often but not always unpaid.)

a. 1921 recession
c. 100-year flood
b. 130-30 fund
d. Taxes

38. In economics, an _____ is any good or commodity, transported from one country to another country in a legitimate fashion, typically for use in trade. _____ goods or services are provided to foreign consumers by domestic producers. _____ is an important part of international trade.

a. Export
c. ACEA agreement
b. ACCRA Cost of Living Index
d. AD-IA Model

39. A variety of measures of national income and output are used in economics to estimate total economic activity in a country or region, including gross domestic product (GDP), _____ , and net national income (NNI.)

There are three main ways of calculating these numbers; the output approach, the income approach and the expenditure approach. In theory, the three must yield the same, because total expenditures on goods and services must equal the total income paid to the producers (GNI), and that must also equal the total value of the output of goods and services (_____.)

a. Purchasing power parity
c. Household final consumption expenditure
b. Gross world product
d. Gross national product

40. In economics, an _____ is any good (e.g. a commodity) or service brought into one country from another country in a legitimate fashion, typically for use in trade. It is a good that is brought in from another country for sale. _____ goods or services are provided to domestic consumers by foreign producers. An _____ in the receiving country is an export to the sending country.

a. Economic integration
c. Import
b. Incoterms
d. Import quota

41. The _____ equals the gross domestic product (GDP) minus depreciation on a country's capital goods.

_____ accounts for capital that has been consumed over the year in the form of housing, vehicle, or machinery deterioration. The depreciation accounted for is often referred to as capital consumption allowance and represents the amount needed in order to replace those depreciated assets.

Chapter 5. Measuring Economic Activity

a. Carrying charge
b. Cass criterion
c. Commodity price shocks
d. Net domestic product

42. _____ is a term used in economics to describe how an economic quantity is related to economic fluctuations. It is the opposite of procyclical. However, it has more than one meaning.

a. Price revolution
b. Countercyclical
c. Mathematical economics
d. Law of comparative advantage

43. A _____ product is a product designed for cheapness and short-term convenience rather than medium to long-term durability, with most products only intended for single use. The term is also sometimes used for products that may last several months (ex. _____ air filters) to distinguish from similar products that last indefinitely (ex.

a. 130-30 fund
b. 1921 recession
c. 100-year flood
d. Disposable

44. _____ is gross income minus income tax on that income.

Discretionary income is income after subtracting taxes and normal expenses (such as rent or mortgage, utilities, insurance, medical, transportation, property maintenance, child support, inflation, food and sundries, 'c.) to maintain a certain standard of living.

a. Disposable income
b. Disposable personal income
c. Taxation as theft
d. Stamp Act

45. _____ is the measure of investment used to compute GDP. This is an important component of GDP because it provides an indicator of the future productive capacity of the economy. It includes replacement purchases plus net additions to capital assets plus investments in inventories.

a. Current account
b. National Income and Product Accounts
c. Compensation of employees
d. Gross private domestic investment

46. Economic _____ is defined as an excess distribution to any factor in a production process above that which is required to induce the factor into the process or any excess above that which is necessary to keep the factor in its current use..

Classical Factor _____ is primarily concerned with the fee paid for the use of fixed (e.g. natural) resources. The classical definition is expressed as any excess payment above that required to induce or provide for production.

a. 1921 recession
b. Rent
c. 100-year flood
d. 130-30 fund

47. _____ refers to internal and external organizing and correcting factors that provide order to market and other types of societal institutions and organizations - economic, political, social and cultural - so that they may function efficiently and effectively as well as repair their failures.

Chapter 5. Measuring Economic Activity

The expression _____ is increasingly found in the title, abstract and text of articles, chapters and papers in the business, management, organization, strategy, social-issues, political-science and sociology literatures. The ABI/Inform Global source located 1748 such uses of both expressions in October 2008, compared with 31 in 1991 and 247 in 2002.

a. Positive statement
b. Total revenue
c. Private Benefits of Control
d. Nonmarket

48. In finance, _____ is investment originating from other countries. See Foreign direct investment.

a. Demand side economics
b. Horizontal merger
c. Preclusive purchasing
d. Foreign investment

49. In economics, _____ is a rise in the general level of prices of goods and services in an economy over a period of time. When the general price level rises, each unit of currency buys fewer goods and services; consequently, _____ is also a decline in the real value of money--a loss of purchasing power in the medium of exchange which is also the monetary unit of account in the economy. A chief measure of general price-level _____ is the general _____ rate, which is the percentage change in a general price index (normally the Consumer Price Index) over time.

a. Opportunity cost
b. Economic
c. Inflation
d. Energy economics

50. In economics, the _____ is a measure of inflation, the rate of increase of a price index (for example, a consumer price index.) It is the percentage rate of change in price level over time. The rate of decrease in the purchasing power of money is approximately equal.

It's used to calculate the real interest rate, as well as real increases in wages, and official measurements of this rate act as input variables to COLA adjustments and Inflation derivatives prices.

a. Equity value
b. Interest rate option
c. Edgeworth paradox
d. Inflation rate

51. _____s (economically referred to as land or raw materials) occur naturally within environments that exist relatively undisturbed by mankind, in a natural form. A _____'s is often characterized by amounts of biodiversity existent in various ecosystems.

Mining, petroleum extraction, fishing, hunting, and forestry are generally considered natural-resource industries.

a. 100-year flood
b. 1921 recession
c. Natural resource
d. 130-30 fund

52. In economics, the _____ is a historical inverse relation between the rate of unemployment and the rate of inflation in an economy. Stated simply, the lower the unemployment in an economy, the higher the rate of increase in nominal wages in the economy. Rate of Change of Wages against Unemployment, United Kingdom 1913-1948 from Phillips (1958)

William Phillips, a New Zealand born economist, wrote a paper in 1958 titled The Relationship between Unemployment and the Rate of Change of Money Wages in the United Kingdom 1861-1957, which was published in the quarterly journal Economica.

a. Lorenz curve
b. Demand curve
c. Cost curve
d. Phillips curve

53. The _____ or black market is a market where all commerce is conducted without regard to taxation, law or regulations of trade. The term is also often known as the underdog, shadow economy, black economy, parallel economy or phantom trades.

In modern societies the _____ covers a vast array of activities.

a. Information economy
b. Information markets
c. Autarky
d. Underground economy

54. _____s is the social science that studies the production, distribution, and consumption of goods and services. The term _____s comes from the Ancient Greek οἰκονομῖα from οἶκος (oikos, 'house') + νόμος (nomos, 'custom' or 'law'), hence 'rules of the house(hold)'. Current _____ models developed out of the broader field of political economy in the late 19th century, owing to a desire to use an empirical approach more akin to the physical sciences.

a. Opportunity cost
b. Economic
c. Inflation
d. Energy economics

55. _____ is the development of economic wealth of countries or regions for the well-being of their inhabitants. It is the process by which a nation improves the economic, political, and social well being of its people. From a policy perspective, _____ can be defined as efforts that seek to improve the economic well-being and quality of life for a community by creating and/or retaining jobs and supporting or growing incomes and the tax base.

a. Inflation
b. Economic methodology
c. Experimental economics
d. Economic development

56. The _____, a unit of the United States Department of Labor, is the principal fact-finding agency for the U.S. government in the broad field of labor economics and statistics. The BLS is an independent national statistical agency that collects, processes, analyzes, and disseminates essential statistical data to the American public, the U.S. Congress, other Federal agencies, State and local governments, business, and labor representatives. The BLS also serves as a statistical resource to the Department of Labor.

a. Bureau of Labor Statistics
b. Gross Regional Product
c. Gross world product
d. Gross national product

57. _____ is a broad label that refers to any individuals or households that use goods and services generated within the economy. The concept of a _____ is used in different contexts, so that the usage and significance of the term may vary.

Typically when business people and economists talk of _____s they are talking about person as _____, an aggregated commodity item with little individuality other than that expressed in the buy/not-buy decision.

Chapter 5. Measuring Economic Activity

a. 1921 recession
c. 100-year flood
b. 130-30 fund
d. Consumer

58. A _____ is a measure of the average price of consumer goods and services purchased by households. A _____ measures a price change for a constant market basket of goods and services from one period to the next within the same area (city, region, or nation.) It is a price index determined by measuring the price of a standard group of goods meant to represent the typical market basket of a typical urban consumer.
   a. Lipstick index
   c. Cost-of-living index
   b. CPI
   d. Consumer price index

59. In economics, _____ is a sustained decrease in the general price level of goods and services. _____ occurs when the annual inflation rate falls below zero percent, resulting in an increase in the real value of money -- a negative inflation rate. This should not be confused with disinflation, a slow-down in the inflation rate (i.e. when the inflation decreases, but still remains positive.)
   a. Tobit model
   c. Price revolution
   b. Literacy rate
   d. Deflation

60. The term _____ or commodity bundle refers to a fixed list of items used specifically to track the progress of inflation in an economy or specific market.

The most common type of _____ is the basket of consumer goods, used to define the Consumer Price Index (CPI.) Other types of baskets are used to define

- Producer Price Index (PPI), previously known as Wholesale Price Index (WPI)
- various commodity price indices

The term _____ analysis in the retail business refers to research that provides the retailer with information to understand the purchase behaviour of a buyer. This information will enable the retailer to understand the buyer's needs and rewrite the store's layout accordingly, develop cross-promotional programs, or even capture new buyers (much like the cross-selling concept.)

   a. Robin Hood index
   c. Category Development Index
   b. Cost-weighted activity index
   d. Market basket

61. A _____ is a hypothetical measure of overall prices for some set of goods and services, in a given region during a given interval, normalized relative to some base set. Typically, a _____ is approximated with a price index.

The classical dichotomy is the assumption that there is a relatively clean distinction between overall increases or decreases in prices and underlying, e;reale; economic variables.

   a. Price elasticity of supply
   c. Price level
   b. Discouraged worker
   d. Discretionary spending

62. An _____ is an economic data figure reflecting price or quantity compared with a standard or base value. The base usually equals 100 and the _____ is usually expressed as 100 times the ratio to the base value. For example, if a commodity costs twice as much in 1970 as it did in 1960, its _____ would be 200 relative to 1960.

Chapter 5. Measuring Economic Activity

a. Index number
b. ACCRA Cost of Living Index
c. Economic depreciation
d. International economics

63. A _____ measures average changes in prices received by domestic producers for their output. It is one of several price indices

Its importance is being undermined by the steady decline in manufactured goods as a share of spending.

A number of countries that now report a _____ previously reported a Wholesale Price Index.

a. Gross national product
b. Visible balance
c. Producer price index
d. Hemline index

64. _____ are the divisions at which tax rates change in a progressive tax system (or an explicitly regressive tax system, although this is much rarer.) Essentially, they are the cutoff values for taxable income -- income past a certain point will be taxed at a higher rate.
a. Tax farming
b. Tax brackets
c. Disposable income
d. Popiwek

Chapter 6. Consumption and Investment

1. The term _____ refers to economy-wide fluctuations in production or economic activity over several months or years. These fluctuations occur around a long-term growth trend, and typically involve shifts over time between periods of relatively rapid economic growth (expansion or boom), and periods of relative stagnation or decline (contraction or recession.)

These fluctuations are often measured using the growth rate of real gross domestic product.

- a. Nominal value
- b. Tobit model
- c. Consumer theory
- d. Business cycle

2. _____ is a broad label that refers to any individuals or households that use goods and services generated within the economy. The concept of a _____ is used in different contexts, so that the usage and significance of the term may vary.

Typically when business people and economists talk of _____s they are talking about person as _____, an aggregated commodity item with little individuality other than that expressed in the buy/not-buy decision.

- a. 1921 recession
- b. 100-year flood
- c. 130-30 fund
- d. Consumer

3. _____ is the degree of optimism that consumers feel about the overall state of the economy and their personal financial situation. How confident people feel about stability of their incomes determines their spending activity and therefore serves as one of the key indicators for the overall shape of the economy. In essence, if _____ is higher, consumers are making more purchases, boosting the economic expansion.
- a. Rule Developing Experimentation
- b. Communal marketing
- c. Consumer behavior
- d. Consumer confidence

4. _____ is a common concept in economics, and gives rise to derived concepts such as consumer debt. Generally _____ is defined by opposition to production. But the precise definition can vary because different schools of economists define production quite differently.
- a. Foreclosure data providers
- b. Federal Reserve Bank Notes
- c. Cash or share options
- d. Consumption

5. The _____ or gross domestic income (GDI), a basic measure of an economy's economic performance, is the market value of all final goods and services produced within the borders of a nation in a year. _____ can be defined in three ways, all of which are conceptually identical. First, it is equal to the total expenditures for all final goods and services produced within the country in a stipulated period of time (usually a 365-day year.)
- a. Gross domestic product
- b. Monopolistic competition
- c. Market structure
- d. Countercyclical

6. _____ is a misspelled phrase from Latin 'pro capite' phrase meaning per head with pro meaning 'per' or 'for each' and capite meaning 'head.' Both words together equate to the phrase 'for each head.'

It is usually used in the field of statistics to indicate the average per person for any given concern, such as income, crime rate, etc.

Chapter 6. Consumption and Investment

It is also used in wills to indicate that each of the named beneficiaries should receive, by devise or bequest, equal shares of the estate. This is in contrast to a per stirpes division, in which each branch of the inheriting family inherits an equal share of the estate.

a. Population statistics
b. False positive rate
c. Sargan test
d. Per capita

7. An _____, in economics, is the amount by which the real Gross domestic product exceeds potential GDP. The real GDP is also known as GDP 'adjusted for inflation', 'constant prices' GDP or 'constant dollar' GDP, because it measures the aggregate output in a country's income accounts in a given year, expressed in base-year prices. On the other hand, the potential GDP is the quantity of real GDP when a country's economy is at full-employment.

a. ACCRA Cost of Living Index
b. AD-IA Model
c. Inflationary gap
d. ACEA agreement

8. _____ or consumer demand or consumption is also known as personal consumption expenditure. It is the largest part of aggregate demand or effective demand at the macroeconomic level. There are two variants of consumption in the aggregate demand model, including induced consumption and autonomous consumption.

a. Potential output
b. Complex multiplier
c. Dishoarding
d. Consumer spending

9. _____s is the social science that studies the production, distribution, and consumption of goods and services. The term _____s comes from the Ancient Greek οἰκονομία from οἶκος (oikos, 'house') + νόμος (nomos, 'custom' or 'law'), hence 'rules of the house(hold)'. Current _____ models developed out of the broader field of political economy in the late 19th century, owing to a desire to use an empirical approach more akin to the physical sciences.

a. Opportunity cost
b. Energy economics
c. Inflation
d. Economic

10. A _____ product is a product designed for cheapness and short-term convenience rather than medium to long-term durability, with most products only intended for single use. The term is also sometimes used for products that may last several months (ex. _____ air filters) to distinguish from similar products that last indefinitely (ex.

a. 130-30 fund
b. 100-year flood
c. 1921 recession
d. Disposable

11. _____ is gross income minus income tax on that income.

Discretionary income is income after subtracting taxes and normal expenses (such as rent or mortgage, utilities, insurance, medical, transportation, property maintenance, child support, inflation, food and sundries, 'c.') to maintain a certain standard of living.

a. Stamp Act
b. Disposable personal income
c. Taxation as theft
d. Disposable income

12. The _____ is 'the basic residential unit in which economic production, consumption, inheritance, child rearing, and shelter are organized and carried out'; [the _____] 'may or may not be synonomous with family'.

Chapter 6. Consumption and Investment

The _____ is the basic unit of analysis in many social, microeconomic and government models. The term refers to all individuals who live in the same dwelling.

a. Family economics
c. 100-year flood
b. 130-30 fund
d. Household

13. In economics, the _____ measures the payments that flow between any individual country and all other countries. It is used to summarize all international economic transactions for that country during a specific time period, usually a year. The _____ is determined by the country's exports and imports of goods, services, and financial capital, as well as financial transfers.

a. Balance of payments
c. Gross domestic product per barrel
b. Gross world product
d. Skyscraper Index

14. A _____ is the transfer of wealth from one party (such as a person or company) to another. A _____ is usually made in exchange for the provision of goods, services or both, or to fulfill a legal obligation.

The simplest and oldest form of _____ is barter, the exchange of one good or service for another.

a. Soft count
c. Going concern
b. Payment
d. Social gravity

15. _____ was the American founder of the Ford Motor Company and father of modern assembly lines used in mass production. His introduction of the Model T automobile revolutionized transportation and American industry. He was a prolific inventor and was awarded 161 U.S. patents.

a. Maximilian Carl Emil Weber
c. Henry Ford
b. George Cabot Lodge II
d. Werner Sombart

16. A _____ is an object whose consumption increases the utility of the consumer, for which the quantity demanded exceeds the quantity supplied at zero price. _____s are usually modeled as having diminishing marginal utility. The first individual purchase has high utility; the second has less.

a. Merit good
c. Pie method
b. Good
d. Composite good

17. In economics, economic output is divided into physical goods and intangible services. Consumption of _____ is assumed to produce utility. It is often used when referring to a _____ Tax.

a. Manufactured goods
c. Private good
b. Composite good
d. Goods and services

18. _____ is a term that is used to describe the overall process of invention, innovation and diffusion of technology or processes. The term is redundant with technological development, technological achievement, and technological progress. In essence _____ is the invention of a technology (or a process), the continuous process of improving a technology (in which it often becomes cheaper) and its diffusion throughout industry or society.

a. 130-30 fund
c. 1921 recession
b. 100-year flood
d. Technological change

Chapter 6. Consumption and Investment

19. _____ in economics refers to metrics and measures of output from production processes, per unit of input. Labor _____, for example, is typically measured as a ratio of output per labor-hour, an input. _____ may be conceived of as a metrics of the technical or engineering efficiency of production.
- a. Productivity
- b. Piece work
- c. Fordism
- d. Production-possibility frontier

20. In economics and business, specifically cost accounting, the _____ point (BEP) is the point at which cost or expenses and revenue are equal: there is no net loss or gain, and one has 'broken even'. A profit or a loss has not been made, although opportunity costs have been paid, and capital has received the risk-adjusted, expected return.

For example, if the business sells less than 200 tables each month, it will make a loss, if it sells more, it will be a profit.

- a. Nonmarket
- b. Buffer stock scheme
- c. Small numbers game
- d. Break-even

21. In economics, the _____ is a single mathematical function used to express consumer spending. It was developed by John Maynard Keynes and detailed most famously in his book The General Theory of Employment, Interest, and Money. The function is used to calculate the amount of total consumption in an economy.
- a. Consumption function
- b. Liquidity preference
- c. Procyclical
- d. DAD-SAS model

22. In algebra, a _____ is a function depending on n that associates a scalar, det(A), to an n×n square matrix A. The fundamental geometric meaning of a _____ is a scale factor for measure when A is regarded as a linear transformation. _____s are important both in calculus, where they enter the substitution rule for several variables, and in multilinear algebra.

For a fixed nonnegative integer n, there is a unique _____ function for the n×n matrices over any commutative ring R. In particular, this function exists when R is the field of real or complex numbers.

- a. 130-30 fund
- b. 100-year flood
- c. Determinant
- d. 1921 recession

23. _____, 1st Baron Keynes was a renowned economist from Britain whose many ideas on economic and political theories as well as on many governments' monetary policies influenced America. He advocated a government that played an active role in the lives of people regarding business, economy, etc. In this role, the government would use fiscal measures to reduce the consequences of recessions, economic depressions and booms.
- a. Adolf Hitler
- b. John Maynard Keynes
- c. Adolph Fischer
- d. Adam Smith

24. In economics, the _____ or marginal physical product is the extra output produced by one more unit of an input (for instance, the difference in output when a firm's labour is increased from five to six units.) Assuming that no other inputs to production change, the _____ of a given input (X) can be expressed as:

_____ = ΔY/ΔX = (the change of Y)/(the change of X.)

-
  -
    - Pending approval by Thomas Sowell***

In neoclassical economics, this is the mathematical derivative of the production function.... Note that the 'product' (Y) is typically defined ignoring external costs and benefits.

a. Factor prices
b. Productive capacity
c. Labor problem
d. Marginal product

25. In economics, the _____ also known as MPL or MPN is the change in output from hiring one additional unit of labor. It is the increase in output added by the last unit of labor. Assuming that no other inputs to production change, the marginal product of a given input (X) can be expressed as:

MP = ΔY/ΔX = (the change of Y)/(the change of X.)

a. Product Pipeline
b. Marginal product
c. Marginal product of labor
d. Production function

26. In economics, the _____ is an empirical metric that quantifies induced consumption, the concept that the increase in personal consumer spending (consumption) that occurs with an increase in disposable income (income after taxes and transfers.) For example, if a household earns one extra dollar of disposable income, and the _____ is 0.65, then of that dollar, the household will spend 65 cents and save 35 cents.

Mathematically, the _____ (MPC) function is expressed as the derivative of the consumption (C) function with respect to disposable income (Y.)

a. Marginal propensity to consume
b. Supply shock
c. Technology shock
d. Marginal propensity to import

27. The _____ refers to the increase in saving (non-purchase of current goods and services) that results from an increase in income. For example, if a household earns one extra dollar, and the _____ is 0.35, then of that dollar, the household will spend 65 cents and save 35 cents. It can also go the other way, referring to the decrease in saving that results from a decrease in income.

a. Real business cycle
b. Solow residual
c. Robertson lag
d. Marginal propensity to save

28. In neoclassical economics and microeconomics, _____ describes the perfect being a market in which there are many small firms, all producing homogeneous goods. In the short term, such markets are productively inefficient as output will not occur where mc is equal to ac, but allocatively efficient, as output under _____ will always occur where mc is equal to mr, and therefore where mc equals ar. However, in the long term, such markets are both allocatively and productively efficient.

a. General equilibrium
b. Co-operative economics
c. Law of supply
d. Perfect competition

29. _____ is the point where a person stops employment completely. A person may also semi-retire and keep some sort of _____ job, out of choice rather than necessity. This usually happens upon reaching a determined age, when physical conditions don't allow the person to work any more (by illness or accident), or even for personal choice (usually in the presence of an adequate pension or personal savings.)
   a. 100-year flood
   b. Layoff
   c. Retirement
   d. Termination of employment

30. A _____ is a public market for the trading of company stock and derivatives at an agreed price; these are securities listed on a stock exchange as well as those only traded privately.

The size of the world _____ was estimated at about $36.6 trillion US at the beginning of October 2008. The total world derivatives market has been estimated at about $791 trillion face or nominal value, 11 times the size of the entire world economy.

   a. Adolf Hitler
   b. Adolph Fischer
   c. Stock market
   d. Adam Smith

31. A _____ is a sudden dramatic decline of stock prices across a significant cross-section of a stock market. Crashes are driven by panic as much as by underlying economic factors. They often follow speculative stock market bubbles.
   a. 1921 recession
   b. Stock market crash
   c. 100-year flood
   d. 130-30 fund

32. The _____ is an economic term, referring to an increase in spending that accompanies an increase or perceived increase in wealth.

The effect would cause changes in the amounts and composition of consumer consumption caused by changes in consumer wealth. People should spend more when one of two things is true: when people actually are richer (by objective measurement, for example, a bonus or a pay raise at work, which would be an income effect), or when people perceive themselves to be 'richer' (for example, the assessed value of their home increases, or a stock they own has gone up in price recently.)

   a. Wealth effect
   b. 130-30 fund
   c. Wealth condensation
   d. 100-year flood

33. In economics, a _____ is a mechanism that allows people to easily buy and sell (trade) financial securities (such as stocks and bonds), commodities (such as precious metals or agricultural goods), and other fungible items of value at low transaction costs and at prices that reflect the efficient-market hypothesis.

_____ s have evolved significantly over several hundred years and are undergoing constant innovation to improve liquidity.

Both general markets (where many commodities are traded) and specialized markets (where only one commodity is traded) exist.

Chapter 6. Consumption and Investment

a. Market anomaly
b. Noise trader
c. Convertible arbitrage
d. Financial market

34. In financial accounting, a _____ or statement of financial position is a summary of a person's or organization's balances. Assets, liabilities and ownership equity are listed as of a specific date, such as the end of its financial year. A _____ is often described as a snapshot of a company's financial condition.

a. 130-30 fund
b. 100-year flood
c. Balance sheet
d. 1921 recession

35. A _____ refers to any type debt instrument, such as a loan, bond, mortgage that does not have a fixed rate of interest over the life of the instrument. Such debt typically uses an index or other base rate for establishing the interest rate for each relevant period. One of the most common rates to use as the basis for applying interest rates is the London Inter-bank Offered Rate, or LIBOR

a. Moneylender
b. Floating interest rate
c. Disposal tax effect
d. Money market

36. _____ is the a method of technical and economic research of the systems for purpose to optimize a parity between system's consumer functions or properties and expenses to achieve those functions or properties.

This methodology for continuous perfection of production, industrial technologies, organizational structures was developed by Juryj Sobolev in 1948 at the 'Perm telephone factory'

- 1948 Juryj Sobolev - the first success in application of a method analysis at the 'Perm telephone factory'.
- 1949 - the first application for the invention as result of use of the new method.

Today in economically developed countries practically each enterprise or the company use methodology of the kind of functional-cost analysis as a practice of the quality management, most full satisfying to principles of standards of series ISO 9000.

- Interest of consumer not in products itself, but the advantage which it will receive from its usage.
- The consumer aspires to reduce his expenses
- Functions needed by consumer can be executed in the various ways, and, hence, with various efficiency and expenses. Among possible alternatives of realization of functions exist such in which the parity of quality and the price is the optimal for the consumer.

The goal of _____ is achievement of the highest consumer satisfaction of production at simultaneous decrease in all kinds of industrial expenses Classical _____ has three English synonyms - Value Engineering, Value Management, Value Analysis.

a. Staple financing
b. Willingness to pay
c. Function cost analysis
d. Monopoly wage

37. _____ is a branch of economics that deals with the performance, structure, and behavior of a national or regional economy as a whole. Along with microeconomics, _____ is one of the two most general fields in economics. It is the study of the behavior and decision-making of entire economies.

Chapter 6. Consumption and Investment

a. Tobit model
c. New Trade Theory
b. Macroeconomics
d. Nominal value

38. The _____ is an expected return that the provider of capital plans to earn on their investment.

Capital (money) used for funding a business should earn returns for the capital providers who risk their capital. For an investment to be worthwhile, the expected return on capital must be greater than the _____.

a. Capital expenditure
c. Modigliani-Miller theorem
b. Cost of capital
d. Capital intensive

39. _____ is the measure of investment used to compute GDP. This is an important component of GDP because it provides an indicator of the future productive capacity of the economy. It includes replacement purchases plus net additions to capital assets plus investments in inventories.

a. Current account
c. National Income and Product Accounts
b. Compensation of employees
d. Gross private domestic investment

40. _____ is a fee paid on borrowed assets. It is the price paid for the use of borrowed money, or, money earned by deposited funds. Assets that are sometimes lent with _____ include money, shares, consumer goods through hire purchase, major assets such as aircraft, and even entire factories in finance lease arrangements.

a. Insolvency
c. Asset protection
b. Internal debt
d. Interest

41. An _____ is the price a borrower pays for the use of money they do not own, for instance a small company might borrow from a bank to kick start their business, and the return a lender receives for deferring the use of funds, by lending it to the borrower. _____s are normally expressed as a percentage rate over the period of one year.

_____s targets are also a vital tool of monetary policy and are used to control variables like investment, inflation, and unemployment.

a. Enterprise value
c. Arrow-Debreu model
b. ACCRA Cost of Living Index
d. Interest rate

42. _____ is an assumption used in many contemporary macroeconomic models, and also in other areas of contemporary economics and game theory and in other applications of rational choice theory.

Since most macroeconomic models today study decisions over many periods, the expectations of workers, consumers, and firms about future economic conditions are an essential part of the model. How to model these expectations has long been controversial, and it is well known that the macroeconomic predictions of the model may differ depending on the assumptions made about expectations

a. Potential output
c. Balanced-growth equilibrium
b. Rational expectations
d. Minimum wage

Chapter 6. Consumption and Investment

43. An _____ is a tax levied on the financial income of people, corporations, or other legal entities. Various _____ systems exist, with varying degrees of tax incidence. Income taxation can be progressive, proportional, or regressive.
    a. AD-IA Model
    b. Income tax
    c. ACCRA Cost of Living Index
    d. ACEA agreement

44. _____ is a concept coined by structuralist inflation theorists. It refers to a situation where all prices in an economy are continuously adjusted with relation to a price index by force of contracts.

    Changes in price indices trigger changes in prices of goods.

    a. Incomes policies
    b. Employment Cost Index
    c. Inflationary Spikes
    d. Inertial inflation

45. In economics, _____ is a rise in the general level of prices of goods and services in an economy over a period of time. When the general price level rises, each unit of currency buys fewer goods and services; consequently, _____ is also a decline in the real value of money--a loss of purchasing power in the medium of exchange which is also the monetary unit of account in the economy. A chief measure of general price-level _____ is the general _____ rate, which is the percentage change in a general price index (normally the Consumer Price Index) over time.
    a. Energy economics
    b. Economic
    c. Opportunity cost
    d. Inflation

46. In economics, _____ is the active redirecting resources from being consumed today so that they may create benefits in the future; the use of assets to earn income or profit._____ is the process of making an investment in order to earn a profit, for example equity investment either through a fund, a 401k plan, or individually. People often invest in order to build up their estate or to accumulate funds for retirement.

    To try to predict good stocks to invest in, two main schools of thought exist: technical analysis and fundamentals analysis.

    a. AD-IA Model
    b. ACCRA Cost of Living Index
    c. Investing
    d. ACEA agreement

47. To _____ is to impose a financial charge or other levy upon a taxpayer by a state or the functional equivalent of a state.

    _____es are also imposed by many subnational entities. _____es consist of direct _____ or indirect _____, and may be paid in money or as its labour equivalent (often but not always unpaid.)

    a. Tax
    b. 1921 recession
    c. 100-year flood
    d. 130-30 fund

48. To tax is to impose a financial charge or other levy upon a taxpayer by a state or the functional equivalent of a state.

    _____ are also imposed by many subnational entities. _____ consist of direct tax or indirect tax, and may be paid in money or as its labour equivalent (often but not always unpaid.)

a. 100-year flood
b. 130-30 fund
c. 1921 recession
d. Taxes

49. Economics:

- _____, the desire to own something and the ability to pay for it
- _____ curve, a graphic representation of a _____ schedule
- _____ deposit, the money in checking accounts
- _____ pull theory, the theory that inflation occurs when _____ for goods and services exceeds existing supplies
- _____ schedule, a table that lists the quantity of a good a person will buy it each different price
- _____ side economics, the school of economics at believes government spending and tax cuts open economy by raising _____

a. Production
b. McKesson ' Robbins scandal
c. Variability
d. Demand

50. In economics, the _____ can be defined as the graph depicting the relationship between the price of a certain commodity, and the amount of it that consumers are willing and able to purchase at that given price. It is a graphic representation of a demand schedule. The _____ for all consumers together follows from the _____ of every individual consumer: the individual demands at each price are added together.

a. Demand curve
b. Cost curve
c. Wage curve
d. Kuznets curve

51. In economics, _____ is the total demand for final goods and services in the economy (Y) at a given time and price level. It is the amount of goods and services in the economy that will be purchased at all possible price levels. This is the demand for the gross domestic product of a country when inventory levels are static.

a. Aggregate expenditure
b. Aggregate supply
c. Aggregation problem
d. Aggregate demand

52. The _____ was an evolution of developed countries from an industrial/manufacturing-based wealth producing economy into a service sector asset based economy, brought about by globalization and currency manipulation by governments and their central banks. Some analysts claimed that this change in the economic structure of the United States had created a state of permanent steady growth, low unemployment, and immunity to boom and bust macroeconomic cycles. They believed that the change rendered obsolete many business practices.

a. 130-30 fund
b. 100-year flood
c. 1921 recession
d. New economy

Chapter 6. Consumption and Investment

53. _____ has several particular meanings:

- in mathematics
    - _____ function
    - Euler _____
    - _____
    - _____ subgroup
    - method of _____s (partial differential equations)
- in physics and engineering
    - any _____ curve that shows the relationship between certain input- and output parameters, e.g.
    - an I-V or current-voltage _____ is the current in a circuit as a function of the applied voltage
    - Receiver-Operator _____
- in fiction
    - in Dungeons ' Dragons, _____ is another name for ability score

a. Technocracy
c. Characteristic
b. Demand
d. Russian financial crisis

54. _____ was an American economist, statistician and public intellectual, and a recipient of the Nobel Memorial Prize in Economic Sciences. He is best known among scholars for his theoretical and empirical research, especially consumption analysis, monetary history and theory, and for his demonstration of the complexity of stabilization policy. A global public followed his restatement of a political philosophy that insisted on minimizing the role of government in favor of the private sector.

a. Adam Smith
c. Milton Friedman
b. Adolph Fischer
d. Adolf Hitler

Chapter 7. Business Fluctuations and the Theory of Aggregate Demand

1. In economics, _____ is the total demand for final goods and services in the economy (Y) at a given time and price level. It is the amount of goods and services in the economy that will be purchased at all possible price levels. This is the demand for the gross domestic product of a country when inventory levels are static.
   a. Aggregate demand
   b. Aggregate expenditure
   c. Aggregate supply
   d. Aggregation problem

2. The term _____ refers to economy-wide fluctuations in production or economic activity over several months or years. These fluctuations occur around a long-term growth trend, and typically involve shifts over time between periods of relatively rapid economic growth (expansion or boom), and periods of relative stagnation or decline (contraction or recession.)

   These fluctuations are often measured using the growth rate of real gross domestic product.

   a. Tobit model
   b. Consumer theory
   c. Business cycle
   d. Nominal value

3. _____ is an economic system in which wealth, and the means of producing wealth, are privately owned. Through _____, the land, labor, and capital are owned, operated, and traded for the purpose of generating profits, without force or fraud, by private individuals either singly or jointly, and investments, distribution, income, production, pricing and supply of goods, commodities and services are determined by voluntary private decision in a market economy. A distinguishing feature of _____ is that each person owns his or her own labor and therefore is allowed to sell the use of it to employers.
   a. Socialism for the rich and capitalism for the poor
   b. Late capitalism
   c. Creative capitalism
   d. Capitalism

4. The _____ was a worldwide economic downturn starting in most places in 1929 and ending at different times in the 1930s or early 1940s for different countries. It was the largest and most important economic depression in the 20th century, and is used in the 21st century as an example of how far the world's economy can fall. The _____ originated in the United States; historians most often use as a starting date the stock market crash on October 29, 1929, known as Black Tuesday.
   a. Jarrow March
   b. British Empire Economic Conference
   c. Wall Street Crash of 1929
   d. Great Depression

5. _____, 1st Baron Keynes was a renowned economist from Britain whose many ideas on economic and political theories as well as on many governments' monetary policies influenced America. He advocated a government that played an active role in the lives of people regarding business, economy, etc. In this role, the government would use fiscal measures to reduce the consequences of recessions, economic depressions and booms.
   a. Adolph Fischer
   b. Adolf Hitler
   c. Adam Smith
   d. John Maynard Keynes

6. _____ and Keynesian Theory) is a macroeconomic theory based on the ideas of 20th-century British economist John Maynard Keynes. _____ argues that private sector decisions sometimes lead to inefficient macroeconomic outcomes and therefore advocates active policy responses by the public sector, including monetary policy actions by the central bank and fiscal policy actions by the government to stabilize output over the business cycle.

   The theories forming the basis of _____ were first presented in The General Theory of Employment, Interest and Money, published in 1936.

Chapter 7. Business Fluctuations and the Theory of Aggregate Demand

a. Market failure
b. Deflation
c. Rational choice theory
d. Keynesian economics

7. The _____ is the largest national economy in the world. Its gross domestic product (GDP) was estimated as $14.2 trillion in 2008. The U.S. economy maintains a high level of output per person (GDP per capita, $46,800 in 2008, ranked at around number ten in the world.)
   a. ACCRA Cost of Living Index
   b. AD-IA Model
   c. ACEA agreement
   d. Economy of the United States

8. In economics, the _____ measures the payments that flow between any individual country and all other countries. It is used to summarize all international economic transactions for that country during a specific time period, usually a year. The _____ is determined by the country's exports and imports of goods, services, and financial capital, as well as financial transfers.
   a. Gross domestic product per barrel
   b. Skyscraper Index
   c. Gross world product
   d. Balance of payments

9. Economics:

   - _____, the desire to own something and the ability to pay for it
   - _____ curve, a graphic representation of a _____ schedule
   - _____ deposit, the money in checking accounts
   - _____ pull theory, the theory that inflation occurs when _____ for goods and services exceeds existing supplies
   - _____ schedule, a table that lists the quantity of a good a person will buy it each different price
   - _____ side economics, the school of economics at believes government spending and tax cuts open economy by raising _____

   a. Demand
   b. Variability
   c. Production
   d. McKesson ' Robbins scandal

10. _____s is the social science that studies the production, distribution, and consumption of goods and services. The term _____s comes from the Ancient Greek oá¼°κονομῖα from oá¼¶κος (oikos, 'house') + vῐΌεμος (nomos, 'custom' or 'law'), hence 'rules of the house(hold)'. Current _____ models developed out of the broader field of political economy in the late 19th century, owing to a desire to use an empirical approach more akin to the physical sciences.
    a. Opportunity cost
    b. Energy economics
    c. Economic
    d. Inflation

11. A _____ is the transfer of wealth from one party (such as a person or company) to another. A _____ is usually made in exchange for the provision of goods, services or both, or to fulfill a legal obligation.

The simplest and oldest form of _____ is barter, the exchange of one good or service for another.

a. Payment
b. Going concern
c. Social gravity
d. Soft count

Chapter 7. Business Fluctuations and the Theory of Aggregate Demand

12. The _____ or gross domestic income (GDI), a basic measure of an economy's economic performance, is the market value of all final goods and services produced within the borders of a nation in a year. _____ can be defined in three ways, all of which are conceptually identical. First, it is equal to the total expenditures for all final goods and services produced within the country in a stipulated period of time (usually a 365-day year.)
    a. Monopolistic competition
    b. Countercyclical
    c. Market structure
    d. Gross domestic product

13. The _____ is a US private, nonprofit research organization dedicated to studying the science and empirics of economics, especially the American economy. It is 'committed to undertaking and disseminating unbiased economic research among public policymakers, business professionals, and the academic community.' It publishes NBER Working Papers and books. The NBER is located in Cambridge, Massachusetts with branch offices in Palo Alto, California, and New York City.
    a. CEFTA
    b. National Bureau of Economic Research
    c. Non-governmental organization
    d. Deutsche Bank

14. An _____, in economics, is the amount by which the real Gross domestic product exceeds potential GDP. The real GDP is also known as GDP 'adjusted for inflation', 'constant prices' GDP or 'constant dollar' GDP, because it measures the aggregate output in a country's income accounts in a given year, expressed in base-year prices. On the other hand, the potential GDP is the quantity of real GDP when a country's economy is at full-employment.
    a. AD-IA Model
    b. Inflationary gap
    c. ACCRA Cost of Living Index
    d. ACEA agreement

15. In economics, a _____ is a general slowdown in economic activity over a sustained period of time, or a business cycle contraction. During _____s, many macroeconomic indicators vary in a similar way. Production as measured by Gross Domestic Product (GDP), employment, investment spending, capacity utilization, household incomes and business profits all fall during _____s.
    a. Treasury View
    b. Monetary economics
    c. Leading indicators
    d. Recession

16. _____ has several particular meanings:

    - in mathematics
        - _____ function
        - Euler _____
        - _____
        - _____ subgroup
        - method of _____s (partial differential equations)
    - in physics and engineering
        - any _____ curve that shows the relationship between certain input- and output parameters, e.g.
        - an I-V or current-voltage _____ is the current in a circuit as a function of the applied voltage
        - Receiver-Operator _____
    - in fiction
        - in Dungeons ' Dragons, _____ is another name for ability score

Chapter 7. Business Fluctuations and the Theory of Aggregate Demand

a. Demand
b. Technocracy
c. Russian financial crisis
d. Characteristic

17. _____ refers to an action or object coming from outside a system. It is the opposite of endogenous, something generated from within the system.

- In an economic model, an _____ change is one that comes from outside the model and is unexplained by the model. For example, in the simple supply and demand model, a change in consumer tastes or preferences is unexplained by the model and also leads to endogenous changes in demand that lead to changes in the equilibrium price. Put another way, an _____ change involves an alteration of a variable that is autonomous, i.e., unaffected by the workings of the model.

- In linear regression, it means that the variable is independent of all other response values.

- In biology, '_____' refers to an action or object coming from the outside of a system. For example, an _____ contrast agent in medical imaging refers to a liquid injected into the patient intravenously that enhances visibility of a pathology, such as a tumor.

a. ACEA agreement
b. AD-IA Model
c. ACCRA Cost of Living Index
d. Exogenous

18. The _____ was an evolution of developed countries from an industrial/manufacturing-based wealth producing economy into a service sector asset based economy, brought about by globalization and currency manipulation by governments and their central banks. Some analysts claimed that this change in the economic structure of the United States had created a state of permanent steady growth, low unemployment, and immunity to boom and bust macroeconomic cycles. They believed that the change rendered obsolete many business practices.

a. 100-year flood
b. 1921 recession
c. 130-30 fund
d. New economy

19. A _____ is a public market for the trading of company stock and derivatives at an agreed price; these are securities listed on a stock exchange as well as those only traded privately.

The size of the world _____ was estimated at about $36.6 trillion US at the beginning of October 2008 . The total world derivatives market has been estimated at about $791 trillion face or nominal value, 11 times the size of the entire world economy.

a. Adolf Hitler
b. Adolph Fischer
c. Adam Smith
d. Stock market

20. The term _____ refers to a great buildup in the price of a particular commodity or, alternately, the localized rise in an economy, often based upon the value of a single commodity, followed by a downturn as the commodity price falls due to a change in economic circumstances or the collapse of unrealistic expectations.

_____ phenomenon have existed for centuries. During a 'boom' period, buyers find themselves paying increasingly higher prices until the 'bust', at which time the goods and commodities for which they have paid inflated prices may end up as valueless or nearly so.

Chapter 7. Business Fluctuations and the Theory of Aggregate Demand

a. Carrying charge
b. Double bottom line
c. Merchant capitalism
d. Boom and bust

21. _____ in economics and business is the result of an exchange and from that trade we assign a numerical monetary value to a good, service or asset. If Alice trades Bob 4 apples for an orange, the _____ of an orange is 4 apples. Inversely, the _____ of an apple is 1/4 oranges.
a. Price
b. Premium pricing
c. Price book
d. Price war

22. In economics, _____ is the total supply of goods and services produced by a national economy during a specific time period. It is the total amount of goods and services in the economy available at all possible price levels.
a. Aggregate demand
b. Aggregation problem
c. Aggregate expenditure
d. Aggregate supply

23. _____ was an American economist, statistician and public intellectual, and a recipient of the Nobel Memorial Prize in Economic Sciences. He is best known among scholars for his theoretical and empirical research, especially consumption analysis, monetary history and theory, and for his demonstration of the complexity of stabilization policy. A global public followed his restatement of a political philosophy that insisted on minimizing the role of government in favor of the private sector.
a. Adolph Fischer
b. Adam Smith
c. Adolf Hitler
d. Milton Friedman

24. _____ is the view within monetary economics that variation in the money supply has major influences on national output in the short run and the price level over longer periods and that objectives of monetary policy are best met by targeting the growth rate of the money supply.

_____ today is mainly associated with the work of Milton Friedman, who was among the generation of economists to accept Keynesian economics and then criticize it on his own terms. Friedman and Anna Schwartz wrote an influential book, Monetary History of the United States 1867-1960, and argued that 'inflation is always and everywhere a monetary phenomenon.' Friedman advocated a central bank policy aimed at keeping the supply and demand for money at equilibrium, as measured by growth in productivity and demand.

a. Monetarism
b. Marginal revenue productivity theory of wages
c. Historical school of economics
d. Complexity economics

25. _____ is the study of questions about the city, government, politics, liberty, justice, property, rights, law and the enforcement of a legal code by authority: what they are, why (or even if) they are needed, what makes a government legitimate, what rights and freedoms it should protect and why, what form it should take and why, what the law is, and what duties citizens owe to a legitimate government, if any, and when it may be legitimately overthrown--if ever. In a vernacular sense, the term '_____' often refers to a general view, or specific ethic, political belief or attitude, about politics that does not necessarily belong to the technical discipline of philosophy.

_____ can also be understood by analysing it through the perspectives of metaphysics, epistemology and axiology thereby unearthing the ultimate reality side, the knowledge or methodical side and the value aspects of politics.

Chapter 7. Business Fluctuations and the Theory of Aggregate Demand

a. Political philosophy
b. Materialism
c. Global justice
d. Deductive logic

26. A _____ is an event that suddenly changes the price of a commodity or service. It may be caused by a sudden increase or decrease in the supply of a particular good. This sudden change affects the equilibrium price.
   a. Supply shock
   b. Demand shock
   c. SIMIC
   d. Friedman rule

27. In economics, the _____ can be defined as the graph depicting the relationship between the price of a certain commodity, and the amount of it that consumers are willing and able to purchase at that given price. It is a graphic representation of a demand schedule. The _____ for all consumers together follows from the _____ of every individual consumer: the individual demands at each price are added together.
   a. Demand curve
   b. Kuznets curve
   c. Cost curve
   d. Wage curve

28. _____s is concerned with the tasks of developing and applying quantitative or statistical methods to the study and elucidation of economic principles. _____s combines economic theory with statistics to analyze and test economic relationships. Theoretical _____s considers questions about the statistical properties of estimators and tests, while applied _____s is concerned with the application of _____ methods to assess economic theories.
   a. Economic
   b. Evolutionary economics
   c. Experimental economics
   d. Econometric

29. _____s are statistical models used in econometrics. An _____ specifies the statistical relationship that is believed to hold between the various economic quantities pertaining a particular economic phenomena under study. An _____ can be derived from a deterministic economic model by allowing for uncertainty or from an economic model which itself is stochastic.
   a. ACCRA Cost of Living Index
   b. Event study
   c. Economic statistics
   d. Econometric model

30. _____ is the process of estimation in unknown situations. Prediction is a similar, but more general term. Both can refer to estimation of time series, cross-sectional or longitudinal data.
   a. Forecasting
   b. 1921 recession
   c. 100-year flood
   d. 130-30 fund

31. The _____ is an American economic index intended to estimate future economic activity. It is calculated by The Conference Board, a non-governmental organization, which determines the value of the index from the values of ten key variables. These variables have historically turned downward before a recession and upward before an expansion.
   a. Atkinson index
   b. Index of dissimilarity
   c. Index of diversity
   d. Index of leading indicators

32. _____ is a misspelled phrase from Latin 'pro capite' phrase meaning per head with pro meaning 'per' or 'for each' and capite meaning 'head.' Both words together equate to the phrase 'for each head.'

It is usually used in the field of statistics to indicate the average per person for any given concern, such as income, crime rate, etc.

It is also used in wills to indicate that each of the named beneficiaries should receive, by devise or bequest, equal shares of the estate. This is in contrast to a per stirpes division, in which each branch of the inheriting family inherits an equal share of the estate.

a. Population statistics
b. Sargan test
c. False positive rate
d. Per capita

33. In economics, _____ are key economic variables that economists used to predict a new phase of the business cycle. A leading indicator is one that changes before the economy does; a lagging indicator is one that changes after the economy has changed. Examples of _____ include stock prices, which often improve or worsen before a similar change in the economy.
a. Macroeconomics
b. Leading indicators
c. Medium of exchange
d. Gross domestic product

34. _____ is a common concept in economics, and gives rise to derived concepts such as consumer debt. Generally _____ is defined by opposition to production. But the precise definition can vary because different schools of economists define production quite differently.
a. Federal Reserve Bank Notes
b. Cash or share options
c. Foreclosure data providers
d. Consumption

35. The term _____ is an acronym for Non-Accelerating Inflation Rate of Unemployment. It is a concept in economic theory significant in the interplay of macroeconomics and microeconomics. This 'full employment' unemployment rate is sometimes termed the 'inflation-threshold unemployment rate': Actual unemployment cannot fall below the _____, and the inflation rate is likely to rise quickly (accelerate) in times of strong labor demands during periods of growth.
a. Cobweb model
b. Coal depletion
c. Social Credit
d. NAIRU

36. In economics, an _____ is any good or commodity, transported from one country to another country in a legitimate fashion, typically for use in trade. _____ goods or services are provided to foreign consumers by domestic producers. _____ is an important part of international trade.
a. AD-IA Model
b. ACEA agreement
c. ACCRA Cost of Living Index
d. Export

37. _____ refers to a business or organization attempting to acquire goods or services to accomplish the goals of the enterprise. Though there are several organizations that attempt to set standards in the _____ process, processes can vary greatly between organizations. Typically the word '_____' is not used interchangeably with the word 'procurement', since procurement typically includes Expediting, Supplier Quality, and Traffic and Logistics (T'L) in addition to _____.
a. Free port
b. Purchasing
c. 130-30 fund
d. 100-year flood

38. _____ is a fee paid on borrowed assets. It is the price paid for the use of borrowed money, or, money earned by deposited funds. Assets that are sometimes lent with _____ include money, shares, consumer goods through hire purchase, major assets such as aircraft, and even entire factories in finance lease arrangements.

Chapter 7. Business Fluctuations and the Theory of Aggregate Demand

a. Asset protection
b. Internal debt
c. Insolvency
d. Interest

39. An _____ is the price a borrower pays for the use of money they do not own, for instance a small company might borrow from a bank to kick start their business, and the return a lender receives for deferring the use of funds, by lending it to the borrower. _____s are normally expressed as a percentage rate over the period of one year.

_____s targets are also a vital tool of monetary policy and are used to control variables like investment, inflation, and unemployment.

a. Enterprise value
b. Interest rate
c. Arrow-Debreu model
d. ACCRA Cost of Living Index

40. In economics, _____ is the total amount of money available in an economy at a particular point in time. There are several ways to define 'money', but standard measures usually include currency in circulation and demand deposits.

_____ data are recorded and published, usually by the government or the central bank of the country.

a. Neutrality of money
b. Veil of money
c. Velocity of money
d. Money supply

41. A _____ is a hypothetical measure of overall prices for some set of goods and services, in a given region during a given interval, normalized relative to some base set. Typically, a _____ is approximated with a price index.

The classical dichotomy is the assumption that there is a relatively clean distinction between overall increases or decreases in prices and underlying, e;reale; economic variables.

a. Discouraged worker
b. Discretionary spending
c. Price elasticity of supply
d. Price level

42. In algebra, a _____ is a function depending on n that associates a scalar, det(A), to an n×n square matrix A. The fundamental geometric meaning of a _____ is a scale factor for measure when A is regarded as a linear transformation. _____s are important both in calculus, where they enter the substitution rule for several variables, and in multilinear algebra.

For a fixed nonnegative integer n, there is a unique _____ function for the n×n matrices over any commutative ring R. In particular, this function exists when R is the field of real or complex numbers.

a. 1921 recession
b. Determinant
c. 100-year flood
d. 130-30 fund

43. _____ is the a method of technical and economic research of the systems for purpose to optimize a parity between system's consumer functions or properties and expenses to achieve those functions or properties.

Chapter 7. Business Fluctuations and the Theory of Aggregate Demand

This methodology for continuous perfection of production, industrial technologies, organizational structures was developed by Juryj Sobolev in 1948 at the 'Perm telephone factory'

- 1948 Juryj Sobolev - the first success in application of a method analysis at the 'Perm telephone factory'.
- 1949 - the first application for the invention as result of use of the new method.

Today in economically developed countries practically each enterprise or the company use methodology of the kind of functional-cost analysis as a practice of the quality management, most full satisfying to principles of standards of series ISO 9000.

- Interest of consumer not in products itself, but the advantage which it will receive from its usage.
- The consumer aspires to reduce his expenses
- Functions needed by consumer can be executed in the various ways, and, hence, with various efficiency and expenses. Among possible alternatives of realization of functions exist such in which the parity of quality and the price is the optimal for the consumer.

The goal of _____ is achievement of the highest consumer satisfaction of production at simultaneous decrease in all kinds of industrial expenses Classical _____ has three English synonyms - Value Engineering, Value Management, Value Analysis.

a. Monopoly wage
b. Staple financing
c. Willingness to pay
d. Function cost analysis

44. _____ is an economic model based on price, utility and quantity in a market. It predicts that in a competitive market, price will function to equalize the quantity demanded by consumers, and the quantity supplied by producers, resulting in an economic equilibrium of price and quantity. The model incorporates other factors changing equilibrium as a shift of demand and/or supply.

a. Deferred gratification
b. Joint demand
c. Rational addiction
d. Supply and demand

45. A _____, reserve bank, or monetary authority is the entity responsible for the monetary policy of a country or of a group of member states. It is a bank that can lend money to other banks in times of need. Its primary responsibility is to maintain the stability of the national currency and money supply, but more active duties include controlling subsidized-loan interest rates, and acting as a lender of last resort to the banking sector during times of financial crisis (private banks often being integral to the national financial system.)

a. 130-30 fund
b. 100-year flood
c. 1921 recession
d. Central bank

Chapter 7. Business Fluctuations and the Theory of Aggregate Demand

46. The _____ is the central banking system of the United States. Created in 1913 by the enactment of the Federal Reserve Act (signed by Woodrow Wilson), it is a quasi-public and quasi-private (government entity with private components) banking system that comprises (1) the presidentially appointed Board of Governors of the _____ in Washington, D.C.; (2) the Federal Open Market Committee; (3) twelve regional Federal Reserve Banks located in major cities throughout the nation acting as fiscal agents for the U.S. Treasury, each with its own nine-member board of directors; (4) numerous other private U.S. member banks, which subscribe to required amounts of non-transferable stock in their regional Federal Reserve Banks; and (5) various advisory councils. Since February 2006, Ben Bernanke has served as the Chairman of the Board of Governors of the _____.

a. Federal Reserve System
b. Monetary Policy Report to the Congress
c. Term auction facility
d. Federal Reserve System Open Market Account

47. The term _____ refers to government debt, expenditures and revenues, or to finance (particularly financial revenue) in general.

- _____ deficit is the budget deficit of federal or local government
- _____ policy is the discretionary spending of governments. Contrasts with monetary policy.
- _____ year and _____ quarter are reporting periods for firms and other agencies.

a. Procter ' Gamble
b. Bucket shop
c. Drawdown
d. Fiscal

48. In economics, _____ is the use of government spending and revenue collection to influence the economy.

_____ can be contrasted with the other main type of economic policy, monetary policy, which attempts to stabilize the economy by controlling interest rates and the supply of money. The two main instruments of _____ are government spending and taxation.

a. Fiscal policy
b. Sustainable investment rule
c. 100-year flood
d. Fiscalism

49. _____ is widely regarded as the first modern school of economic thought. It is the idea that free markets can regulate themselves. Its major developers include Adam Smith, David Ricardo, Thomas Malthus and John Stuart Mill. Sometimes the definition of _____ is expanded to include William Petty, Johann Heinrich von Thünen.

a. Classical economics
b. Tendency of the rate of profit to fall
c. Schools of economic thought
d. Marginalism

50. _____ is a term that is used to describe the overall process of invention, innovation and diffusion of technology or processes. The term is redundant with technological development, technological achievement, and technological progress. In essence _____ is the invention of a technology (or a process), the continuous process of improving a technology (in which it often becomes cheaper) and its diffusion throughout industry or society.

a. Technological change
b. 100-year flood
c. 1921 recession
d. 130-30 fund

51. In economics, a _____ is a sudden event that increases or decreases demand for goods or services temporarily. A positive _____ increases demand and a negative _____ decreases demand. Prices of goods and services are affected in both cases.
   a. Lucas-Islands model
   b. Robertson lag
   c. War economy
   d. Demand shock

Chapter 8. The Multiplier Model

1. The term _____ refers to economy-wide fluctuations in production or economic activity over several months or years. These fluctuations occur around a long-term growth trend, and typically involve shifts over time between periods of relatively rapid economic growth (expansion or boom), and periods of relative stagnation or decline (contraction or recession.)

These fluctuations are often measured using the growth rate of real gross domestic product.

   a. Business cycle
   b. Consumer theory
   c. Nominal value
   d. Tobit model

2. _____, 1st Baron Keynes was a renowned economist from Britain whose many ideas on economic and political theories as well as on many governments' monetary policies influenced America. He advocated a government that played an active role in the lives of people regarding business, economy, etc. In this role, the government would use fiscal measures to reduce the consequences of recessions, economic depressions and booms.
   a. Adam Smith
   b. Adolph Fischer
   c. Adolf Hitler
   d. John Maynard Keynes

3. _____ and Keynesian Theory) is a macroeconomic theory based on the ideas of 20th-century British economist John Maynard Keynes. _____ argues that private sector decisions sometimes lead to inefficient macroeconomic outcomes and therefore advocates active policy responses by the public sector, including monetary policy actions by the central bank and fiscal policy actions by the government to stabilize output over the business cycle.

The theories forming the basis of _____ were first presented in The General Theory of Employment, Interest and Money, published in 1936.

   a. Market failure
   b. Keynesian economics
   c. Rational choice theory
   d. Deflation

4. _____ is a common concept in economics, and gives rise to derived concepts such as consumer debt. Generally _____ is defined by opposition to production. But the precise definition can vary because different schools of economists define production quite differently.
   a. Consumption
   b. Cash or share options
   c. Foreclosure data providers
   d. Federal Reserve Bank Notes

5. In economics, the _____ is a single mathematical function used to express consumer spending. It was developed by John Maynard Keynes and detailed most famously in his book The General Theory of Employment, Interest, and Money. The function is used to calculate the amount of total consumption in an economy.
   a. Liquidity preference
   b. Procyclical
   c. DAD-SAS model
   d. Consumption function

6. _____ refers to an action or object coming from outside a system. It is the opposite of endogenous, something generated from within the system.

- In an economic model, an _____ change is one that comes from outside the model and is unexplained by the model. For example, in the simple supply and demand model, a change in consumer tastes or preferences is unexplained by the model and also leads to endogenous changes in demand that lead to changes in the equilibrium price. Put another way, an _____ change involves an alteration of a variable that is autonomous, i.e., unaffected by the workings of the model.

- In linear regression, it means that the variable is independent of all other response values.

- In biology, '_____' refers to an action or object coming from the outside of a system. For example, an _____ contrast agent in medical imaging refers to a liquid injected into the patient intravenously that enhances visibility of a pathology, such as a tumor.

a. ACCRA Cost of Living Index
b. AD-IA Model
c. ACEA agreement
d. Exogenous

7. The _____ or gross domestic income (GDI), a basic measure of an economy's economic performance, is the market value of all final goods and services produced within the borders of a nation in a year. _____ can be defined in three ways, all of which are conceptually identical. First, it is equal to the total expenditures for all final goods and services produced within the country in a stipulated period of time (usually a 365-day year.)

a. Monopolistic competition
b. Market structure
c. Countercyclical
d. Gross domestic product

8. _____ is a misspelled phrase from Latin 'pro capite' phrase meaning per head with pro meaning 'per' or 'for each' and capite meaning 'head.' Both words together equate to the phrase 'for each head.'

It is usually used in the field of statistics to indicate the average per person for any given concern, such as income, crime rate, etc.

It is also used in wills to indicate that each of the named beneficiaries should receive, by devise or bequest, equal shares of the estate. This is in contrast to a per stirpes division, in which each branch of the inheriting family inherits an equal share of the estate.

a. False positive rate
b. Population statistics
c. Sargan test
d. Per capita

9. An _____, in economics, is the amount by which the real Gross domestic product exceeds potential GDP. The real GDP is also known as GDP 'adjusted for inflation', 'constant prices' GDP or 'constant dollar' GDP, because it measures the aggregate output in a country's income accounts in a given year, expressed in base-year prices. On the other hand, the potential GDP is the quantity of real GDP when a country's economy is at full-employment.

a. AD-IA Model
b. ACEA agreement
c. Inflationary gap
d. ACCRA Cost of Living Index

Chapter 8. The Multiplier Model

10. In algebra, a _____ is a function depending on n that associates a scalar, det(A), to an n×n square matrix A. The fundamental geometric meaning of a _____ is a scale factor for measure when A is regarded as a linear transformation. _____s are important both in calculus, where they enter the substitution rule for several variables, and in multilinear algebra.

For a fixed nonnegative integer n, there is a unique _____ function for the n×n matrices over any commutative ring R. In particular, this function exists when R is the field of real or complex numbers.

a. 1921 recession
c. 130-30 fund
b. 100-year flood
d. Determinant

11. In economics, the _____ or spending multiplier is the idea that an initial amount of spending (usually by the government) leads to increased consumption spending and so results in an increase in national income greater than the initial amount of spending. In other words, an initial change in aggregate demand causes a change in aggregate output for the economy that is a multiple of the initial change.

The existence of a _____ was initially proposed by Ralph George Hawtrey in 1931.

a. Magical triangle
c. Spending multiplier
b. Keynesian cross
d. Multiplier effect

12. In economics, the multiplier effect or _____ is the idea that an initial amount of spending (usually by the government) leads to increased consumption spending and so results in an increase in national income greater than the initial amount of spending. In other words, an initial change in aggregate demand causes a change in aggregate output for the economy that is a multiple of the initial change.

The existence of a multiplier effect was initially proposed by Ralph George Hawtrey in 1931.

a. Multiplier effect
c. Keynesian formula
b. Neo-Keynesian economics
d. Spending Multiplier

13. _____ is an economic concept with commonplace familiarity. It is the price that a good or service is offered at, or will fetch, in the marketplace. It is of interest mainly in the study of microeconomics.
a. Noisy market hypothesis
c. Paper trading
b. Market anomaly
d. Market price

14. In economics, _____ refers to the highest level of real Gross Domestic Product output that can be sustained over the long term. The existence of a limit is due to natural and institutional constraints. If actual GDP rises and stays above _____, then (in the absence of wage and price controls) inflation tends to increase as demand exceeds supply.
a. Monetary conditions index
c. Monetary policy reaction function
b. Fundamental psychological law
d. Potential output

15. _____ is widely regarded as the first modern school of economic thought. It is the idea that free markets can regulate themselves.Its major developers include Adam Smith, David Ricardo, Thomas Malthus and John Stuart Mill. Sometimes the definition of _____ is expanded to include William Petty, Johann Heinrich von Thünen.

a. Schools of economic thought
b. Classical economics
c. Marginalism
d. Tendency of the rate of profit to fall

16. _____s is the social science that studies the production, distribution, and consumption of goods and services. The term _____s comes from the Ancient Greek oá¼°κονομῖα from oá¼¶κος (oikos, 'house') + vÍŒμος (nomos, 'custom' or 'law'), hence 'rules of the house(hold)'. Current _____ models developed out of the broader field of political economy in the late 19th century, owing to a desire to use an empirical approach more akin to the physical sciences.
a. Inflation
b. Economic
c. Energy economics
d. Opportunity cost

17. _____ is the increase in the amount of the goods and services produced by an economy over time. It is conventionally measured as the percent rate of increase in real gross domestic product, or real GDP. Growth is usually calculated in real terms, i.e. inflation-adjusted terms, in order to net out the effect of inflation on the price of the goods and services produced.
a. ACCRA Cost of Living Index
b. Economic growth
c. AD-IA Model
d. ACEA agreement

18. _____ in economics and business is the result of an exchange and from that trade we assign a numerical monetary value to a good, service or asset. If Alice trades Bob 4 apples for an orange, the _____ of an orange is 4 apples. Inversely, the _____ of an apple is 1/4 oranges.
a. Premium pricing
b. Price book
c. Price
d. Price war

19. The term _____ refers to government debt, expenditures and revenues, or to finance (particularly financial revenue) in general.

- _____ deficit is the budget deficit of federal or local government
- _____ policy is the discretionary spending of governments. Contrasts with monetary policy.
- _____ year and _____ quarter are reporting periods for firms and other agencies.

a. Drawdown
b. Bucket shop
c. Procter ' Gamble
d. Fiscal

20. In economics, _____ is the use of government spending and revenue collection to influence the economy.

_____ can be contrasted with the other main type of economic policy, monetary policy, which attempts to stabilize the economy by controlling interest rates and the supply of money. The two main instruments of _____ are government spending and taxation.

a. Sustainable investment rule
b. Fiscalism
c. 100-year flood
d. Fiscal policy

21. _____ are the inflation-indexed bonds issued by the U.S. Treasury. The principal is adjusted to the Consumer Price Index, the commonly used measure of inflation. The coupon rate is constant, but generates a different amount of interest when multiplied by the inflation-adjusted principal, thus protecting the holder against inflation.
   a. 130-30 fund
   b. 1921 recession
   c. 100-year flood
   d. Treasury Inflation-Protected Securities

94   *Chapter 8. The Multiplier Model*

22.   A _____ is:

- Rewrite _____, in generative grammar and computer science
- Standardization, a formal and widely-accepted statement, fact, definition, or qualification
- Operation, a determinate _____ for performing a mathematical operation and obtaining a certain result (Mathematics, Logic)
    - Unary operation
    - Binary operation
- _____ of inference, a function from sets of formulae to formulae (Mathematics, Logic)
- _____ of thumb, principle with broad application that is not intended to be strictly accurate or reliable for every situation. Also often simply referred to as a _____
- Moral, an atomic element of a moral code for guiding choices in human behavior
- Heuristic, a quantized '_____' which shows a tendency or probability for successful function
- A regulation, as in sports
- A Production _____, as in computer science
- Procedural law, a _____ set governing the application of laws to cases
    - A law, which may informally be called a '_____'
    - A court ruling, a decision by a court
- In the U.S. Government, a regulation mandated by Congress, but written or expanded upon by the Executive Branch.
- Norm (sociology), an informal but widely accepted _____, concept, truth, definition, or qualification (social norms, legal norms, coding norms)
- Norm (philosophy), a kind of sentence or a reason to act, feel or believe
- 'Rulership' is the concept of governance by a government:
    - Military _____, governance by a military body
    - Monastic _____, a collection of precepts that guides the life of monks or nuns in a religious order where the superior holds the place of Christ
- Slide _____

- '_____,' a song by Ayumi Hamasaki
- '_____,' a song by rapper Nas
- '_____s,' an album by the band The Whitest Boy Alive
- _____s: Pyaar Ka Superhit Formula, a 2003 Bollywood film
- ruler, an instrument for measuring lengths
- _____, a component of an astrolabe, circumferator or similar instrument
- The _____s, a bestselling self-help book
- _____ Project (Run Up-to-date Linux Everywhere), a project that aims to use up-to-date Linux software on old PCs
- _____ engine, a software system that helps managing business _____s
- Ja _____, a hip hop artist
    - R.U.L.E., a 2005 greatest hits album by rapper Ja _____
- '_____s,' a KMFDM song

a. Demand   b. Rule
c. Procter ' Gamble   d. Technocracy

Chapter 8. The Multiplier Model

23. A _____ product is a product designed for cheapness and short-term convenience rather than medium to long-term durability, with most products only intended for single use. The term is also sometimes used for products that may last several months (ex. _____ air filters) to distinguish from similar products that last indefinitely (ex.
    a. 100-year flood
    b. 1921 recession
    c. 130-30 fund
    d. Disposable

24. _____ is gross income minus income tax on that income.

Discretionary income is income after subtracting taxes and normal expenses (such as rent or mortgage, utilities, insurance, medical, transportation, property maintenance, child support, inflation, food and sundries, 'c.) to maintain a certain standard of living.

    a. Taxation as theft
    b. Disposable income
    c. Stamp Act
    d. Disposable personal income

25. A _____ is a tax that is a fixed amount no matter what the change in circumstance of the taxed entity. (A lump-sum subsidy or lump-sum redistribution is defined similarly.) It is a regressive tax, such that the lower income is, the higher percentage of income applicable to the tax.
    a. Grant-in-aid
    b. Budget deficit
    c. Lump-sum tax
    d. Funding body

26. _____ refers to a business or organization attempting to acquire goods or services to accomplish the goals of the enterprise. Though there are several organizations that attempt to set standards in the _____ process, processes can vary greatly between organizations. Typically the word '_____' is not used interchangeably with the word 'procurement', since procurement typically includes Expediting, Supplier Quality, and Traffic and Logistics (T'L) in addition to _____.
    a. 100-year flood
    b. Purchasing
    c. 130-30 fund
    d. Free port

27. To _____ is to impose a financial charge or other levy upon a taxpayer by a state or the functional equivalent of a state.

    _____es are also imposed by many subnational entities. _____es consist of direct _____ or indirect _____, and may be paid in money or as its labour equivalent (often but not always unpaid.)

    a. Tax
    b. 100-year flood
    c. 1921 recession
    d. 130-30 fund

28. To tax is to impose a financial charge or other levy upon a taxpayer by a state or the functional equivalent of a state.

    _____ are also imposed by many subnational entities. _____ consist of direct tax or indirect tax, and may be paid in money or as its labour equivalent (often but not always unpaid.)

    a. Taxes
    b. 130-30 fund
    c. 1921 recession
    d. 100-year flood

Chapter 8. The Multiplier Model

29. In economics, _____ is the total demand for final goods and services in the economy (Y) at a given time and price level. It is the amount of goods and services in the economy that will be purchased at all possible price levels. This is the demand for the gross domestic product of a country when inventory levels are static.
    a. Aggregate demand
    b. Aggregate expenditure
    c. Aggregation problem
    d. Aggregate supply

30. Economics:

    - _____, the desire to own something and the ability to pay for it
    - _____ curve, a graphic representation of a _____ schedule
    - _____ deposit, the money in checking accounts
    - _____ pull theory, the theory that inflation occurs when _____ for goods and services exceeds existing supplies
    - _____ schedule, a table that lists the quantity of a good a person will buy it each different price
    - _____ side economics, the school of economics at believes government spending and tax cuts open economy by raising _____

    a. Production
    b. McKesson ' Robbins scandal
    c. Demand
    d. Variability

31. In macroeconomics, _____ is a condition of the national economy, where all or nearly all persons willing and able to work at the prevailing wages and working conditions are able to do so. It is defined either as 0% unemployment, literally, no unemployment (the rate of unemployment is the fraction of the work force unable to find work), as by James Tobin, or as the level of employment rates when there is no cyclical unemployment. It is defined by the majority of mainstream economists as being an acceptable level of natural unemployment above 0%, the discrepancy from 0% being due to non-cyclical types of unemployment.
    a. Harrod-Johnson diagram
    b. Full employment
    c. Demand shock
    d. Marginal propensity to consume

32. The _____ was a worldwide economic downturn starting in most places in 1929 and ending at different times in the 1930s or early 1940s for different countries. It was the largest and most important economic depression in the 20th century, and is used in the 21st century as an example of how far the world's economy can fall. The _____ originated in the United States; historians most often use as a starting date the stock market crash on October 29, 1929, known as Black Tuesday.
    a. Wall Street Crash of 1929
    b. Jarrow March
    c. Great Depression
    d. British Empire Economic Conference

33. _____ was a global military conflict which involved a majority of the world's nations, including all of the great powers, organized into two opposing military alliances: the Allies and the Axis. The war involved the mobilization of over 100 million military personnel, making it the most widespread war in history. In a state of 'total war', the major participants placed their entire economic, industrial, and scientific capabilities at the service of the war effort, erasing the distinction between civilian and military resources.
    a. 130-30 fund
    b. 100-year flood
    c. 1921 recession
    d. World War II

Chapter 8. The Multiplier Model

34. A _____ occurs when an entity spends more money than it takes in. The opposite of a _____ is a budget surplus. Debt is essentially an accumulated flow of deficits.
   a. Lump-sum tax
   b. Budget deficit
   c. Public Financial Management
   d. Funding body

35. A _____ is a situation in which the government takes in more than it spends.
   a. 130-30 fund
   b. 100-year flood
   c. Budget set
   d. Budget surplus

36. _____ is a school of macroeconomic thought that argues that economic growth can be most effectively created using incentives for people to produce (supply) goods and services, such as adjusting income tax and capital gains tax rates, and by allowing greater flexibility by reducing regulation. Consumers will then benefit from a greater supply of goods and services at lower prices.

The term _____ was coined by journalist Jude Wanniski in 1975, and popularized the ideas of economists Robert Mundell and Arthur Laffer.

   a. Commodity trading advisors
   b. Clap note
   c. Fiscal stimulus plans
   d. Supply-side economics

37. A _____ is a reduction in taxes. Economic stimulus via _____s, along with interest rate intervention and deficit spending, are one of the central tenets of Keynesian economics.

The immediate effects of a _____ are, generally, a decrease in the real income of the government and an increase in the real income of those whose tax rate has been lowered.

   a. Direct taxes
   b. Withholding tax
   c. Popiwek
   d. Tax cut

38. _____, or a _____ is the concept of a resulting effect (cf. cause and effect, arising from another action. In general terms, it is used to indicate that all human actions, particularly crime and sin, have profound effects.
   a. Variability
   b. Consequence
   c. Rule
   d. Solved

39. _____s is concerned with the tasks of developing and applying quantitative or statistical methods to the study and elucidation of economic principles. _____s combines economic theory with statistics to analyze and test economic relationships. Theoretical _____s considers questions about the statistical properties of estimators and tests, while applied _____s is concerned with the application of _____ methods to assess economic theories.
   a. Experimental economics
   b. Econometric
   c. Economic
   d. Evolutionary economics

40. _____s are statistical models used in econometrics. An _____ specifies the statistical relationship that is believed to hold between the various economic quantities pertaining a particular economic phenomena under study. An _____ can be derived from a deterministic economic model by allowing for uncertainty or from an economic model which itself is stochastic.

Chapter 8. The Multiplier Model

a. Econometric model
b. ACCRA Cost of Living Index
c. Economic statistics
d. Event study

41. An _____ or Ä"conomic system is a system that involves the production, distribution and consumption of goods and services between the entities in a particular society. It is the method used by society to produce and distribute goods and services. The _____ is composed of people and institutions, including their relationships to productive resources, such as through the convention of property.
    a. Indicative planning
    b. Information economy
    c. Intention economy
    d. Economic system

42. A _____ or directed economy is an economic system in which the government or workers' councils manages the economy. It is an economic system in which the central government makes all decisions on the production and consumption of goods and services. Its most extensive form is referred to as a _____, centrally planned economy, or command and control economy.
    a. Transition economy
    b. Nutritional Economics
    c. Command economy
    d. Subsistence economy

43. The _____ is a book published by John Maynard Keynes. Keynes attended the Versailles Conference as a delegate of the British Treasury and argued for a much more generous peace. It was a best seller throughout the world and was critical in establishing a general opinion that the Versailles Treaty was a 'Carthaginian peace'.
    a. Economic Consequences of the Peace
    b. ACCRA Cost of Living Index
    c. ACEA agreement
    d. AD-IA Model

44. The _____ is the apparent contradiction that although water is on the whole more useful, in terms of survival, than diamonds, diamonds command a higher price in the market. The economist Adam Smith is often considered to be the classic presenter of this paradox. Nicolaus Copernicus, John Locke, John Law and others had previously tried to explain the disparity.
    a. 130-30 fund
    b. 100-year flood
    c. St. Petersburg paradox
    d. Paradox of value

45. The _____ is a paradox of economics propounded by John Maynard Keynes. The paradox states that if everyone saves more money during times of recession, then aggregate demand will fall and will in turn lower total savings in the population because of the decrease in consumption and economic growth.

The argument is that, in equilibrium, total income (and thus demand) must equal total output, and that total investment must equal total saving.

    a. Keynesian cross
    b. Spending multiplier
    c. Speculative demand
    d. Paradox of thrift

46. A _____ association is a financial institution that specializes in accepting savings deposits and making mortgage and other loans. The S'L or thrift term is mainly used in the United States; similar institutions in the United Kingdom, Ireland and some Commonwealth countries include building societies and trustee savings banks.

They are often mutually held, meaning that the depositors and borrowers are members with voting rights, and have the ability to direct the financial and managerial goals of the organization, similar to the policyholders of a mutual insurance company.

a. Collective investment scheme
c. Fonds commun de placement
b. Savings and Loan
d. Participating policy

1.

A _____ is a type of financial intermediary and a type of bank. Commercial banking is also known as business banking. It is a bank that provides checking accounts, savings accounts, and money market accounts and that accepts time deposits.

a. Daylight overdraft
b. Bought deal
c. Commercial bank
d. Lombard banking

2. In finance, the _____ is the system that allows the transfer of money between savers and borrowers.

Put another way: the _____ is a set of complex and closely interconnected financial institutions, markets, instruments, services, practices, and transactions.

a. Hedonimetry
b. Foreign investment
c. Lean consumption
d. Financial system

3. In business and accounting, _____ are everything of value that is owned by a person or company. It is a claim on the property your income of a borrower. The balance sheet of a firm records the monetary value of the _____ owned by the firm.

a. ACEA agreement
b. ACCRA Cost of Living Index
c. Amortization schedule
d. Assets

4. _____ is a fee paid on borrowed assets. It is the price paid for the use of borrowed money, or, money earned by deposited funds. Assets that are sometimes lent with _____ include money, shares, consumer goods through hire purchase, major assets such as aircraft, and even entire factories in finance lease arrangements.

a. Insolvency
b. Internal debt
c. Interest
d. Asset protection

5. An _____ is the price a borrower pays for the use of money they do not own, for instance a small company might borrow from a bank to kick start their business, and the return a lender receives for deferring the use of funds, by lending it to the borrower. _____s are normally expressed as a percentage rate over the period of one year.

_____s targets are also a vital tool of monetary policy and are used to control variables like investment, inflation, and unemployment.

a. Interest rate
b. Enterprise value
c. ACCRA Cost of Living Index
d. Arrow-Debreu model

6. The _____ is the central banking system of the United States. Created in 1913 by the enactment of the Federal Reserve Act (signed by Woodrow Wilson), it is a quasi-public and quasi-private (government entity with private components) banking system that comprises (1) the presidentially appointed Board of Governors of the _____ in Washington, D.C.; (2) the Federal Open Market Committee; (3) twelve regional Federal Reserve Banks located in major cities throughout the nation acting as fiscal agents for the U.S. Treasury, each with its own nine-member board of directors; (4) numerous other private U.S. member banks, which subscribe to required amounts of non-transferable stock in their regional Federal Reserve Banks; and (5) various advisory councils. Since February 2006, Ben Bernanke has served as the Chairman of the Board of Governors of the _____.

Chapter 9. Financial Markets and the Special Case of Money   101

a. Monetary Policy Report to the Congress
b. Federal Reserve System Open Market Account
c. Federal Reserve System
d. Term auction facility

7. _____s are cash, evidence of an ownership interest in an entity or deliver, cash or another _____.

_____s can be categorized by form depending on whether they are cash instruments or derivative instruments:

- Cash instruments are _____s whose value is determined directly by markets. They can be divided into securities, which are readily transferable, and other cash instruments such as loans and deposits, where both borrower and lender have to agree on a transfer.
- Derivative instruments are _____s which derive their value from the value and characteristics of one or more underlying assets. They can be divided into exchange-traded derivatives and over-the-counter (OTC) derivatives.

Alternatively, _____s can be categorized by 'asset class' depending on whether they are equity based (reflecting ownership of the issuing entity) or debt based (reflecting a loan the investor has made to the issuing entity.) If it is debt, it can be further categorised into short term (less than one year) or long term.

Foreign Exchange instruments and transactions are neither debt nor equity based and belong in their own category.

a. Municipal Bond Arbitrage
b. Fundamentally based indexes
c. Market liquidity
d. Financial instrument

8. _____s are financial contracts whose values are derived from the value of something else (known as the underlying.) The underlying value on which a _____ is based can be an asset (e.g., commodities, equities (stocks), residential mortgages, commercial real estate, loans, bonds), an index (e.g., interest rates, exchange rates, stock market indices, consumer price index (CPI) -- see inflation _____s), weather conditions bonds or other forms of credit.

a. 130-30 fund
b. 100-year flood
c. Second derivative
d. Derivative

9. The cost advantages of using _____ include:

- Reconciling conflicting preferences of lenders and borrowers

- Risk aversion- intermediaries help spread out and decrease the risks

- Economies of scale- using _____ reduces the costs of lending and borrowing

- Economies of scope- intermediaries concentrate on the demands of the lenders and borrowers and are able to enhance their products and services (use same inputs to produce different outputs)

_____ include:

- Banks
- Building societies
- Credit unions
- Financial advisers or brokers
- Insurance companies
- Collective investment schemes
- Pension funds

Financial institutions (intermediaries) perform the vital role of bringing together those economic agents with surplus funds who want to lend, with those with a shortage of funds who want to borrow.

In doing this they offer the major benefits of maturity and risk transformation. It is possible for this to be done by direct contact between the ultimate borrowers, but there are major cost disadvantages of direct finance.

Indeed, one explanation of the existence of specialist _____ is that they have a related (cost) advantage in offering financial services, which not only enables them to make profit, but also raises the overall efficiency of the economy.

a. Broker-dealer
b. SICAV
c. Collective investment scheme
d. Financial intermediaries

10. In economics, a _____ is a mechanism that allows people to easily buy and sell (trade) financial securities (such as stocks and bonds), commodities (such as precious metals or agricultural goods), and other fungible items of value at low transaction costs and at prices that reflect the efficient-market hypothesis.

_____s have evolved significantly over several hundred years and are undergoing constant innovation to improve liquidity.

Both general markets (where many commodities are traded) and specialized markets (where only one commodity is traded) exist.

a. Market anomaly
b. Noise trader
c. Convertible arbitrage
d. Financial market

11. _____, in law and economics, is a form of risk management primarily used to hedge against the risk of a contingent loss. _____ is defined as the equitable transfer of the risk of a loss, from one entity to another, in exchange for a premium, and can be thought of as a guaranteed small loss to prevent a large, possibly devastating loss. An insurer is a company selling the _____; an insured or policyholder is the person or entity buying the _____.

a. ACCRA Cost of Living Index
b. AD-IA Model
c. Insurance
d. ACEA agreement

12. The accounting equation relates assets, _____, and owner's equity:

Assets = _____ + Owner's Equity

The accounting equation is the mathematical structure of the balance sheet.

The Australian Accounting Research Foundation defines _____ as: 'future sacrifice of economic benefits that the entity is presently obliged to make to other entities as a result of past transactions and other past events.'

Probably the most accepted accounting definition of liability is the one used by the International Accounting Standards Board (IASB.) The following is a quotation from IFRS Framework:

A liability is a present obligation of the enterprise arising from past events, the settlement of which is expected to result in an outflow from the enterprise of resources embodying economic benefits

-

Regulations as to the recognition of _____ are different all over the world, but are roughly similar to those of the IASB.

a. Coase theorem
c. Community property

b. Competition law theory
d. Liabilities

13. _____ is the process by which money is produced or issued. There are three different ways to create money:

- manufacturing a new monetary unit, such as paper currency or metal coins (_____)
- loaning out a physical monetary unit multiple times through fractional-reserve lending (credit creation)
- buying of government securities or other financial instruments by central bank through Open market operations (electronic creation)

Coins are produced by manufacturing metal in a factory called a mint.

Banknotes and bank account balances are financial securities issued by a bank.

Similarly, money destruction, i.e., the reverse of _____, can occur in two different ways, depending on how the money was created.

a. Shadow Open Market Committee
c. Second-round effect

b. Monetary policy of Sweden
d. Money creation

14. A _____ is a professionally managed type of collective investment scheme that pools money from many investors and invests it in stocks, bonds, short-term money market instruments, and/or other securities. The _____ will have a fund manager that trades the pooled money on a regular basis. As of early 2008, the worldwide value of all _____s totals more than $26 trillion.

a. Self-invested personal pension
c. Mutual fund
b. Dark pools of liquidity
d. Participating policy

15. _____ is the revenue to a brokerage firm when commissioned securities and insurance salespeople sell a product, whether it is an investment like stocks, bonds or insurance like life insurance or long term care insurance. The commission that the agent receives is usually a percentage of this figure, although some firms like Merrill Lynch use figures called Production Credits, usually smaller than _____, to determine payouts and retain more revenue.

For example, a mutual fund with a 5.75% sales charge is sold to someone who invests $10,000.

a. Number of Shares
c. Monopoly price
b. Discretionary policy
d. Gross Dealer Concession

16. In general, a _____ is an arrangement to provide people with an income when they are no longer earning a regular income from employment.

The terms retirement plan or superannuation refer to a _____ granted upon retirement . Retirement plans may be set up by employers, insurance companies, the government or other institutions such as employer associations or trade unions.

a. Real wage
c. Profit-sharing agreement
b. Superannuation
d. Pension

17. _____ is the identification, assessment, and prioritization of risks followed by coordinated and economical application of resources to minimize, monitor, and control the probability and/or impact of unfortunate events.. Risks can come from uncertainty in financial markets, project failures, legal liabilities, credit risk, accidents, natural causes and disasters as well as deliberate attacks from an adversary. Several _____ standards have been developed including the Project Management Institute, the National Institute of Science ' Technology, actuarial societies, and ISO standards.

a. Regression toward the mean
c. Penny stock
b. Risk management
d. Kanban

18. A security is a fungible, negotiable instrument representing financial value. _____ are broadly categorized into debt _____; equity _____, e.g., common stocks; and derivative (finance) contracts such as forwards, futures, options and swaps. The company or other entity issuing the security is called the issuer.

a. Settlement risk
c. Pass-Through Certificates
b. Red herring prospectus
d. Securities

19. The _____ is 'the basic residential unit in which economic production, consumption, inheritance, child rearing, and shelter are organized and carried out'; [the _____] 'may or may not be synonomous with family'.

The _____ is the basic unit of analysis in many social, microeconomic and government models. The term refers to all individuals who live in the same dwelling.

a. Family economics
c. 130-30 fund
b. 100-year flood
d. Household

Chapter 9. Financial Markets and the Special Case of Money

20. _____ in economics and business is the result of an exchange and from that trade we assign a numerical monetary value to a good, service or asset. If Alice trades Bob 4 apples for an orange, the _____ of an orange is 4 apples. Inversely, the _____ of an apple is 1/4 oranges.
    a. Price
    b. Price book
    c. Premium pricing
    d. Price war

21. _____ is a life of security. It may also refer to the final payment date of a loan or other financial instrument, at which point all remaining interest and principal is due to be paid.

    1, 3, 6 months _____ band can be calculated by using 30-day per month periods.

    a. Future-oriented
    b. Future value
    c. Maturity
    d. Refinancing risk

22. _____ is the value on a given date of a future payment or series of future payments, discounted to reflect the time value of money and other factors such as investment risk. _____ calculations are widely used in business and economics to provide a means to compare cash flows at different times on a meaningful 'like to like' basis.

    Money value fluctuates over time: $100 today are not worth $100 in five years.

    a. Future value
    b. Present value of costs
    c. Tax shield
    d. Present value

23. In economics, _____ is a sustained decrease in the general price level of goods and services. _____ occurs when the annual inflation rate falls below zero percent, resulting in an increase in the real value of money -- a negative inflation rate. This should not be confused with disinflation, a slow-down in the inflation rate (i.e. when the inflation decreases, but still remains positive.)
    a. Literacy rate
    b. Deflation
    c. Price revolution
    d. Tobit model

24. _____ is the a method of technical and economic research of the systems for purpose to optimize a parity between system's consumer functions or properties and expenses to achieve those functions or properties.

    This methodology for continuous perfection of production, industrial technologies, organizational structures was developed by Juryj Sobolev in 1948 at the 'Perm telephone factory'

    - 1948 Juryj Sobolev - the first success in application of a method analysis at the 'Perm telephone factory' .
    - 1949 - the first application for the invention as result of use of the new method.

Chapter 9. Financial Markets and the Special Case of Money

Today in economically developed countries practically each enterprise or the company use methodology of the kind of functional-cost analysis as a practice of the quality management, most full satisfying to principles of standards of series ISO 9000.

- Interest of consumer not in products itself, but the advantage which it will receive from its usage.
- The consumer aspires to reduce his expenses
- Functions needed by consumer can be executed in the various ways, and, hence, with various efficiency and expenses. Among possible alternatives of realization of functions exist such in which the parity of quality and the price is the optimal for the consumer.

The goal of _____ is achievement of the highest consumer satisfaction of production at simultaneous decrease in all kinds of industrial expenses Classical _____ has three English synonyms - Value Engineering, Value Management, Value Analysis.

a. Willingness to pay
c. Function cost analysis
b. Staple financing
d. Monopoly wage

25. Market _____ is a business, economics or investment term that refers to an asset's ability to be easily converted through an act of buying or selling without causing a significant movement in the price and with minimum loss of value. Money, or cash on hand, is the most liquid asset. An act of exchange of a less liquid asset with a more liquid asset is called liquidation.

a. 100-year flood
c. 130-30 fund
b. Liquidity
d. 1921 recession

26. In finance, a _____ is a debt security, in which the authorized issuer owes the holders a debt and, depending on the terms of the _____, is obliged to pay interest (the coupon) and/or to repay the principal at a later date, termed maturity. A _____ is a formal contract to repay borrowed money with interest at fixed intervals.

Thus a _____ is like a loan: the issuer is the borrower (debtor), the holder is the lender (creditor), and the coupon is the interest.

a. Zero-coupon
c. Bond
b. Callable
d. Prize Bond

27. A _____ is a bond issued by a corporation. It is a bond that a corporation issues to raise money in order to expand its business. The term is usually applied to longer-term debt instruments, generally with a maturity date falling at least a year after their issue date.

a. Bond valuation
c. Dirty price
b. Bond fund
d. Corporate bond

28. In economics, _____ is a rise in the general level of prices of goods and services in an economy over a period of time. When the general price level rises, each unit of currency buys fewer goods and services; consequently, _____ is also a decline in the real value of money--a loss of purchasing power in the medium of exchange which is also the monetary unit of account in the economy. A chief measure of general price-level _____ is the general _____ rate, which is the percentage change in a general price index (normally the Consumer Price Index) over time.

a. Inflation
b. Economic
c. Opportunity cost
d. Energy economics

29. In economics, the _____ is a measure of inflation, the rate of increase of a price index (for example, a consumer price index.)It is the percentage rate of change in price level over time. The rate of decrease in the purchasing power of money is approximately equal.

It's used to calculate the real interest rate, as well as real increases in wages, and official measurements of this rate act as input variables to COLA adjustments and Inflation derivatives prices.

a. Inflation rate
b. Interest rate option
c. Equity value
d. Edgeworth paradox

30. In finance and economics _____ or nominal rate of interest refers to the rate of interest before adjustment for inflation (in contrast with the real interest rate); or, for interest rates 'as stated' without adjustment for the full effect of compounding (also referred to as the nominal annual rate.) An interest rate is called nominal if the frequency of compounding (e.g. a month) is not identical to the basic time unit (normally a year.)

The real interest rate includes compensation for the lender's lost value due to inflation, whereas the _____ excludes inflation.

a. London Interbank Offered Rate
b. Risk-free interest rate
c. Fixed interest
d. Nominal interest rate

31. The '_____' is approximately the nominal interest rate minus the inflation rate Since the inflation rate over the course of a loan is not known initially, volatility in inflation represents a risk to both the lender and the borrower.

In economics and finance, an individual who lends money for repayment at a later point in time expects to be compensated for the time value of money, or not having the use of that money while it is lent.

a. Core inflation
b. Cost-push inflation
c. Reflation
d. Real interest rate

32. _____ is a broad label that refers to any individuals or households that use goods and services generated within the economy. The concept of a _____ is used in different contexts, so that the usage and significance of the term may vary.

Typically when business people and economists talk of _____s they are talking about person as _____, an aggregated commodity item with little individuality other than that expressed in the buy/not-buy decision.

a. Consumer
b. 1921 recession
c. 100-year flood
d. 130-30 fund

Chapter 9. Financial Markets and the Special Case of Money

33. A _____ is a measure of the average price of consumer goods and services purchased by households. A _____ measures a price change for a constant market basket of goods and services from one period to the next within the same area (city, region, or nation.) It is a price index determined by measuring the price of a standard group of goods meant to represent the typical market basket of a typical urban consumer.
    a. Cost-of-living index
    b. CPI
    c. Lipstick index
    d. Consumer price index

34. _____ are the inflation-indexed bonds issued by the U.S. Treasury. The principal is adjusted to the Consumer Price Index, the commonly used measure of inflation. The coupon rate is constant, but generates a different amount of interest when multiplied by the inflation-adjusted principal, thus protecting the holder against inflation.
    a. 1921 recession
    b. 130-30 fund
    c. Treasury inflation-protected securities
    d. 100-year flood

35. A _____ is a normalized average (typically a weighted average) of prices for a given class of goods or services in a given region, during a given interval of time. It is a statistic designed to help to compare how these prices, taken as a whole, differ between time periods or geographical locations.

    Price indices have several potential uses.

    a. Two-part tariff
    b. Price index
    c. Transactional Net Margin Method
    d. Product sabotage

36. A _____, reserve bank, or monetary authority is the entity responsible for the monetary policy of a country or of a group of member states. It is a bank that can lend money to other banks in times of need. Its primary responsibility is to maintain the stability of the national currency and money supply, but more active duties include controlling subsidized-loan interest rates, and acting as a lender of last resort to the banking sector during times of financial crisis (private banks often being integral to the national financial system.)
    a. 1921 recession
    b. 100-year flood
    c. Central bank
    d. 130-30 fund

37. _____ is the process by which the government, central bank (ii) availability of money, and (iii) cost of money or rate of interest, in order to attain a set of objectives oriented towards the growth and stability of the economy. Monetary theory provides insight into how to craft optimal _____.

    _____ is referred to as either being an expansionary policy where an expansionary policy increases the total supply of money in the economy, and a contractionary policy decreases the total money supply.

    a. 100-year flood
    b. 1921 recession
    c. Monetary policy
    d. 130-30 fund

38. Bartering is a medium in which goods or services are directly exchanged for other goods and/or services, without the use of money. It can be bilateral or multilateral, and usually exists parallel to monetary systems in most developed countries, though to a very limited extent. _____ usually replaces money as the method of exchange in times of monetary crisis, when the currency is unstable and devalued by hyperinflation.

Chapter 9. Financial Markets and the Special Case of Money

a. Meitheal
b. Community-based economics
c. Barter
d. New Economics Foundation

39. A _____ is something for which there is demand, but which is supplied without qualitative differentiation across a market. It is a product that is the same no matter who produces it, such as petroleum, notebook paper, or milk. In other words, copper is copper.
   a. Hard commodity
   b. 100-year flood
   c. Soft commodity
   d. Commodity

40. _____ is money whose value comes from a commodity out of which it is made. It is objects that have value in themselves as well as for use as money.

Examples of commodities that have been used as mediums of exchange include gold, silver, copper, salt, peppercorns, large stones, decorated belts, shells, alcohol, cigarettes, cannabis, candy, barley etc.

   a. Currency competition
   b. Fiat money
   c. Reserve currency
   d. Commodity money

41. The _____ problem (often 'double _____') is an important category of transaction costs that impose severe limitations on economies lacking money and thus dominated by barter or other in-kind transactions. The problem is caused by the improbability of the wants, needs or events that cause or motivate a transaction occurring at the same time and the same place.

In-kind transactions have several problems, most notably timing constraints.

   a. Going concern
   b. Coincidence of Wants
   c. Buy-sell agreement
   d. RFM

42. _____ refers to money or scrip which is exchanged only electronically. Typically, this involves use of computer networks, the internet and digital stored value systems. Electronic Funds Transfer and direct deposit are examples of _____.
   a. ACEA agreement
   b. Electronic money
   c. AD-IA Model
   d. ACCRA Cost of Living Index

43. _____ is money declared by a government to be legal tender. The term derives from the Latin fiat, meaning 'let it be done'. _____ achieves value because a government accepts it in payment of taxes and says it can be used within the country as a 'tender' to pay all debts.
   a. Currency board
   b. Devaluation
   c. World currency
   d. Fiat money

44. _____ or forced tender is payment that, by law, cannot be refused in settlement of a debt.

_____ is variously defined in different jurisdictions. Formally, it is anything which when offered in payment extinguishes the debt.

Chapter 9. Financial Markets and the Special Case of Money

a. Patent portfolio
b. Leave of absence
c. Landsbanki Freezing Order 2008
d. Legal tender

45. In economics, _____ is the total amount of money available in an economy at a particular point in time. There are several ways to define 'money', but standard measures usually include currency in circulation and demand deposits.

_____ data are recorded and published, usually by the government or the central bank of the country.

a. Veil of money
b. Velocity of money
c. Money supply
d. Neutrality of money

46. In economics, _____ is the widest measurement of the money supply. It is generally

'One measure of the money supply that includes M1, plus savings and small time deposits, overnight repos at commercial banks, and non-institutional money market accounts. This is a key economic indicator used to forecast inflation, since it is not as narrow as M1 and still relatively easy to track.

a. Club goods
b. Buy-side analyst
c. Flight-to-quality
d. Broad Money

47. _____ is money accepted for exchange of goods in an economy. The prevalence of one money over another arises, usually, when a government designates through decrees that the government shall accept only particular notes and coins in payment for taxes. Typically, money of _____ consists of stamped coins and minted paper bills.

a. Local currency
b. Security thread
c. Totnes pound
d. Currency

48. A _____ is a kind of negotiable instrument, a promissory note made by a bank payable to the bearer on demand, used as money, and in many jurisdictions is legal tender. Along with coins, _____s make up the cash or bearer forms of all modern money. With the exception of non-circulating high-value or precious metal commemorative issues, coins are generally used for lower valued monetary units, while _____s are used for higher values.

a. Microprinting
b. Banknote
c. Security thread
d. Local currency

49. A _____ is an intermediary used in trade to avoid the inconveniences of a pure barter system.

By contrast, as William Stanley Jevons argued, in a barter system there must be a coincidence of wants before two people can trade - one must want exactly what the other has to offer, when and where it is offered, so that the exchange can occur. A _____ permits the value of goods to be assessed and rendered in terms of the intermediary, most often, a form of money widely accepted to buy any other good.

a. Price revolution
b. Consumer theory
c. Labour economics
d. Medium of exchange

50. A _____ is a standard monetary unit of measurement of the market value/cost of goods, services, or assets. It is one of three well-known functions of money. It lends meaning to profits, losses, liability, or assets.

Chapter 9. Financial Markets and the Special Case of Money

a. AD-IA Model
b. ACEA agreement
c. ACCRA Cost of Living Index
d. Unit of account

51. In economics, _____ is the total demand for final goods and services in the economy (Y) at a given time and price level. It is the amount of goods and services in the economy that will be purchased at all possible price levels. This is the demand for the gross domestic product of a country when inventory levels are static.
    a. Aggregate expenditure
    b. Aggregation problem
    c. Aggregate supply
    d. Aggregate demand

52. _____ is the branch of economics concerned with 'the allocation and deployment of economic resources, both spatially and across time, in an uncertain environment' . It is additionally characterised by its 'concentration on monetary activities', in which 'money of one type or another is likely to appear on both sides of a trade' . The questions within _____ are typically framed in terms of 'time, uncertainty, options and information' .
    a. Public economics
    b. Price revolution
    c. Fixed exchange rate
    d. Financial economics

53. _____ or economic opportunity loss is the value of the next best alternative foregone as the result of making a decision. _____ analysis is an important part of a company's decision-making processes but is not treated as an actual cost in any financial statement. The next best thing that a person can engage in is referred to as the _____ of doing the best thing and ignoring the next best thing to be done.
    a. Industrial organization
    b. Opportunity cost
    c. Economic
    d. Economic ideology

54. _____ is an economic model based on price, utility and quantity in a market. It predicts that in a competitive market, price will function to equalize the quantity demanded by consumers, and the quantity supplied by producers, resulting in an economic equilibrium of price and quantity. The model incorporates other factors changing equilibrium as a shift of demand and/or supply.
    a. Supply and demand
    b. Rational addiction
    c. Joint demand
    d. Deferred gratification

55. _____ is the demand for financial assets, e.g., securities, money or foreign currency. It is used for purposes of business transactions and personal consumption.

The need to accommodate a firm's expected cash transactions.

    a. Multiplier effect
    b. Transactions demand
    c. Keynesian cross
    d. Spending multiplier

Chapter 9. Financial Markets and the Special Case of Money

56. Economics:

- _____, the desire to own something and the ability to pay for it
- _____ curve, a graphic representation of a _____ schedule
- _____ deposit, the money in checking accounts
- _____ pull theory, the theory that inflation occurs when _____ for goods and services exceeds existing supplies
- _____ schedule, a table that lists the quantity of a good a person will buy it each different price
- _____ side economics, the school of economics at believes government spending and tax cuts open economy by raising _____

a. McKesson ' Robbins scandal
b. Variability
c. Production
d. Demand

57. The _____ is the desired holding of money balances in the form of cash or bank deposits.

Money is dominated as store of value by interest bearing assets. However, money is necessary to carry out transactions, or in other words, it provides liquidity.

a. Market neutral
b. Borrowing base
c. Conglomerate merger
d. Demand for money

58. _____s is the social science that studies the production, distribution, and consumption of goods and services. The term _____s comes from the Ancient Greek οἰκονομῑα from οἶκος (oikos, 'house') + νόμος (nomos, 'custom' or 'law'), hence 'rules of the house(hold)'. Current _____ models developed out of the broader field of political economy in the late 19th century, owing to a desire to use an empirical approach more akin to the physical sciences.

a. Inflation
b. Energy economics
c. Opportunity cost
d. Economic

59. In financial accounting, a _____ or statement of financial position is a summary of a person's or organization's balances. Assets, liabilities and ownership equity are listed as of a specific date, such as the end of its financial year. A _____ is often described as a snapshot of a company's financial condition.

a. 1921 recession
b. Balance sheet
c. 100-year flood
d. 130-30 fund

60. In business, _____ is the total liabilitiess minus total outside assets of an individual or a company. For a company, this is called shareholders' prefernce and may be referred to as book value. _____ is stated as at a particular year in time.

a. Post earnings announcement drift
b. Sinking fund
c. Bond credit rating
d. Net worth

61. _____ is the banking practice in which banks keep only a fraction of their deposits in reserve (as cash and other highly liquid assets) and lend out the remainder, while maintaining the simultaneous obligation to redeem all these deposits upon demand. Fractional reserve banking necessarily occurs when banks lend out any fraction of the funds received from demand deposits. This practice is universal in modern banking.

Chapter 9. Financial Markets and the Special Case of Money 113

a. Fractional-reserve banking
c. Certificate of deposit
b. Lender of last resort
d. Bank roll

62. In economics, economic equilibrium is simply a state of the world where economic forces are balanced and in the absence of external influences the (equilibrium) values of economic variables will not change. It is the point at which quantity demanded and quantity supplied are equal. _____, for example, refers to a condition where a market price is established through competition such that the amount of goods or services sought by buyers is equal to the amount of goods or services produced by sellers.
a. Regulated market
c. Marketization
b. Product-Market Growth Matrix
d. Market equilibrium

63. In banking, _____ are bank reserves in excess of the reserve requirement set by a central bank (in the United States, the Federal Reserve System, called the Fed; in Canada, the Bank of Canada.) They are reserves of cash more than the required amounts. Holding _____ is generally considered costly and uneconomical as no interest is earned on the excess amount.
a. Universal bank
c. Annual percentage rate
b. Origination fee
d. Excess reserves

64. The _____ was a worldwide economic downturn starting in most places in 1929 and ending at different times in the 1930s or early 1940s for different countries. It was the largest and most important economic depression in the 20th century, and is used in the 21st century as an example of how far the world's economy can fall. The _____ originated in the United States; historians most often use as a starting date the stock market crash on October 29, 1929, known as Black Tuesday.
a. Great Depression
c. British Empire Economic Conference
b. Jarrow March
d. Wall Street Crash of 1929

65. A _____ is an institution willing to extend credit when no one else will.

Originally the term referred to a reserve financial institution that secured other banks or eligible institutions, as a last resort; most often the central bank of a country. The purpose of this loan and lender is to prevent the collapse of institutions that are experiencing financial difficulty, most often near collapse.

a. Capital requirement
c. Time deposit
b. Transactional account
d. Lender of last resort

66. The _____ is an American stock exchange. It is the largest electronic screen-based equity securities trading market in the United States. With approximately 3,800 companies, it has more trading volume per hour than any other stock exchange in the world.
a. 1921 recession
c. 100-year flood
b. NASDAQ
d. 130-30 fund

67. _____ is an equity (stock) exchange located at 11 Wall Street in lower Manhattan, New York, USA. It is the largest stock exchange in the world by dollar value of its listed companies' securities. As of October 2008, the combined capitalization of all domestic _____ listed companies was US$10.1 trillion.

a. 100-year flood
b. 1921 recession
c. 130-30 fund
d. New York Stock Exchange

68. The _____ percentage shows how profitable a company's assets are in generating revenue.

_____ can be computed as:

$$\text{ROA} = \frac{\text{Net Income - Interest Expense - Interest Tax savings}}{\text{Average Total Assets}}$$

This number tells you what the company can do with what it has, i.e. how many dollars of earnings they derive from each dollar of assets they control. Its a useful number for comparing competing companies in the same industry.

a. Capital recovery factor
b. Return on assets
c. Sustainable growth rate
d. Jaws ratio

69. In probability theory and statistics, _____ is a measure of the variability or dispersion of a population, a data set, or a probability distribution. A low _____ indicates that the data points tend to be very close to the same value (the mean), while high _____ indicates that the data are 'spread out' over a large range of values.

For example, the average height for adult men in the United States is about 70 inches, with a _____ of around 3 inches.

a. 130-30 fund
b. 100-year flood
c. 1921 recession
d. Standard deviation

70. A _____ is a corporation or mutual organization which provides trading facilities for stock brokers and traders, to trade stocks and other securities. It may be a physical trading room where the traders gather, or a formalised communications network. Creation of a _____ is a strategy of economic development.

a. SEAQ
b. Primary shares
c. 100-year flood
d. Stock Exchange

71. A _____ is a public market for the trading of company stock and derivatives at an agreed price; these are securities listed on a stock exchange as well as those only traded privately.

The size of the world _____ was estimated at about $36.6 trillion US at the beginning of October 2008 . The total world derivatives market has been estimated at about $791 trillion face or nominal value, 11 times the size of the entire world economy.

a. Adolf Hitler
b. Stock market
c. Adolph Fischer
d. Adam Smith

Chapter 9. Financial Markets and the Special Case of Money

72. _____, 1st Baron Keynes was a renowned economist from Britain whose many ideas on economic and political theories as well as on many governments' monetary policies influenced America. He advocated a government that played an active role in the lives of people regarding business, economy, etc. In this role, the government would use fiscal measures to reduce the consequences of recessions, economic depressions and booms.

   a. Adolf Hitler
   b. Adam Smith
   c. Adolph Fischer
   d. John Maynard Keynes

73. A _____ is a type of economic bubble taking place in stock markets when price of stocks rise and become overvalued by any measure of stock valuation.

The existence of _____s is at odds with the assumptions of efficient market theory which assumes rational investor behaviour. Behavioral finance theory attribute _____s to cognitive biases that lead to groupthink and herd behavior.

   a. Fill or kill
   b. Scrip issue
   c. Growth investing
   d. Stock market bubble

74. The _____ is one of several stock market indices, created by nineteenth-century Wall Street Journal editor and Dow Jones ' Company co-founder Charles Dow. It is an index that shows how certain stocks have traded. Dow compiled the index to gauge the performance of the industrial sector of the American stock market.

   a. Fama-French three factor model
   b. Dow Jones Industrial Average
   c. Federal Reserve Bank Notes
   d. Commodity fetishism

75. _____ is an American economist and was the Chairman of the Federal Reserve of the United States from 1987 to 2006. He currently works as a private advisor and providing consulting for firms through his company, Greenspan Associates LLC.

First appointed Federal Reserve chairman by President Ronald Reagan in August 1987, he was reappointed at successive four-year intervals until retiring on January 31, 2006 after the second-longest tenure in the position.

   a. Adolf Hitler
   b. Adolph Fischer
   c. Adam Smith
   d. Alan Greenspan

76. '_____' is a phrase used by former Federal Reserve Board Chairman Alan Greenspan in a speech given at the American Enterprise Institute during the stock market boom of the 1990s. The phrase was interpreted by financial pundits as a typical extraordinary economy.

Greenspan's comment was made on December 5, 1996 (emphasis added in excerpt):

The presence of the short comment--not repeated by Greenspan since--within a rather dry and complex speech would not normally have been so memorable; however, it was followed by immediate slumps in stock markets worldwide, provoking a strong reaction in financial circles and making its way into colloquial speech.

   a. AD-IA Model
   b. ACCRA Cost of Living Index
   c. Irrational exuberance
   d. ACEA agreement

Chapter 9. Financial Markets and the Special Case of Money

77. The _____ was a British joint stock company that traded in South America during the 18th century. Founded in 1711, the company was granted a monopoly to trade in Spain's South American colonies as part of a treaty during the War of Spanish Succession. In return, the company assumed the national debt England had incurred during the war.
   a. South Sea Company
   b. Financial Crimes Enforcement Network
   c. Trade adjustment assistance
   d. Delancey Street Foundation

78. A _____ is a sudden dramatic decline of stock prices across a significant cross-section of a stock market. Crashes are driven by panic as much as by underlying economic factors. They often follow speculative stock market bubbles.
   a. 100-year flood
   b. Stock market crash
   c. 130-30 fund
   d. 1921 recession

79. _____ is a concept with somewhat disparate meanings in several fields. It also has a common meaning which has a loose connection with some of those more definite meanings.

   Casually, it is typically used to denote a lack of order, or purpose, or cause.

   a. 100-year flood
   b. Randomness
   c. 1921 recession
   d. 130-30 fund

80. A _____, sometimes denoted _____, is a mathematical formalization of a trajectory that consists of taking successive random steps. The results of _____ analysis have been applied to computer science, physics, ecology, economics, and a number of other fields as a fundamental model for random processes in time. For example, the path traced by a molecule as it travels in a liquid or a gas, the search path of a foraging animal, the price of a fluctuating stock and the financial status of a gambler can all be modeled as _____s.
   a. 100-year flood
   b. 130-30 fund
   c. 1921 recession
   d. Random walk

81. An _____ or index tracker is a collective investment scheme (usually a mutual fund or exchange-traded fund) that aims to replicate the movements of an index of a specific financial market regardless of market conditions.

   Tracking can be achieved by trying to hold all of the securities in the index, in the same proportions as the index. Other methods include statistically sampling the market and holding 'representative' securities.

   a. Investment trust
   b. Unit trust
   c. Asset management company
   d. Index fund

82. _____ was an American economist, statistician and public intellectual, and a recipient of the Nobel Memorial Prize in Economic Sciences. He is best known among scholars for his theoretical and empirical research, especially consumption analysis, monetary history and theory, and for his demonstration of the complexity of stabilization policy. A global public followed his restatement of a political philosophy that insisted on minimizing the role of government in favor of the private sector.
   a. Adolph Fischer
   b. Milton Friedman
   c. Adolf Hitler
   d. Adam Smith

Chapter 10. Central Banking and Monetary Policy

1. The _____ is the central banking system of the United States. Created in 1913 by the enactment of the Federal Reserve Act (signed by Woodrow Wilson), it is a quasi-public and quasi-private (government entity with private components) banking system that comprises (1) the presidentially appointed Board of Governors of the _____ in Washington, D.C.; (2) the Federal Open Market Committee; (3) twelve regional Federal Reserve Banks located in major cities throughout the nation acting as fiscal agents for the U.S. Treasury, each with its own nine-member board of directors; (4) numerous other private U.S. member banks, which subscribe to required amounts of non-transferable stock in their regional Federal Reserve Banks; and (5) various advisory councils. Since February 2006, Ben Bernanke has served as the Chairman of the Board of Governors of the _____.

   a. Monetary Policy Report to the Congress
   b. Federal Reserve System Open Market Account
   c. Term auction facility
   d. Federal Reserve System

2. A _____, reserve bank, or monetary authority is the entity responsible for the monetary policy of a country or of a group of member states. It is a bank that can lend money to other banks in times of need. Its primary responsibility is to maintain the stability of the national currency and money supply, but more active duties include controlling subsidized-loan interest rates, and acting as a lender of last resort to the banking sector during times of financial crisis (private banks often being integral to the national financial system.)
   a. 130-30 fund
   b. 100-year flood
   c. 1921 recession
   d. Central bank

3. The Federal Reserve System (also the Federal Reserve; informally The Fed) is the central banking system of the United States. Created in 1913 by the enactment of the Federal Reserve Act (signed by Woodrow Wilson), it is a quasi-public and quasi-private (government entity with private components) banking system that comprises (1) the presidentially appointed Board of Governors of the Federal Reserve System in Washington, D.C.; (2) the Federal Open Market Committee; (3) twelve regional _____ located in major cities throughout the nation acting as fiscal agents for the U.S. Treasury, each with its own nine-member board of directors; (4) numerous other private U.S. member banks, which subscribe to required amounts of non-transferable stock in their regional _____; and (5) various advisory councils. Since February 2006, Ben Bernanke has served as the Chairman of the Board of Governors of the Federal Reserve System.
   a. Fed Funds Probability
   b. Federal funds
   c. Federal Open Market Committee
   d. Federal Reserve Banks

4. In economics, _____ is the total demand for final goods and services in the economy (Y) at a given time and price level. It is the amount of goods and services in the economy that will be purchased at all possible price levels. This is the demand for the gross domestic product of a country when inventory levels are static.
   a. Aggregate expenditure
   b. Aggregation problem
   c. Aggregate supply
   d. Aggregate demand

5. Economics:

   - _____, the desire to own something and the ability to pay for it
   - _____ curve, a graphic representation of a _____ schedule
   - _____ deposit, the money in checking accounts
   - _____ pull theory, the theory that inflation occurs when _____ for goods and services exceeds existing supplies
   - _____ schedule, a table that lists the quantity of a good a person will buy it each different price
   - _____ side economics, the school of economics at believes government spending and tax cuts open economy by raising _____

a. Demand	b. Production
c. McKesson ' Robbins scandal	d. Variability

6. In economics, _____ is a rise in the general level of prices of goods and services in an economy over a period of time. When the general price level rises, each unit of currency buys fewer goods and services; consequently, _____ is also a decline in the real value of money--a loss of purchasing power in the medium of exchange which is also the monetary unit of account in the economy. A chief measure of general price-level _____ is the general _____ rate, which is the percentage change in a general price index (normally the Consumer Price Index) over time.

a. Energy economics	b. Opportunity cost
c. Inflation	d. Economic

7. _____ is the process by which the government, central bank (ii) availability of money, and (iii) cost of money or rate of interest, in order to attain a set of objectives oriented towards the growth and stability of the economy. Monetary theory provides insight into how to craft optimal _____.

_____ is referred to as either being an expansionary policy where an expansionary policy increases the total supply of money in the economy, and a contractionary policy decreases the total money supply.

a. 130-30 fund	b. 100-year flood
c. 1921 recession	d. Monetary policy

8. The _____, a component of the Federal Reserve System, is charged under United States law with overseeing the nation's open market operations. It is the Federal Reserve Committee that makes key decisions about interest rates and the growth jam of the United States money supply. It is the principal organ of United States national monetary policy.

a. Primary Dealer Credit Facility	b. Fed Funds Probability
c. Federal Reserve Transparency Act	d. Federal Open Market Committee

9. _____ is an American economist and was the Chairman of the Federal Reserve of the United States from 1987 to 2006. He currently works as a private advisor and providing consulting for firms through his company, Greenspan Associates LLC.

First appointed Federal Reserve chairman by President Ronald Reagan in August 1987, he was reappointed at successive four-year intervals until retiring on January 31, 2006 after the second-longest tenure in the position.

a. Adolf Hitler	b. Adolph Fischer
c. Adam Smith	d. Alan Greenspan

10. In economics, the _____ is the term used to refer to the environment in which bonds are bought and sold between a central bank ' its regulated banks. It is not a free market process.

- To intervene in the 'business cycle', a central bank may choose to go into the _____ and buy or sell government bonds, which is known as _____ operations to increase reserves.

a. Outside money	b. Open Market
c. ACCRA Cost of Living Index	d. Inside money

Chapter 10. Central Banking and Monetary Policy

11. In financial accounting, a _____ or statement of financial position is a summary of a person's or organization's balances. Assets, liabilities and ownership equity are listed as of a specific date, such as the end of its financial year. A _____ is often described as a snapshot of a company's financial condition.
    a. 130-30 fund
    b. 100-year flood
    c. 1921 recession
    d. Balance sheet

12. _____ are banks' holdings of deposits in accounts with their central bank (for instance the European Central Bank or the Federal Reserve, in the latter case including federal funds), plus currency that is physically held in bank vaults (vault cash.) The central banks of some nations set minimum reserve requirements. Even when no requirements are set, banks commonly wish to hold some reserves, called desired reserves, against unexpected events.
    a. Bilateral netting
    b. Structuring
    c. Sweep account
    d. Bank reserves

13. Discounting is a financial mechanism in which a debtor obtains the right to delay payments to a creditor, for a defined period of time, in exchange for a charge or fee. Essentially, the party that owes money in the present purchases the right to delay the payment until some future date. The _____, or charge, is simply the difference between the original amount owed in the present and the amount that has to be paid in the future to settle the debt.
    a. Reinsurance
    b. Discount
    c. Certified Risk Manager
    d. Reliability theory

14. The _____ is an interest rate a central bank charges depository institutions that borrow reserves from it.

    The term _____ has two meanings:

    - the same as interest rate; the term 'discount' does not refer to the meaning of the word, but to the purpose of using the quantity, such as computations of present value, e.g. net present value or discounted cash flow

    - the annual effective _____, which is the annual interest divided by the capital including that interest; this rate is lower than the interest rate; it corresponds to using the value after a year as the nominal value, and seeing the initial value as the nominal value minus a discount; it is used for Treasury Bills and similar financial instruments

    The annual effective _____ is the annual interest divided by the capital including that interest, which is the interest rate divided by 100% plus the interest rate. It is the annual discount factor to be applied to the future cash flow, to find the discount, subtracted from a future value to find the value one year earlier.

    For example, suppose there is a government bond that sells for $95 and pays $100 in a year's time.

    a. Discount rate
    b. Johansen test
    c. Stochastic volatility
    d. Perpetuity

15. _____ is a fee paid on borrowed assets. It is the price paid for the use of borrowed money, or, money earned by deposited funds. Assets that are sometimes lent with _____ include money, shares, consumer goods through hire purchase, major assets such as aircraft, and even entire factories in finance lease arrangements.

a. Interest
c. Insolvency
b. Asset protection
d. Internal debt

16. An _____ is the price a borrower pays for the use of money they do not own, for instance a small company might borrow from a bank to kick start their business, and the return a lender receives for deferring the use of funds, by lending it to the borrower. _____s are normally expressed as a percentage rate over the period of one year.

_____s targets are also a vital tool of monetary policy and are used to control variables like investment, inflation, and unemployment.

a. Interest rate
c. ACCRA Cost of Living Index
b. Arrow-Debreu model
d. Enterprise value

17. The accounting equation relates assets, _____, and owner's equity:

Assets = _____ + Owner's Equity

The accounting equation is the mathematical structure of the balance sheet.

The Australian Accounting Research Foundation defines _____ as: 'future sacrifice of economic benefits that the entity is presently obliged to make to other entities as a result of past transactions and other past events.'

Probably the most accepted accounting definition of liability is the one used by the International Accounting Standards Board (IASB.) The following is a quotation from IFRS Framework:

A liability is a present obligation of the enterprise arising from past events, the settlement of which is expected to result in an outflow from the enterprise of resources embodying economic benefits

-

Regulations as to the recognition of _____ are different all over the world, but are roughly similar to those of the IASB.

a. Community property
c. Coase theorem
b. Liabilities
d. Competition law theory

18. _____ are the means of implementing monetary policy by which a central bank controls its national money supply by buying and selling government securities, or other financial instruments. Monetary targets, such as interest rates or exchange rates, are used to guide this implementation.

Since most money is now in the form of electronic records, rather than paper records such as banknotes, _____ are conducted simply by electronically increasing or decreasing ('crediting' or 'debiting') the amount of money that a bank has, e.g., in its reserve account at the central bank, in exchange for a bank selling or buying a financial instrument.

a. ACEA agreement	b. ACCRA Cost of Living Index
c. AD-IA Model	d. Open market operations

19. A _____ is a currency which is held in significant quantities by many governments and institutions as part of their foreign exchange reserves. It also tends to be the international pricing currency for products traded on a global market, such as oil, gold, etc.

This permits the issuing country to purchase the commodities at a marginally cheaper rate than other nations, which must exchange their currency with each purchase and pay a transaction cost.

a. Texas redbacks	b. Currency board
c. Reserve currency	d. World currency

20. _____ is money accepted for exchange of goods in an economy. The prevalence of one money over another arises, usually, when a government designates through decrees that the government shall accept only particular notes and coins in payment for taxes. Typically, money of _____ consists of stamped coins and minted paper bills.

a. Local currency	b. Totnes pound
c. Currency	d. Security thread

21. In economics, _____ is the total amount of money available in an economy at a particular point in time. There are several ways to define 'money', but standard measures usually include currency in circulation and demand deposits.

_____ data are recorded and published, usually by the government or the central bank of the country.

a. Neutrality of money	b. Velocity of money
c. Money supply	d. Veil of money

22. In the United States, _____ are overnight borrowings by banks to maintain their bank reserves at the Federal Reserve. Banks keep reserves at Federal Reserve Banks to meet their reserve requirements and to clear financial transactions. Transactions in the _____ market enable depository institutions with reserve balances in excess of reserve requirements to lend reserves to institutions with reserve deficiencies.

a. Federal funds rate	b. Federal Reserve Transparency Act
c. Term auction facility	d. Federal funds

23. In the United States, the _____ is the interest rate at which private depository institutions (mostly banks) lend balances (federal funds) at the Federal Reserve to other depository institutions, usually overnight. It is the interest rate banks charge each other for loans. Changing the target rate is one way the Chairman of the Federal Reserve can influence the supply of money in the U.S. economy..

a. Term auction facility	b. Federal banking
c. Monetary Policy Report to the Congress	d. Federal funds rate

24. _____ is a financial mechanism in which a debtor obtains the right to delay payments to a creditor, for a defined period of time, in exchange for a charge or fee. Essentially, the party that owes money in the present purchases the right to delay the payment until some future date. The discount, or charge, is simply the difference between the original amount owed in the present and the amount that has to be paid in the future to settle the debt.

Chapter 10. Central Banking and Monetary Policy

a. Maximum life span
b. Generalized linear model
c. Certified Risk Manager
d. Discounting

25. The _____ is a bank regulation that sets the minimum reserves each bank must hold to customer deposits and notes. It would normally be in the form of fiat currency stored in a bank vault (vault cash), or with a central bank.

The reserve ratio is sometimes used as a tool in the monetary policy, influencing the country's economy, borrowing, and interest rates.

a. Reserve requirement
b. Fractional-reserve banking
c. Private money
d. Probability of default

26. The _____ is an instrument of monetary policy (usually controlled by central banks) that allows eligible institutions to borrow money from the central bank, usually on a short-term basis, to meet temporary shortages of liquidity caused by internal or external disruptions. The term originated with the practice of sending a bank representative to a reserve bank teller window when a bank needed to borrow money.

The interest rate charged on such loans by a central bank is called the discount rate, base rate, repo rate, or primary rate.

a. Private money
b. Capital requirement
c. Prime rate
d. Discount window

27. _____ is the banking practice in which banks keep only a fraction of their deposits in reserve (as cash and other highly liquid assets) and lend out the remainder, while maintaining the simultaneous obligation to redeem all these deposits upon demand. Fractional reserve banking necessarily occurs when banks lend out any fraction of the funds received from demand deposits. This practice is universal in modern banking.

a. Lender of last resort
b. Certificate of deposit
c. Bank roll
d. Fractional-reserve banking

28. A _____ is an expression that compares quantities relative to each other. The most common examples involve two quantities, but any number of quantities can be compared. _____s are represented mathematically by separating each quantity with a colon, for example the _____ 2:3, which is read as the _____ 'two to three'.

a. Y-intercept
b. 100-year flood
c. 130-30 fund
d. Ratio

29. The reserve requirement (or required _____) is a bank regulation that sets the minimum reserves each bank must hold to customer deposits and notes. It would normally be in the form of fiat currency stored in a bank vault (vault cash), or with a central bank.

The _____ is sometimes used as a tool in the monetary policy, influencing the country's economy, borrowing, and interest rates.

a. First player wins
b. Reserve ratio
c. Dividend unit
d. Bank-State-Branch

Chapter 10. Central Banking and Monetary Policy

30. The _____ was a worldwide economic downturn starting in most places in 1929 and ending at different times in the 1930s or early 1940s for different countries. It was the largest and most important economic depression in the 20th century, and is used in the 21st century as an example of how far the world's economy can fall. The _____ originated in the United States; historians most often use as a starting date the stock market crash on October 29, 1929, known as Black Tuesday.
    a. British Empire Economic Conference
    b. Wall Street Crash of 1929
    c. Great Depression
    d. Jarrow March

31. _____s are a form of government regulation which subject banks to certain requirements, restrictions and guidelines.

The objectives of _____, and the emphasis, varies between jurisdiction. The most common objectives are:

1. Prudential -- to reduce the level of risk bank creditors are exposed to (i.e. to protect depositors)
2. Systemic risk reduction -- to reduce the risk of disruption resulting from adverse trading conditions for banks causing multiple or major bank failures
3. Avoid misuse of banks -- to reduce the risk of banks being used for criminal purposes, e.g. laundering the proceeds of crime
4. To protect banking confidentiality
5. Credit allocation -- to direct credit to favored sectors

Banking regulations can vary widely across nations and jurisdictions

    a. Buydown
    b. Patent portfolio
    c. Property right
    d. Bank regulation

32. The term '_____' refers to the concept of collecting information and attempting to spot a pattern in the information. In some fields of study, the term '_____' has more formally-defined meanings.

In project management _____ is a mathematical technique that uses historical results to predict future outcome.

    a. Coefficient of determination
    b. Quantile regression
    c. Probit model
    d. Trend analysis

33. In business and accounting, _____ are everything of value that is owned by a person or company. It is a claim on the property your income of a borrower. The balance sheet of a firm records the monetary value of the _____ owned by the firm.
    a. ACEA agreement
    b. ACCRA Cost of Living Index
    c. Amortization schedule
    d. Assets

34. A _____ occurs when a large number of bank customers withdraw their deposits because they believe the bank is insolvent. As a _____ progresses, it generates its own momentum, in a kind of self-fulfilling prophecy: as more people withdraw their deposits, the likelihood of default increases, and this encourages further withdrawals. This can destabilize the bank to the point where it faces bankruptcy.

a. Fractional-reserve banking
b. Funds Transfer Pricing
c. Tier 1 capital
d. Bank run

35. The _____ consists of a number of economic theories which describe the nature of the firm, company including its existence, its behaviour, and its relationship with the market.

In simplified terms, the _____ aims to answer these questions:

1. Existence - why do firms emerge, why are not all transactions in the economy mediated over the market?
2. Boundaries - why the boundary between firms and the market is located exactly there? Which transactions are performed internally and which are negotiated on the market?
3. Organization - why are firms structured in such specific way? What is the interplay of formal and informal relationships?

Despite looking simple, these questions are not answered by the established economic theory, which usually views firms as given, and treats them as black boxes without any internal structure.

The First World War period saw a change of emphasis in economic theory away from industry-level analysis which mainly included analysing markets to analysis at the level of the firm, as it became increasingly clear that perfect competition was no longer an adequate model of how firms behaved. Economic theory till then had focussed on trying to understand markets alone and there had been little study on understanding why firms or organisations exist.

a. Khazzoom-Brookes postulate
b. Technology gap
c. Policy Ineffectiveness Proposition
d. Theory of the firm

36. The _____ is a United States government corporation created by the Glass-Steagall Act of 1933. It provides deposit insurance, which guarantees the safety of deposits in member banks, currently up to $250,000 per depositor per bank. Funds in non-interest bearing transaction accounts are fully insured, with no limit, under the temporary Transaction Account Guarantee Program.

a. Foreign direct investment
b. Great Leap Forward
c. Federal Deposit Insurance Corporation
d. Luxembourg Income Study

37. _____, in law and economics, is a form of risk management primarily used to hedge against the risk of a contingent loss. _____ is defined as the equitable transfer of the risk of a loss, from one entity to another, in exchange for a premium, and can be thought of as a guaranteed small loss to prevent a large, possibly devastating loss. An insurer is a company selling the _____; an insured or policyholder is the person or entity buying the _____.

a. AD-IA Model
b. ACCRA Cost of Living Index
c. Insurance
d. ACEA agreement

38. An _____ is an economy in which people, including businesses, can trade in goods and services with other people and businesses in the international community at large. This contrasts with a closed economy in which international trade cannot take place.

The act of selling goods or services to a foreign country is called exporting.

Chapter 10. Central Banking and Monetary Policy

a. Attention work
b. Information economy
c. Indicative planning
d. Open economy

39. _____ is a common concept in economics, and gives rise to derived concepts such as consumer debt. Generally _____ is defined by opposition to production. But the precise definition can vary because different schools of economists define production quite differently.

a. Foreclosure data providers
b. Cash or share options
c. Federal Reserve Bank Notes
d. Consumption

40. The _____ is an economic and political union of 27 member states, located primarily in Europe. It was established by the Treaty of Maastricht on 1 November 1993, upon the foundations of the pre-existing European Economic Community. With a population of almost 500 million, the _____ generates an estimated 30% share (US$18.4 trillion in 2008) of the nominal gross world product.

a. ACCRA Cost of Living Index
b. ACEA agreement
c. European Court of Justice
d. European Union

41. A _____, sometimes called a pegged exchange rate, is a type of exchange rate regime wherein a currency's value is matched to the value of another single currency or to a basket of other currencies such as gold.

A _____ is usually used to stabilize the value of a currency, vis-a-vis the currency it is pegged to. This facilitates trade and investments between the two countries, and is especially useful for small economies where external trade forms a large part of their GDP.

a. Law of supply
b. Monetary economics
c. Leading indicators
d. Fixed exchange rate

42. A fixed exchange rate, sometimes called a _____, is a type of exchange rate regime wherein a currency's value is matched to the value of another single currency or to a basket of other currencies such as gold.

A fixed exchange rate is usually used to stabilize the value of a currency, vis-a-vis the currency it is pegged to. This facilitates trade and investments between the two countries, and is especially useful for small economies where external trade forms a large part of their GDP.

a. Mainstream economics
b. Recession
c. Leading indicators
d. Pegged exchange rate

43. In economics, the _____ measures the payments that flow between any individual country and all other countries. It is used to summarize all international economic transactions for that country during a specific time period, usually a year. The _____ is determined by the country's exports and imports of goods, services, and financial capital, as well as financial transfers.

a. Balance of payments
b. Gross domestic product per barrel
c. Gross world product
d. Skyscraper Index

44. _____ is an economic system in which wealth, and the means of producing wealth, are privately owned. Through _____, the land, labor, and capital are owned, operated, and traded for the purpose of generating profits, without force or fraud, by private individuals either singly or jointly, and investments, distribution, income, production, pricing and supply of goods, commodities and services are determined by voluntary private decision in a market economy. A distinguishing feature of _____ is that each person owns his or her own labor and therefore is allowed to sell the use of it to employers.

- a. Creative capitalism
- b. Late capitalism
- c. Capitalism
- d. Socialism for the rich and capitalism for the poor

45. _____ is a negative term describing an claimed capitalist economy in which success in business depends on close relationships between businesspeople and government officials. It may be exhibited in the distribution of legal permits, government grants, special tax breaks, and so forth.

_____ is believed to arise when political cronyism spills over into the business world; self-serving friendships and family ties between businessmen and the government influence the economy and society to the extent that it corrupts public-serving economic and political ideals.

- a. 100-year flood
- b. Crony capitalism
- c. Good governance
- d. 130-30 fund

46. A _____ is a monetary authority which is required to maintain a fixed exchange rate with a foreign currency. This policy objective requires the conventional objectives of a central bank to be subordinated to the exchange rate target.

The main qualities of an orthodox _____ are:

- A _____'s foreign currency reserves must be sufficient to ensure that all holders of its notes and coins (and all banks creditor of a Reserve Account at the _____) can convert them into the reserve currency (usually 110-115% of the monetary base M0.)
- A _____ maintains absolute, unlimited convertibility between its notes and coins and the currency against which they are pegged (the anchor currency), at a fixed rate of exchange, with no restrictions on current-account or capital-account transactions.
- A _____ only earns profit from interests on foreign reserves (less the expense of note-issuing), and does not engage in forward-exchange transactions. These foreign reserves exist (1) because local notes have been issued in exchange, or (2) because commercial banks must by regulation deposit a minimum reserve at the _____. (1) generates a seignorage revenue. (2) is the revenue on minimum reserves (revenue of investment activities less cost of minimum reserves remuneration)
- A _____ has no discretionary powers to effect monetary policy and does not lend to the government. Governments cannot print money, and can only tax or borrow to meet their spending commitments.
- A _____ does not act as a lender of last resort to commercial banks, and does not regulate reserve requirements.
- A _____ does not attempt to manipulate interest rates by establishing a discount rate like a central bank. The peg with the foreign currency tends to keep interest rates and inflation very closely aligned to those in the country against whose currency the peg is fixed.

The _____ in question will no longer issue fiat money but instead will only issue one unit of local currency for each unit (or decided amount) of foreign currency it has in its vault (often a hard currency such as the U.S. dollar or the euro.) The surplus on the balance of payments of that country is reflected by higher deposits local banks hold at the central bank as well as (initially) higher deposits of the (net) exporting firms at their local banks.

a. Petrodollar
c. Reserve currency
b. Currency board
d. Currency competition

47. In finance, the _____s between two currencies specifies how much one currency is worth in terms of the other. It is the value of a foreign natione;s currency in terms of the home natione;s currency. For example an _____ of 102 Japanese yen to the United States dollar means that JPY 102 is worth the same as USD 1.

a. Interbank market
c. Exchange rate
b. ACEA agreement
d. ACCRA Cost of Living Index

48. The term _____ is applied broadly to a variety of situations in which some financial institutions or assets suddenly lose a large part of their value. In the 19th and early 20th centuries, many financial crises were associated with banking panics, and many recessions coincided with these panics. Other situations that are often called financial crises include stock market crashes and the bursting of other financial bubbles, currency crises, and sovereign defaults.

a. Market failure
c. Co-operative economics
b. Macroeconomics
d. Financial crisis

49. Market _____ is a business, economics or investment term that refers to an asset's ability to be easily converted through an act of buying or selling without causing a significant movement in the price and with minimum loss of value. Money, or cash on hand, is the most liquid asset. An act of exchange of a less liquid asset with a more liquid asset is called liquidation.

a. 100-year flood
c. 130-30 fund
b. 1921 recession
d. Liquidity

50. A _____ is the transfer of wealth from one party (such as a person or company) to another. A _____ is usually made in exchange for the provision of goods, services or both, or to fulfill a legal obligation.

The simplest and oldest form of _____ is barter, the exchange of one good or service for another.

a. Soft count
c. Going concern
b. Payment
d. Social gravity

51. _____ in economics and business is the result of an exchange and from that trade we assign a numerical monetary value to a good, service or asset. If Alice trades Bob 4 apples for an orange, the _____ of an orange is 4 apples. Inversely, the _____ of an apple is 1/4 oranges.

a. Premium pricing
c. Price book
b. Price war
d. Price

52. In finance, the _____ is the global financial market for short-term borrowing and lending. It provides short-term liquidity funding for the global financial system. The _____ is where short-term obligations such as Treasury bills, commercial paper and bankers' acceptances are bought and sold.

Chapter 10. Central Banking and Monetary Policy

a. T-Model
b. Deferred compensation
c. Consignment stock
d. Money market

53. _____ is an economic model based on price, utility and quantity in a market. It predicts that in a competitive market, price will function to equalize the quantity demanded by consumers, and the quantity supplied by producers, resulting in an economic equilibrium of price and quantity. The model incorporates other factors changing equilibrium as a shift of demand and/or supply.

a. Supply and demand
b. Deferred gratification
c. Rational addiction
d. Joint demand

54. The _____ is the desired holding of money balances in the form of cash or bank deposits.

Money is dominated as store of value by interest bearing assets. However, money is necessary to carry out transactions, or in other words, it provides liquidity.

a. Market neutral
b. Conglomerate merger
c. Demand for Money
d. Borrowing base

55. In economics, a _____ is a table that lists the quantity of a good a person will buy it each different price See Demand curve.

a. Federal Reserve districts
b. Free contract
c. Rational irrationality
d. Demand schedule

56. _____ is the process by which money is produced or issued. There are three different ways to create money:

- manufacturing a new monetary unit, such as paper currency or metal coins (_____)
- loaning out a physical monetary unit multiple times through fractional-reserve lending (credit creation)
- buying of government securities or other financial instruments by central bank through Open market operations (electronic creation)

Coins are produced by manufacturing metal in a factory called a mint.

Banknotes and bank account balances are financial securities issued by a bank.

Similarly, money destruction, i.e., the reverse of _____, can occur in two different ways, depending on how the money was created.

a. Monetary policy of Sweden
b. Shadow Open Market Committee
c. Second-round effect
d. Money creation

57. _____s is the social science that studies the production, distribution, and consumption of goods and services. The term _____s comes from the Ancient Greek οἰκονομία from οἶκος (oikos, 'house') + νόμος (nomos, 'custom' or 'law'), hence 'rules of the house(hold)'. Current _____ models developed out of the broader field of political economy in the late 19th century, owing to a desire to use an empirical approach more akin to the physical sciences.

Chapter 10. Central Banking and Monetary Policy

a. Inflation
b. Opportunity cost
c. Energy economics
d. Economic

58. The _____ or gross domestic income (GDI), a basic measure of an economy's economic performance, is the market value of all final goods and services produced within the borders of a nation in a year. _____ can be defined in three ways, all of which are conceptually identical. First, it is equal to the total expenditures for all final goods and services produced within the country in a stipulated period of time (usually a 365-day year.)
  a. Countercyclical
  b. Gross domestic product
  c. Market structure
  d. Monopolistic competition

59. _____ is a misspelled phrase from Latin 'pro capite' phrase meaning per head with pro meaning 'per' or 'for each' and capite meaning 'head.' Both words together equate to the phrase 'for each head.'

It is usually used in the field of statistics to indicate the average per person for any given concern, such as income, crime rate, etc.

It is also used in wills to indicate that each of the named beneficiaries should receive, by devise or bequest, equal shares of the estate. This is in contrast to a per stirpes division, in which each branch of the inheriting family inherits an equal share of the estate.

  a. Per capita
  b. False positive rate
  c. Sargan test
  d. Population statistics

60. An _____, in economics, is the amount by which the real Gross domestic product exceeds potential GDP. The real GDP is also known as GDP 'adjusted for inflation', 'constant prices' GDP or 'constant dollar' GDP, because it measures the aggregate output in a country's income accounts in a given year, expressed in base-year prices. On the other hand, the potential GDP is the quantity of real GDP when a country's economy is at full-employment.
  a. AD-IA Model
  b. Inflationary gap
  c. ACCRA Cost of Living Index
  d. ACEA agreement

61. In economics, _____ is a sustained decrease in the general price level of goods and services. _____ occurs when the annual inflation rate falls below zero percent, resulting in an increase in the real value of money -- a negative inflation rate. This should not be confused with disinflation, a slow-down in the inflation rate (i.e. when the inflation decreases, but still remains positive.)
  a. Literacy rate
  b. Deflation
  c. Price revolution
  d. Tobit model

62. In economics, a _____ is a sudden event that increases or decreases demand for goods or services temporarily. A positive _____ increases demand and a negative _____ decreases demand. Prices of goods and services are affected in both cases.
  a. Robertson lag
  b. Lucas-Islands model
  c. Demand shock
  d. War economy

63. _____ is a term used in economics to describe how an economic quantity is related to economic fluctuations. It is the opposite of procyclical. However, it has more than one meaning.

130 Chapter 10. Central Banking and Monetary Policy

a. Law of comparative advantage
b. Mathematical economics
c. Countercyclical
d. Price revolution

64. _____ is exchange of capital, goods, and services across international borders or territories. In most countries, it represents a significant share of gross domestic product (GDP.) While _____ has been present throughout much of history, its economic, social, and political importance has been on the rise in recent centuries.
   a. Import license
   b. Incoterms
   c. Intra-industry trade
   d. International trade

65. In economics, a _____ is a general slowdown in economic activity over a sustained period of time, or a business cycle contraction. During _____s, many macroeconomic indicators vary in a similar way. Production as measured by Gross Domestic Product (GDP), employment, investment spending, capacity utilization, household incomes and business profits all fall during _____s.
   a. Monetary economics
   b. Leading indicators
   c. Recession
   d. Treasury View

66. In economics, _____ is the total supply of goods and services produced by a national economy during a specific time period. It is the total amount of goods and services in the economy available at all possible price levels.
   a. Aggregate expenditure
   b. Aggregation problem
   c. Aggregate demand
   d. Aggregate supply

67. _____ is monetary policy that seeks to reduce the size of the money supply. They are fiscal policies, like lower spending and higher taxes, that reduce economic growth. In most nations, monetary policy is controlled by either a central bank or a finance ministry.
   a. Contractionary monetary policy
   b. Shadow Open Market Committee
   c. Monetary policy of Sweden
   d. Money creation

68. The _____ is one of the world's most important central banks, responsible for monetary policy covering the 16 member States of the Eurozone. It was established by the European Union (EU) in 1998 with its headquarters in Frankfurt, Germany.

The predecessor to the _____ was the European Monetary Institute.

   a. ACEA agreement
   b. AD-IA Model
   c. European Central Bank
   d. ACCRA Cost of Living Index

69. _____ is monetary policy that seeks to increase the size of the money supply. In most nations, monetary policy is controlled by either a central bank or a finance ministry

Neoclassical and Keynesian economics significantly differ on the effects and effectiveness of monetary policy on influencing the real economy; there is no clear consensus on how monetary policy affects real economic variables (aggregate output or income, employment.) Both economic schools accept that monetary policy affects monetary variables (price levels, interest rates.)

Chapter 10. Central Banking and Monetary Policy

a. Expansionary monetary policy
b. AD-IA Model
c. ACCRA Cost of Living Index
d. ACEA agreement

70. _____ is widely regarded as the first modern school of economic thought. It is the idea that free markets can regulate themselves. Its major developers include Adam Smith, David Ricardo, Thomas Malthus and John Stuart Mill. Sometimes the definition of _____ is expanded to include William Petty, Johann Heinrich von Thünen.
    a. Tendency of the rate of profit to fall
    b. Schools of economic thought
    c. Marginalism
    d. Classical economics

71. _____ refers to an action or object coming from outside a system. It is the opposite of endogenous, something generated from within the system.

    - In an economic model, an _____ change is one that comes from outside the model and is unexplained by the model. For example, in the simple supply and demand model, a change in consumer tastes or preferences is unexplained by the model and also leads to endogenous changes in demand that lead to changes in the equilibrium price. Put another way, an _____ change involves an alteration of a variable that is autonomous, i.e., unaffected by the workings of the model.

    - In linear regression, it means that the variable is independent of all other response values.

    - In biology, '_____' refers to an action or object coming from the outside of a system. For example, an _____ contrast agent in medical imaging refers to a liquid injected into the patient intravenously that enhances visibility of a pathology, such as a tumor.

    a. AD-IA Model
    b. ACCRA Cost of Living Index
    c. ACEA agreement
    d. Exogenous

72. In economic models, the _____ time frame assumes no fixed factors of production. Firms can enter or leave the marketplace, and the cost (and availability) of land, labor, raw materials, and capital goods can be assumed to vary. In contrast, in the short-run time frame, certain factors are assumed to be fixed, because there is not sufficient time for them to change.
    a. Long-run
    b. Productivity world
    c. Diseconomies of scale
    d. Price/performance ratio

73. _____ is an economic concept with commonplace familiarity. It is the price that a good or service is offered at, or will fetch, in the marketplace. It is of interest mainly in the study of microeconomics.
    a. Market price
    b. Market anomaly
    c. Noisy market hypothesis
    d. Paper trading

74. A _____ is a hypothetical measure of overall prices for some set of goods and services, in a given region during a given interval, normalized relative to some base set. Typically, a _____ is approximated with a price index.

The classical dichotomy is the assumption that there is a relatively clean distinction between overall increases or decreases in prices and underlying, e;reale; economic variables.

a. Price level
b. Discretionary spending
c. Price elasticity of supply
d. Discouraged worker

75. The term _____ is used in macroeconomics to refer to a situation where a country's nominal interest rate has been lowered nearly to or equal to zero to avoid a recession, but the liquidity in the market created by these low interest rates does not stimulate the economy to full employment. In this situation, any further increase in the money supply will not stimulate the economy any further. This is because any further injection of liquidity will no longer lower the nominal interest rate, as the nominal interest rate cannot drop below zero.

a. Liquidity trap
b. Macroeconomic models
c. Robertson lag
d. Minimum wage

Chapter 11. The Process of Economic Growth

1. _____s is the social science that studies the production, distribution, and consumption of goods and services. The term _____s comes from the Ancient Greek oá¼°κονομῖα from oá¼¶κος (oikos, 'house') + vÏŒμος (nomos, 'custom' or 'law'), hence 'rules of the house(hold)'. Current _____ models developed out of the broader field of political economy in the late 19th century, owing to a desire to use an empirical approach more akin to the physical sciences.
    a. Inflation
    b. Energy economics
    c. Opportunity cost
    d. Economic

2. _____ is the increase in the amount of the goods and services produced by an economy over time. It is conventionally measured as the percent rate of increase in real gross domestic product, or real GDP. Growth is usually calculated in real terms, i.e. inflation-adjusted terms, in order to net out the effect of inflation on the price of the goods and services produced.
    a. Economic growth
    b. ACEA agreement
    c. ACCRA Cost of Living Index
    d. AD-IA Model

3. The _____ or gross domestic income (GDI), a basic measure of an economy's economic performance, is the market value of all final goods and services produced within the borders of a nation in a year. _____ can be defined in three ways, all of which are conceptually identical. First, it is equal to the total expenditures for all final goods and services produced within the country in a stipulated period of time (usually a 365-day year.)
    a. Gross domestic product
    b. Monopolistic competition
    c. Countercyclical
    d. Market structure

4. In economic models, the _____ time frame assumes no fixed factors of production. Firms can enter or leave the marketplace, and the cost (and availability) of land, labor, raw materials, and capital goods can be assumed to vary. In contrast, in the short-run time frame, certain factors are assumed to be fixed, because there is not sufficient time for them to change.
    a. Productivity world
    b. Price/performance ratio
    c. Diseconomies of scale
    d. Long-run

5. _____ is a misspelled phrase from Latin 'pro capite' phrase meaning per head with pro meaning 'per' or 'for each' and capite meaning 'head.' Both words together equate to the phrase 'for each head.'

It is usually used in the field of statistics to indicate the average per person for any given concern, such as income, crime rate, etc.

It is also used in wills to indicate that each of the named beneficiaries should receive, by devise or bequest, equal shares of the estate. This is in contrast to a per stirpes division, in which each branch of the inheriting family inherits an equal share of the estate.

    a. Per capita
    b. Population statistics
    c. False positive rate
    d. Sargan test

6. An _____, in economics, is the amount by which the real Gross domestic product exceeds potential GDP. The real GDP is also known as GDP 'adjusted for inflation', 'constant prices' GDP or 'constant dollar' GDP, because it measures the aggregate output in a country's income accounts in a given year, expressed in base-year prices. On the other hand, the potential GDP is the quantity of real GDP when a country's economy is at full-employment.

a. ACCRA Cost of Living Index
b. ACEA agreement
c. Inflationary gap
d. AD-IA Model

7. In economics, the _____ measures the payments that flow between any individual country and all other countries. It is used to summarize all international economic transactions for that country during a specific time period, usually a year. The _____ is determined by the country's exports and imports of goods, services, and financial capital, as well as financial transfers.
   a. Balance of payments
   b. Gross domestic product per barrel
   c. Gross world product
   d. Skyscraper Index

8. A _____ is the transfer of wealth from one party (such as a person or company) to another. A _____ is usually made in exchange for the provision of goods, services or both, or to fulfill a legal obligation.

The simplest and oldest form of _____ is barter, the exchange of one good or service for another.

   a. Going concern
   b. Payment
   c. Soft count
   d. Social gravity

9. _____ is the period of time that an individual spends at paid occupational labor. Unpaid labors such as housework are not considered part of the working week. Many countries regulate the work week by law, such as stipulating minimum daily rest periods, annual holidays and a maximum number of working hours per week.
   a. Working time
   b. 100-year flood
   c. 130-30 fund
   d. 1921 recession

10. In economics, accounting and Marxian economics, _____ is often equated with investment of profit income, especially in real capital goods. The concentration and centralisation of capital are two of the results of such accumulation

But _____ can refer variously to

- working and consuming less than earned
- relying on the effects of compound interest to increase initial capital
- real investment in tangible means of production.
- financial investment in assets represented on paper.
- investment in non-productive physical assets such as residential real estate that appreciate in value.
- consuming less than produced by productive assets like farm land--saving or accumulating the residual
- 'human _____,' i.e., new education and training increasing the skills of the labour force.

Non-financial and financial _____ is usually needed for economic growth, since additional production usually requires additional funds to enlarge the scale of production. Smarter and more productive organization of production can also increase production without increased capital.

   a. Capital accumulation
   b. Cultural Marxism
   c. Marxian economics
   d. Productive force

11. _____ is a term used in national accounts statistics and macroeconomics. It basically refers to the net additions to the (physical) capital stock in an accounting period, or, to the value of the increase of the capital stock; though it may occasionally also refer to the (growth of the) total stock of capital formed.

Thus, in UNSNA, _____ equals fixed capital investment, the increase in the value of inventories held, plus (net) lending to foreign countries, during an accounting period.

a. Consumption of fixed capital
b. Capital intensity
c. Capital flight
d. Capital formation

12. In Marxian economics, _____ originally referred to the means of production. Individuals, organizations and governments use _____ in the production of other goods or commodities. _____ include factories, machinery, tools, equipment, and various buildings which are used to produce other products for consumption.

a. Capital intensive
b. Capital goods
c. Wealth inequality in the United States
d. Capital deepening

13. _____ is the development of economic wealth of countries or regions for the well-being of their inhabitants. It is the process by which a nation improves the economic, political, and social well being of its people. From a policy perspective, _____ can be defined as efforts that seek to improve the economic well-being and quality of life for a community by creating and/or retaining jobs and supporting or growing incomes and the tax base.

a. Experimental economics
b. Economic development
c. Inflation
d. Economic methodology

14. The _____ was a period in the late 18th and early 19th centuries when major changes in agriculture, manufacturing, mining, and transportation had a profound effect on the socioeconomic and cultural conditions in Britain. The changes subsequently spread throughout Europe, North America, and eventually the world. The onset of the _____ marked a major turning point in human society; almost every aspect of daily life was eventually influenced in some way.

a. Adam Smith
b. Adolf Hitler
c. Industrial Revolution
d. Adolph Fischer

15. _____ is the term denoting either an entrance or changes which are inserted into a system and which activate/modify a process. It is an abstract concept, used in the modeling, system(s) design and system(s) exploitation. It is usually connected with other terms, e.g., _____ field, _____ variable, _____ parameter, _____ value, _____ signal, _____ device and _____ file.

a. Input
b. ACCRA Cost of Living Index
c. ACEA agreement
d. AD-IA Model

16. _____s (economically referred to as land or raw materials) occur naturally within environments that exist relatively undisturbed by mankind, in a natural form. A _____'s is often characterized by amounts of biodiversity existent in various ecosystems.

Mining, petroleum extraction, fishing, hunting, and forestry are generally considered natural-resource industries.

a. 100-year flood
b. 1921 recession
c. 130-30 fund
d. Natural resource

Chapter 11. The Process of Economic Growth

17. _____ in economics refers to metrics and measures of output from production processes, per unit of input. Labor _____, for example, is typically measured as a ratio of output per labor-hour, an input. _____ may be conceived of as a metrics of the technical or engineering efficiency of production.
   a. Productivity
   b. Production-possibility frontier
   c. Fordism
   d. Piece work

18. In business and accounting, _____ are everything of value that is owned by a person or company. It is a claim on the property your income of a borrower. The balance sheet of a firm records the monetary value of the _____ owned by the firm.
   a. ACCRA Cost of Living Index
   b. ACEA agreement
   c. Assets
   d. Amortization schedule

19. A _____ is an object whose consumption increases the utility of the consumer, for which the quantity demanded exceeds the quantity supplied at zero price. _____s are usually modeled as having diminishing marginal utility. The first individual purchase has high utility; the second has less.
   a. Pie method
   b. Good
   c. Merit good
   d. Composite good

20. _____ is a type of private equity investment, most often a minority investment, in relatively mature companies that are looking for capital to expand or restructure operations, enter new markets or finance a significant acquisition without a change of control of the business.

    Companies that seek _____, will often do so in order to finance a transformational event in their lifecycle. These companies are likely to be more mature than venture capital funded companies, able to generate revenue and operating profits but unable to generate sufficient cash to fund major expansions, acquisitions or other investments.

   a. Club deal
   b. Seed money
   c. Startup company
   d. Growth Capital

21. In microeconomics, _____ is quite simply the conversion of inputs into outputs. It is an economic process that uses resources to create a good or service that is suitable for exchange. This can include manufacturing, storing, shipping, and packaging.
   a. Production
   b. MET
   c. Red Guards
   d. Solved

22. In economics, a _____ is a function that specifies the output of a firm, an industry, or an entire economy for all combinations of inputs. A meta-_____ compares the practice of the existing entities converting inputs X into output y to determine the most efficient practice _____ of the existing entities, whether the most efficient feasible practice production or the most efficient actual practice production. In either case, the maximum output of a technologically-determined production process is a mathematical function of input factors of production.
   a. Constant elasticity of substitution
   b. Short-run
   c. Production function
   d. Post-Fordism

Chapter 11. The Process of Economic Growth

23. A _____ is an expression that compares quantities relative to each other. The most common examples involve two quantities, but any number of quantities can be compared. _____s are represented mathematically by separating each quantity with a colon, for example the _____ 2:3, which is read as the _____ 'two to three'.
    a. 100-year flood
    b. 130-30 fund
    c. Y-intercept
    d. Ratio

24. _____ is a term that is used to describe the overall process of invention, innovation and diffusion of technology or processes. The term is redundant with technological development, technological achievement, and technological progress. In essence _____ is the invention of a technology (or a process), the continuous process of improving a technology (in which it often becomes cheaper) and its diffusion throughout industry or society.
    a. 100-year flood
    b. 130-30 fund
    c. 1921 recession
    d. Technological change

25. _____ , as defined by the _____ Association of America (Information technologyAA), is 'the study, design, development, implementation, support or management of computer-based information systems, particularly software applications and computer hardware.' _____ deals with the use of electronic computers and computer software to convert, store, protect, process, transmit, and securely retrieve information.

    Today, the term _____ has ballooned to encompass many aspects of computing and technology, and the term has become very recognizable. The _____ umbrella can be quite large, covering many fields.

    a. Information technology
    b. ACEA agreement
    c. ACCRA Cost of Living Index
    d. AD-IA Model

26. In economics and sociology, an _____ is any factor (financial or non-financial) that enables or motivates a particular course of action, or counts as a reason for preferring one choice to the alternatives. It is an expectation that encourages people to behave in a certain way. Since human beings are purposeful creatures, the study of _____ structures is central to the study of all economic activity (both in terms of individual decision-making and in terms of co-operation and competition within a larger institutional structure.)
    a. Isocost
    b. Epstein-Zin preferences
    c. Incentive
    d. Economic reform

27. _____ was a survey conducted by the U.S. Department of Justice to gauge the prevalence of alcohol and illegal drug use among prior arrestees. It was a reformulation of the prior Drug Use Forecasting (DUF) program, focused on five drugs in particular: cocaine, marijuana, methamphetamine, opiates, and PCP.

    Participants were randomly selected from arrest records in major metropolitan areas; because no personally identifying information is taken from each record chosen, the resulting data can be correlated to arrest rates, but not to the total population of persons charged.

    a. ACCRA Cost of Living Index
    b. AD-IA Model
    c. ACEA agreement
    d. Arrestee Drug Abuse Monitoring

28. _____ is widely regarded as the first modern school of economic thought. It is the idea that free markets can regulate themselves. Its major developers include Adam Smith, David Ricardo, Thomas Malthus and John Stuart Mill. Sometimes the definition of _____ is expanded to include William Petty, Johann Heinrich von Thünen.

Chapter 11. The Process of Economic Growth

a. Marginalism
b. Classical economics
c. Schools of economic thought
d. Tendency of the rate of profit to fall

29. _____ was a Scottish moral philosopher and a pioneer of political economy. One of the key figures of the Scottish Enlightenment, Smith is the author of The Theory of Moral Sentiments and An Inquiry into the Nature and Causes of the Wealth of Nations. The latter, usually abbreviated as The Wealth of Nations, is considered his magnum opus and the first modern work of economics.

a. Adam Smith
b. Adolph Fischer
c. Adolf Hitler
d. Alan Greenspan

30. An Inquiry into the Nature and Causes of the _____ is the magnum opus of the Scottish economist Adam Smith. It is a clearly written account of economics at the dawn of the Industrial Revolution, as well as a rhetorical piece written for the generally educated individual of the 18th century - advocating a free market economy as more productive and more beneficial to society.

The work is credited as a watershed in history and economics due to its comprehensive, largely accurate characterization of economic mechanisms that survive in modern economics; and also for its effective use of rhetorical technique, including structuring the work to contrast real world examples of free and fettered markets.

a. Black Book of Communism
b. The Bell Curve
c. The Rise and Fall of the Great Powers
d. Wealth of Nations

31. The _____ is a derogatory alternative name for economics devised by the Victorian historian Thomas Carlyle in the 19th century. The term is an inversion of the phrase 'gay science,' meaning 'life-enhancing knowledge.' This was a familiar expression at the time, and was later adopted as the title of a book by Nietzsche

It is often stated that Carlyle gave economics the nickname '_____' as a response to the late 18th century writings of The Reverend Thomas Robert Malthus, who grimly predicted that starvation would result as projected population growth exceeded the rate of increase in the food supply.

a. 130-30 fund
b. 100-year flood
c. 1921 recession
d. Dismal science

32. _____ is any long-term change in the patterns of average weather of a specific region or the Earth as a whole. _____ reflects abnormal variations to the Earth's climate and subsequent effects on other parts of the Earth, such as in the ice caps over durations ranging from decades to millions of years.

In recent usage, especially in the context of environmental policy, _____ usually refers to changes in modern climate

a. Climate change
b. 1921 recession
c. 130-30 fund
d. 100-year flood

Chapter 11. The Process of Economic Growth

33. The _____ is a 1972 book modeling the consequences of a rapidly growing world population and finite resource supplies, commissioned by the Club of Rome. Its authors were Donella H. Meadows, Dennis L. Meadows, Jørgen Randers, and William W. Behrens III. The book used the World3 model to simulate the consequence of interactions between the Earth's and human systems.

   a. Principles of Political Economy and Taxation
   b. Fail-Safe Investing
   c. The Wealth of Nations
   d. Limits to growth

34. The _____ was a phase of the Industrial Revolution; sometimes labeled as the separate Technical Revolution. From a technological and a social point of view there is no clean break between the two.

Major innovations during the period occurred in the chemical, electrical, petroleum, and steel industries.

   a. 100-year flood
   b. 1921 recession
   c. 130-30 fund
   d. Second Industrial Revolution

35. _____ is a term used in economics to describe an economy where capital per worker is increasing. A process of increasing the amount of capital per worker. It is an increase in the capital intensity.

   a. Firm-specific infrastructure
   b. Capital expenditure
   c. Capital formation
   d. Capital deepening

36. _____ are the prices that the factors of production of a finished item attract.

There has been some economic debate as to what determines these prices. Classical and Marxist economists argued that the _____ decided the value of a product and so value was intrinsic within the product.

   a. Marginal product
   b. Productivity model
   c. Marginal product of labor
   d. Factor prices

37. In economics, the _____ or marginal physical product is the extra output produced by one more unit of an input (for instance, the difference in output when a firm's labour is increased from five to six units.) Assuming that no other inputs to production change, the _____ of a given input (X) can be expressed as:

   _____ = ΔY/ΔX = (the change of Y)/(the change of X.)

-
  -
    - Pending approval by Thomas Sowell***

In neoclassical economics, this is the mathematical derivative of the production function.... Note that the 'product' (Y) is typically defined ignoring external costs and benefits.

   a. Labor problem
   b. Productive capacity
   c. Factor prices
   d. Marginal product

38. _____ is the additional output resulting from the use of an additional unit of capital (ceteris paribus assuming all other factors are fixed.) It equals to 1 divided by the Incremental Capital-Output Ratio.

a. Buy-write
b. CAN SLIM
c. Loan officer
d. Marginal product of capital

39. _____ in economics and business is the result of an exchange and from that trade we assign a numerical monetary value to a good, service or asset. If Alice trades Bob 4 apples for an orange, the _____ of an orange is 4 apples. Inversely, the _____ of an apple is 1/4 oranges.
   a. Price war
   b. Price book
   c. Premium pricing
   d. Price

40. In economics, endogenous growth theory or _____ was developed in the 1980s as a response to criticism of the neo-classical growth model.

In neo-classical growth models, the long-run rate of growth is exogenously determined by either assuming a savings rate (the Harrod-Domar model) or a rate of technical progress (Solow model.) However, the savings rate and rate of technological progress remain unexplained.

   a. Real prices and ideal prices
   b. Cobweb model
   c. Kondratiev waves
   d. New growth theory

41. In economics, a _____ is a good that is non-rivaled and non-excludable. This means, respectively, that consumption of the good by one individual does not reduce availability of the good for consumption by others; and that no one can be effectively excluded from using the good. In the real world, there may be no such thing as an absolutely non-rivaled and non-excludable good; but economists think that some goods approximate the concept closely enough for the analysis to be economically useful.
   a. Happiness economics
   b. Demand-pull theory
   c. Neoclassical synthesis
   d. Public good

42. _____ is that which is owed; usually referencing assets owed, but the term can also cover moral obligations and other interactions not requiring money. In the case of assets, _____ is a means of using future purchasing power in the present before a summation has been earned. Some companies and corporations use _____ as a part of their overall corporate finance strategy.
   a. Hard money loan
   b. Debt
   c. Debenture
   d. Collateral Management

43. _____ are legal property rights over creations of the mind, both artistic and commercial, and the corresponding fields of law. Under _____ law, owners are granted certain exclusive rights to a variety of intangible assets, such as musical, literary, and artistic works; ideas, discoveries and inventions; and words, phrases, symbols, and designs. Common types of _____ include copyrights, trademarks, patents, industrial design rights and trade secrets.
   a. Expedited Funds Availability Act
   b. Independent contractor
   c. Intellectual property
   d. Ease of Doing Business Index

44. In economics, a _____ exists when the production or use of goods and services by the market is not efficient. That is, there exists another outcome where all involved can be made better off. _____s can be viewed as scenarios where individuals' pursuit of pure self-interest leads to results that are not efficient - that can be improved upon from the societal point-of-view.

a. Financial economics
b. Fixed exchange rate
c. General equilibrium
d. Market failure

45. _____ is that part of the total debt in a country that is owed to creditors outside the country. The debtors can be the government, corporations or private households. The debt includes money owed to private commercial banks, other governments, or international financial institutions such as the IMF and World Bank.

a. Internal debt
b. International debt collection
c. Asset protection
d. External debt

46. _____ is the change in population over time, and can be quantified as the change in the number of individuals in a population using 'per unit time' for measurement. The term _____ can technically refer to any species, but almost always refers to humans, and it is often used informally for the more specific demographic term _____ rate , and is often used to refer specifically to the growth of the population of the world.

Simple models of _____ include the Malthusian Growth Model and the logistic model.

a. Population dynamics
b. 100-year flood
c. Population growth
d. 130-30 fund

47. A _____ is the exclusive authority to determine how a resource is used, whether that resource is owned by government or by individuals. All economic goods have a _____s attribute. This attribute has three broad components

1. The right to use the good
2. The right to earn income from the good
3. The right to transfer the good to others

The concept of _____s as used by economists and legal scholars are related but distinct. The distinction is largely seen in the economists' focus on the ability of an individual or collective to control the use of the good.

a. Post-sale restraint
b. Property right
c. High-reeve
d. Holder in due course

48. The '_____' is approximately the nominal interest rate minus the inflation rate Since the inflation rate over the course of a loan is not known initially, volatility in inflation represents a risk to both the lender and the borrower.

In economics and finance, an individual who lends money for repayment at a later point in time expects to be compensated for the time value of money, or not having the use of that money while it is lent.

a. Reflation
b. Core inflation
c. Cost-push inflation
d. Real interest rate

49. _____ is a fee paid on borrowed assets. It is the price paid for the use of borrowed money , or, money earned by deposited funds . Assets that are sometimes lent with _____ include money, shares, consumer goods through hire purchase, major assets such as aircraft, and even entire factories in finance lease arrangements.

a. Asset protection
b. Insolvency
c. Internal debt
d. Interest

50. An _____ is the price a borrower pays for the use of money they do not own, for instance a small company might borrow from a bank to kick start their business, and the return a lender receives for deferring the use of funds, by lending it to the borrower. _____s are normally expressed as a percentage rate over the period of one year.

_____s targets are also a vital tool of monetary policy and are used to control variables like investment, inflation, and unemployment.

a. Interest rate
b. Arrow-Debreu model
c. ACCRA Cost of Living Index
d. Enterprise value

51. In business, _____, Overhead cost or _____ expense refers to an ongoing expense of operating a business. The term _____ is usually used to group expenses that are necessary to the continued functioning of the business, but do not directly generate profits.

_____ expenses are all costs on the income statement except for direct labor and direct materials.

a. AD-IA Model
b. Overhead
c. ACCRA Cost of Living Index
d. ACEA agreement

52. The term '_____' refers to the concept of collecting information and attempting to spot a pattern in the information. In some fields of study, the term '_____' has more formally-defined meanings.

In project management _____ is a mathematical technique that uses historical results to predict future outcome.

a. Quantile regression
b. Probit model
c. Coefficient of determination
d. Trend analysis

53. _____ is a procedure used in economics to measure the contribution of different factors to economic growth and to indirectly compute the rate of technological progress, measured as a residual, in an economy.

_____ decomposes the growth rate of economy's total output into that which is due to increases in the amount of factors used - usually the increase in the amount of capital and labor - and that which cannot be accounted for by observable changes in factor utilization. The unexplained part of growth in GDP is then taken to represent increases in productivity (getting more output with the same amounts of inputs) or a measure of broadly defined technological progress.

a. Growth accounting
b. Spillover effect
c. Reaganomics
d. Cobb-Douglas

Chapter 11. The Process of Economic Growth

54. In economics, _____ are the resources employed to produce goods and services. They facilitate production but do not become part of the product (as with raw materials) or significantly transformed by the production process (as with fuel used to power machinery.) To 19th century economists, the _____ were land (natural resources, gifts from nature), labor (the ability to work), and capital goods (human-made tools and equipment.)
   a. Factors of production
   b. Long-run
   c. Product Pipeline
   d. Hicks-neutral technical change

55. In economics, _____ (TFP) is a variable which accounts for effects in total output not caused by inputs. For example, a year with unusually good weather will tend to have higher output, because bad weather hinders agricultural output. A variable like weather does not directly relate to unit inputs, so weather is considered a _____ variable.
   a. Human rights
   b. Total-factor productivity
   c. 35-hour working week
   d. Flow to Equity-Approach

56. _____ or amortisation is the process of increasing an amount over a period of time. The word comes from Middle English amortisen to kill, alienate in mortmain, from Anglo-French amorteser, alteration of amortir, from Vulgar Latin admortire to kill, from Latin ad- + mort-, mors death. Particular instances of the term include:

   - _____, the allocation of a lump sum amount to different time periods, particularly for loans and other forms of finance, including related interest or other finance charges.
     o _____ schedule, a table detailing each periodic payment on a loan (typically a mortgage), as generated by an _____ calculator.
     o Negative _____, an _____ schedule where the loan amount actually increases through not paying the full interest
   - Amortized analysis, analyzing the execution cost of algorithms over a sequence of operations.
   - _____ of capital expenditures of certain assets under accounting rules, particularly intangible assets, in a manner analogous to depreciation.
   - _____ (tax law)

_____ is also used in the context of zoning regulations and describes the time in which a property owner has to relocate when the property's use constitutes a preexisting nonconforming use under zoning regulations.

   a. Augmentation
   b. Amortization
   c. Economic miracle
   d. Oslo Agreements

57. The term _____s refers to wages that have been adjusted for inflation. This term is used in contrast to nominal wages or unadjusted wages.

The use of adjusted figures is in undertaking some form of economic analysis.

   a. Living wage
   b. Federal Wage System
   c. Profit sharing
   d. Real wage

58. _____ is an American economist and was the Chairman of the Federal Reserve of the United States from 1987 to 2006. He currently works as a private advisor and providing consulting for firms through his company, Greenspan Associates LLC.

First appointed Federal Reserve chairman by President Ronald Reagan in August 1987, he was reappointed at successive four-year intervals until retiring on January 31, 2006 after the second-longest tenure in the position.

a. Adam Smith
b. Adolf Hitler
c. Adolph Fischer
d. Alan Greenspan

59. The _____ was an evolution of developed countries from an industrial/manufacturing-based wealth producing economy into a service sector asset based economy, brought about by globalization and currency manipulation by governments and their central banks. Some analysts claimed that this change in the economic structure of the United States had created a state of permanent steady growth, low unemployment, and immunity to boom and bust macroeconomic cycles. They believed that the change rendered obsolete many business practices.

a. 1921 recession
b. 130-30 fund
c. 100-year flood
d. New economy

Chapter 12. The Challenge of Economic Development

1. _____s is the social science that studies the production, distribution, and consumption of goods and services. The term _____s comes from the Ancient Greek οἰκονομία from οἶκος (oikos, 'house') + νόμος (nomos, 'custom' or 'law'), hence 'rules of the house(hold)'. Current _____ models developed out of the broader field of political economy in the late 19th century, owing to a desire to use an empirical approach more akin to the physical sciences.
   a. Inflation
   b. Opportunity cost
   c. Energy economics
   d. Economic

2. _____ is the development of economic wealth of countries or regions for the well-being of their inhabitants. It is the process by which a nation improves the economic, political, and social well being of its people. From a policy perspective, _____ can be defined as efforts that seek to improve the economic well-being and quality of life for a community by creating and/or retaining jobs and supporting or growing incomes and the tax base.
   a. Economic development
   b. Economic methodology
   c. Experimental economics
   d. Inflation

3. _____ is a common concept in economics, and gives rise to derived concepts such as consumer debt. Generally _____ is defined by opposition to production. But the precise definition can vary because different schools of economists define production quite differently.
   a. Cash or share options
   b. Federal Reserve Bank Notes
   c. Foreclosure data providers
   d. Consumption

4. In algebra, a _____ is a function depending on n that associates a scalar, det(A), to an n×n square matrix A. The fundamental geometric meaning of a _____ is a scale factor for measure when A is regarded as a linear transformation. _____s are important both in calculus, where they enter the substitution rule for several variables, and in multilinear algebra.

For a fixed nonnegative integer n, there is a unique _____ function for the n×n matrices over any commutative ring R. In particular, this function exists when R is the field of real or complex numbers.

   a. 130-30 fund
   b. 100-year flood
   c. 1921 recession
   d. Determinant

5. _____ is the increase in the amount of the goods and services produced by an economy over time. It is conventionally measured as the percent rate of increase in real gross domestic product, or real GDP. Growth is usually calculated in real terms, i.e. inflation-adjusted terms, in order to net out the effect of inflation on the price of the goods and services produced.
   a. ACEA agreement
   b. ACCRA Cost of Living Index
   c. AD-IA Model
   d. Economic growth

6. The _____ or gross domestic income (GDI), a basic measure of an economy's economic performance, is the market value of all final goods and services produced within the borders of a nation in a year. _____ can be defined in three ways, all of which are conceptually identical. First, it is equal to the total expenditures for all final goods and services produced within the country in a stipulated period of time (usually a 365-day year.)
   a. Countercyclical
   b. Market structure
   c. Monopolistic competition
   d. Gross domestic product

7. _____ is a misspelled phrase from Latin 'pro capite' phrase meaning per head with pro meaning 'per' or 'for each' and capite meaning 'head.' Both words together equate to the phrase 'for each head.'

It is usually used in the field of statistics to indicate the average per person for any given concern, such as income, crime rate, etc.

It is also used in wills to indicate that each of the named beneficiaries should receive, by devise or bequest, equal shares of the estate. This is in contrast to a per stirpes division, in which each branch of the inheriting family inherits an equal share of the estate.

a. Population statistics
b. Sargan test
c. Per capita
d. False positive rate

8. _____ refers to a business or organization attempting to acquire goods or services to accomplish the goals of the enterprise. Though there are several organizations that attempt to set standards in the _____ process, processes can vary greatly between organizations. Typically the word '_____' is not used interchangeably with the word 'procurement', since procurement typically includes Expediting, Supplier Quality, and Traffic and Logistics (T'L) in addition to _____.

a. Purchasing
b. 130-30 fund
c. Free port
d. 100-year flood

9. _____ is the number of goods/services that can be purchased with a unit of currency. For example, if you had taken one dollar to a store in the 1950s, you would have been able to buy a greater number of items than you would today, indicating that you would have had a greater _____ in the 1950s. Currency can be either a commodity money, like gold or silver, or fiat currency like US dollars.

a. Compliance cost
b. Genuine progress indicator
c. Purchasing power
d. Human Poverty Index

10. The _____ theory uses the long-term equilibrium exchange rate of two currencies to equalize their purchasing power. Developed by Gustav Cassel in 1920, it is based on the law of one price: the theory states that, in ideally efficient markets, identical goods should have only one price.

This purchasing power SEM rate equalizes the purchasing power of different currencies in their home countries for a given basket of goods.

a. Bureau of Labor Statistics
b. Measures of national income and output
c. Gross national product
d. Purchasing power parity

11. _____ is the use of statistics to analyze characteristics or changes to a population. It is related to social demography and demography.

_____ can analyze anything from global demographic changes to local small scale changes.

a. Dynamic Bayesian network
b. Markov logic network
c. Population statistics
d. Nonparametric regression

12. In microeconomics, _____ is quite simply the conversion of inputs into outputs. It is an economic process that uses resources to create a good or service that is suitable for exchange. This can include manufacturing, storing, shipping, and packaging.

a. Production
b. Red Guards
c. Solved
d. MET

13. In economics, a _____ is a function that specifies the output of a firm, an industry, or an entire economy for all combinations of inputs. A meta-_____ compares the practice of the existing entities converting inputs X into output y to determine the most efficient practice _____ of the existing entities, whether the most efficient feasible practice production or the most efficient actual practice production. In either case, the maximum output of a technologically-determined production process is a mathematical function of input factors of production.
   a. Post-Fordism
   b. Constant elasticity of substitution
   c. Short-run
   d. Production function

14. _____ is a voluntary transfer of resources from one country to another, given at least partly with the objective of benefiting the recipient country. It may have other functions as well: it may be given as a signal of diplomatic approval, or to strengthen a military ally, to reward a government for behaviour desired by the donor, to extend the donor's cultural influence, to provide infrastructure needed by the donor for resource extraction from the recipient country, or to gain other kinds of commercial access. Humanitarianism and altruism are, nevertheless, significant motivations for the giving of _____.
   a. ACCRA Cost of Living Index
   b. AID
   c. AD-IA Model
   d. ACEA agreement

15. A security is a fungible, negotiable instrument representing financial value. _____ are broadly categorized into debt _____; equity _____, e.g., common stocks; and derivative (finance) contracts such as forwards, futures, options and swaps. The company or other entity issuing the security is called the issuer.
   a. Red herring prospectus
   b. Settlement risk
   c. Pass-Through Certificates
   d. Securities

16. _____ is a socioeconomic structure and political ideology that promotes the establishment of an egalitarian, classless, stateless society based on common ownership and control of the means of production and property in general. In political science, the term '_____' is sometimes used to refer to communist states, a form of government in which the state operates under a one-party system and declares allegiance to Marxism-Leninism or a derivative thereof, even if the party does not actually claim that it has already reached _____.

Forerunners of communist ideas existed in antiquity and particularly in the 18th and early 19th century France, with thinkers such as Jean-Jacques Rousseau and the more radical Gracchus Babeuf.

   a. Democratic centralism
   b. Social fascism
   c. New Communist Movement
   d. Communism

17. Crude _____ is the nativity or childbirths per 1,000 people per year.

It can be represented by number of childbirths in that year, and p is the current population. This figure is combined with the crude death rate to produce the rate of natural population growth (natural in that it does not take into account net migration.)

   a. Depensation
   b. Neo-Malthusianism
   c. Malthusian equilibrium
   d. Birth rate

Chapter 12. The Challenge of Economic Development

18. _____ data refers to selected population characteristics as used in government, marketing or opinion research, or the _____ profiles used in such research. Note the distinction from the term 'demography' Commonly-used _____s include race, age, income, disabilities, mobility (in terms of travel time to work or number of vehicles available), educational attainment, home ownership, employment status, and even location.
   a. Generation Z
   b. NEET
   c. Demographic warfare
   d. Demographic

19. The _____ model (Demographic transitionM) is a model used to represent the process of explaining the transformation of countries from high birth rates and high death rates to low birth rates and low death rates as part of the economic development of a country from a pre-industrial to an industrialized economy. It is based on an interpretation begun in 1929 by the American demographer Warren Thompson of prior observed changes, or transitions, in birth and death rates in industrialized societies over the past two hundred years.

Most developed countries are beyond stage three of the model; the majority of developing countries are in stage 2 or stage 3.

   a. Demographic economics
   b. Population mobility
   c. Healthy Life Years
   d. Demographic transition

20. _____ refers to the stock of skills and knowledge embodied in the ability to perform labor so as to produce economic value. It is the skills and knowledge gained by a worker through education and experience.Many early economic theories refer to it simply as labor, one of three factors of production, and consider it to be a fungible resource -- homogeneous and easily interchangeable. Other conceptions of labor dispense with these assumptions.
   a. Human capital
   b. Price theory
   c. Law of increasing costs
   d. General equilibrium

21. The traditional definition of _____ is considered to be the ability to use language to read, write, listen, and speak. In modern contexts, the word refers to reading and writing at a level adequate for communication, or at a level that lets one understand and communicate ideas in a literate society, so as to take part in that society. The United Nations Educational, Scientific and Cultural Organization (UNESCO) has drafted the following definition: "_____' is the ability to identify, understand, interpret, create, communicate, compute and use printed and written materials associated with varying contexts.
   a. 130-30 fund
   b. 100-year flood
   c. 1921 recession
   d. Literacy

22. _____ is a term used in national accounts statistics and macroeconomics. It basically refers to the net additions to the (physical) capital stock in an accounting period, or, to the value of the increase of the capital stock; though it may occasionally also refer to the (growth of the) total stock of capital formed.

Thus, in UNSNA, _____ equals fixed capital investment, the increase in the value of inventories held, plus (net) lending to foreign countries, during an accounting period.

   a. Capital flight
   b. Consumption of fixed capital
   c. Capital intensity
   d. Capital formation

Chapter 12. The Challenge of Economic Development

23. _____s (economically referred to as land or raw materials) occur naturally within environments that exist relatively undisturbed by mankind, in a natural form. A _____'s is often characterized by amounts of biodiversity existent in various ecosystems.

Mining, petroleum extraction, fishing, hunting, and forestry are generally considered natural-resource industries.

a. 130-30 fund
c. 100-year flood
b. 1921 recession
d. Natural resource

24. _____ is a specific term used in companies' financial reporting from the company-whole point of view. Because that use excludes the effects of changing ownership interest, an economic measure of _____ is necessary for financial analysis from the shareholders' point of view

_____ is defined by the Financial Accounting Standards Board, or FASB, as e;the change in equity [net assets] of a business enterprise during a period from transactions and other events and circumstances from nonowner sources. It includes all changes in equity during a period except those resulting from investments by owners and distributions to owners.e;

_____ is the sum of net income and other items that must bypass the income statement because they have not been realized, including items like an unrealized holding gain or loss from available for sale securities and foreign currency translation gains or losses.

a. Windfall gain
c. Net national income
b. Real income
d. Comprehensive income

25. The term _____ is used to describe a nation's social or business activity in the process of rapid growth and industrialization. Currently, there are approximately 28 _____ in the world, with the economies of China and India considered to be two of the largest. According to The Economist many people find the term dated, but a new term has yet to gain much traction.

a. Asymmetric price transmission
c. Occupational welfare
b. Affinity diagram
d. Emerging markets

26. The _____ is an international organization that oversees the global financial system by following the macroeconomic policies of its member countries, in particular those with an impact on exchange rates and the balance of payments. It is an organization formed to stabilize international exchange rates and facilitate development. It also offers financial and technical assistance to its members, making it an international lender of last resort.

a. ACCRA Cost of Living Index
c. ACEA agreement
b. International Monetary Fund
d. Office of Thrift Supervision

27. _____ is a term that is used to describe the overall process of invention, innovation and diffusion of technology or processes. The term is redundant with technological development, technological achievement, and technological progress. In essence _____ is the invention of a technology (or a process), the continuous process of improving a technology (in which it often becomes cheaper) and its diffusion throughout industry or society.

a. 100-year flood
c. 1921 recession
b. Technological change
d. 130-30 fund

Chapter 12. The Challenge of Economic Development

28. In business and accounting, _____ are everything of value that is owned by a person or company. It is a claim on the property your income of a borrower. The balance sheet of a firm records the monetary value of the _____ owned by the firm.
    a. ACEA agreement
    b. ACCRA Cost of Living Index
    c. Amortization schedule
    d. Assets

29. _____ is an economic system in which wealth, and the means of producing wealth, are privately owned. Through _____, the land, labor, and capital are owned, operated, and traded for the purpose of generating profits, without force or fraud, by private individuals either singly or jointly, and investments, distribution, income, production, pricing and supply of goods, commodities and services are determined by voluntary private decision in a market economy. A distinguishing feature of _____ is that each person owns his or her own labor and therefore is allowed to sell the use of it to employers.
    a. Late capitalism
    b. Capitalism
    c. Socialism for the rich and capitalism for the poor
    d. Creative capitalism

30. _____ is a negative term describing an claimed capitalist economy in which success in business depends on close relationships between businesspeople and government officials. It may be exhibited in the distribution of legal permits, government grants, special tax breaks, and so forth.

    _____ is believed to arise when political cronyism spills over into the business world; self-serving friendships and family ties between businessmen and the government influence the economy and society to the extent that it corrupts public-serving economic and political ideals.
    a. Good governance
    b. 130-30 fund
    c. 100-year flood
    d. Crony capitalism

31. The term financial crisis is applied broadly to a variety of situations in which some financial institutions or assets suddenly lose a large part of their value. In the 19th and early 20th centuries, many _____ were associated with banking panics, and many recessions coincided with these panics. Other situations that are often called _____ include stock market crashes and the bursting of other financial bubbles, currency crises, and sovereign defaults.
    a. Financial crises
    b. Georgism
    c. Microeconomics
    d. General equilibrium

32. The term _____ is applied broadly to a variety of situations in which some financial institutions or assets suddenly lose a large part of their value. In the 19th and early 20th centuries, many financial crises were associated with banking panics, and many recessions coincided with these panics. Other situations that are often called financial crises include stock market crashes and the bursting of other financial bubbles, currency crises, and sovereign defaults.
    a. Co-operative economics
    b. Market failure
    c. Macroeconomics
    d. Financial crisis

33. The _____ percentage shows how profitable a company's assets are in generating revenue.

_____ can be computed as:

$$\text{ROA} = \frac{\text{Net Income - Interest Expense - Interest Tax savings}}{\text{Average Total Assets}}$$

This number tells you what the company can do with what it has, i.e. how many dollars of earnings they derive from each dollar of assets they control. Its a useful number for comparing competing companies in the same industry.

a. Capital recovery factor
b. Jaws ratio
c. Sustainable growth rate
d. Return on assets

34. _____ according to Onuoha (2007) is the practice of starting new organizations or revitalizing mature organizations, particularly new businesses generally in response to identified opportunities. _____ is often a difficult undertaking, as a vast majority of new businesses fail. Entrepreneurial activities are substantially different depending on the type of organization that is being started.
a. Intrapreneurship
b. ACCRA Cost of Living Index
c. ACEA agreement
d. Entrepreneurship

35. _____ ndustrialization in North America, is the process of social and economic change whereby a human group is transformed from a pre-industrial society into an industrial one. _____ t is a part of a wider modernisation process, where social change and economic development are closely related with technological innovation, particularly with the development of large-scale energy and metallurgy production. _____ t is the extensive organisation of an economy for the purpose of manufacturing.
a. AD-IA Model
b. ACEA agreement
c. ACCRA Cost of Living Index
d. Industrialization

36. _____ is the shortage of common things such as food, clothing, shelter and safe drinking water, all of which determine the quality of life. It may also include the lack of access to opportunities such as education and employment which aid the escape from _____ and/or allow one to enjoy the respect of fellow citizens. According to Mollie Orshansky who developed the _____ measurements used by the U.S. government, 'to be poor is to be deprived of those goods and services and pleasures which others around us take for granted.' Ongoing debates over causes, effects and best ways to measure _____, directly influence the design and implementation of _____-reduction programs and are therefore relevant to the fields of public administration and international development.
a. Poverty map
b. Poverty
c. Growth Elasticity of Poverty
d. Liberal welfare reforms

37. In economics, the _____ measures the payments that flow between any individual country and all other countries. It is used to summarize all international economic transactions for that country during a specific time period, usually a year. The _____ is determined by the country's exports and imports of goods, services, and financial capital, as well as financial transfers.
a. Gross domestic product per barrel
b. Balance of payments
c. Gross world product
d. Skyscraper Index

Chapter 12. The Challenge of Economic Development

38. _____ in the Soviet Union was a policy pursued under Stalin, between 1928 and 1940, to consolidate individual land and labour into collective farms . The Soviet leadership was confident that the replacement of individual peasant farms by kolkhozy would immediately increase food supplies for the urban population, the supply of raw materials for processing industry, and agricultural exports generally. _____ was thus regarded as the solution to the crisis in agricultural distribution that had developed since 1927 and was becoming more acute as the Soviet Union pressed ahead with its ambitious industrialization program.

- a. 100-year flood
- b. 130-30 fund
- c. 1921 recession
- d. Collectivization

39. A _____ is the transfer of wealth from one party (such as a person or company) to another. A _____ is usually made in exchange for the provision of goods, services or both, or to fulfill a legal obligation.

The simplest and oldest form of _____ is barter, the exchange of one good or service for another.

- a. Social gravity
- b. Soft count
- c. Payment
- d. Going concern

40. A economically backward economy is defined as one which makes less progress than normal. USSR leader Gorbachev once said e;If you done;t move forward, sooner or later you begin to move backward.e; The _____ model is a theory of economic growth created by Alexander Gerschenkron. The model postulates that the more backward an economy is at the outset of economic development, the more likely certain conditions are to occur.

- a. Triangle model
- b. Baker Cube
- c. LoopCo
- d. Backwardness

41. _____ was a German lawyer, politician, scholar, political economist and sociologist, who profoundly influenced sociological theory.

Weber's major works deal with rationalization in sociology of religion, government, organizational theory, and behavior. His most famous work is his essay The Protestant Ethic and the Spirit of Capitalism, which began his work in the sociology of religion.

- a. George Cabot Lodge II
- b. Martin Luther
- c. Maximilian Carl Emil Weber
- d. Peter Ferdinand Drucker

42. In economics, an _____ is any good (e.g. a commodity) or service brought into one country from another country in a legitimate fashion, typically for use in trade.It is a good that is brought in from another country for sale. _____ goods or services are provided to domestic consumers by foreign producers. An _____ in the receiving country is an export to the sending country.

- a. Import
- b. Import quota
- c. Economic integration
- d. Incoterms

Chapter 12. The Challenge of Economic Development

43. _____ industrialization is a trade and economic policy based on the premise that a country should attempt to reduce its foreign dependency through the local production of industrialized products. Adopted in many Latin American countries from the 1930s until the late 1980s, and in some Asian and African countries from the 1950s on, Import substitutionl was theoretically organized in the works of Raúl Prebisch, Hans Singer, Celso Furtado and other structural economic thinkers, and gained prominence with the creation of the United Nations Economic Commission for Latin America and the Caribbean . Insofar as its suggestion of state-induced industrialization through governmental spending, it is largely influenced by Keynesian thinking, as well as the infant industry arguments adopted by some highly industrialized countries, such as the United States, until the 1940s.

a. ACEA agreement
b. Import substitution
c. ACCRA Cost of Living Index
d. AD-IA Model

44. An _____ is an economy in which people, including businesses, can trade in goods and services with other people and businesses in the international community at large. This contrasts with a closed economy in which international trade cannot take place.

The act of selling goods or services to a foreign country is called exporting.

a. Information economy
b. Attention work
c. Indicative planning
d. Open economy

45. A _____ is a general term that describes any government policy or regulation that restricts international trade. The barriers can take many forms, including the following terms that include many restrictions in international trade within multiple countries that import and export any items of trade.

- Import duty
- Import licenses
- Export licenses
- Import quotas
- Tariffs
- Subsidies
- Non-tariff barriers to trade
- Voluntary Export Restraints
- Local Content Requirements
- Embargo

Most _____s work on the same principle: the imposition of some sort of cost on trade that raises the price of the traded products. If two or more nations repeatedly use _____s against each other, then a trade war results.

a. Certificate of origin
b. National Foreign Trade Council
c. Global financial system
d. Trade barrier

46. _____ is a term used in economics to describe how an economic quantity is related to economic fluctuations. It is the opposite of procyclical. However, it has more than one meaning.

a. Mathematical economics
b. Law of comparative advantage
c. Price revolution
d. Countercyclical

47. An autarky is an economy that is self-sufficient and does not take part in international trade, or severely limits trade with the outside world. Likewise the term refers to an ecosystem not affected by influences from the outside, which relies entirely on its own resources. In the economic meaning, it is also referred to as a _____.
   a. Transition economy
   b. Network Economy
   c. Digital economy
   d. Closed economy

48. A _____ or directed economy is an economic system in which the government or workers' councils manages the economy. It is an economic system in which the central government makes all decisions on the production and consumption of goods and services. Its most extensive form is referred to as a _____, centrally planned economy, or command and control economy.
   a. Nutritional Economics
   b. Transition economy
   c. Subsistence economy
   d. Command economy

49. An _____ or Å"conomic system is a system that involves the production, distribution and consumption of goods and services between the entities in a particular society. It is the method used by society to produce and distribute goods and services. The _____ is composed of people and institutions, including their relationships to productive resources, such as through the convention of property.
   a. Information economy
   b. Indicative planning
   c. Intention economy
   d. Economic system

50. A _____ is an economy based on the division of labor in which the prices of goods and services are determined in a free price system set by supply and demand. This is often contrasted with a planned economy, in which a central government determines the price of goods and services using a fixed price system. Market economies are contrasted with mixed economy where the price system is not entirely free but under some government control that is not extensive enough to constitute a planned economy.
   a. Nutritional Economics
   b. Commons-based peer production
   c. Network Economy
   d. Market economy

51. _____ in political thought refers to economic theories of social organization advocating collective ownership and administration of the means of production and distribution of goods, and a society characterized by equality for all individuals, with an egalitarian method of compensation. Modern _____ originated in the late 19th-century intellectual and working class political movement that criticized the effects of industrialization and private ownership on society. Karl Marx posited that _____ would be achieved via class struggle and a proletarian revolution after a transitional stage from capitalism called the dictatorship of the proletariat.
   a. Socialism
   b. Adam Smith
   c. Adolph Fischer
   d. Adolf Hitler

52. The _____ is an international financial institution that provides financial and technical assistance to developing countries for development programs (e.g. bridges, roads, schools, etc.) with the stated goal of reducing poverty.

Chapter 12. The Challenge of Economic Development

The _____ differs from the _____ Group, in that the _____ comprises only two institutions:

- International Bank for Reconstruction and Development (IBRD)
- International Development Association (IDA)

Whereas the latter incorporates these two in addition to three more:

- International Finance Corporation (IFC)
- Multilateral Investment Guarantee Agency (MIGA)
- International Centre for Settlement of Investment Disputes (ICSID)

John Maynard Keynes (right) represented the UK at the conference, and Harry Dexter White represented the US.

The _____ is one of two major financial institutions created as a result of the Bretton Woods Conference in 1944. The International Monetary Fund, a related but separate institution, is the second.

a. World Bank
b. Flow to Equity-Approach
c. Bank-State-Branch
d. Financial costs of the 2003 Iraq War

53. The Great Proletarian _____ in the People's Republic of China was a period of widespread social and political upheaval; the nation-wide chaos and economic disarray engulfed much of Chinese society between 1966 and 1976.

It was launched by Mao Zedong, the chairman of the Communist Party of China, on May 16, 1966, who alleged that liberal bourgeoisie elements were dominating the party and insisted that they needed to be removed through post-revolutionary class struggle by mobilizing the thoughts and actions of China's youth, who formed Red Guards groups around the country. Although Mao himself officially declared the _____ to have ended in 1969, today it is widely believed that the power struggles and political instability between 1969 and the arrest of the Gang of Four as well as the death of Mao in 1976 were also part of the Revolution.

a. Cultural Revolution
b. 100-year flood
c. 1921 recession
d. 130-30 fund

54. An _____, in economics, is the amount by which the real Gross domestic product exceeds potential GDP. The real GDP is also known as GDP 'adjusted for inflation', 'constant prices' GDP or 'constant dollar' GDP, because it measures the aggregate output in a country's income accounts in a given year, expressed in base-year prices. On the other hand, the potential GDP is the quantity of real GDP when a country's economy is at full-employment.

a. AD-IA Model
b. ACCRA Cost of Living Index
c. ACEA agreement
d. Inflationary gap

Chapter 12. The Challenge of Economic Development

55. _____ has several particular meanings:

- in mathematics
    - _____ function
    - Euler _____
    - _____
    - _____ subgroup
    - method of _____s (partial differential equations)
- in physics and engineering
    - any _____ curve that shows the relationship between certain input- and output parameters, e.g.
    - an I-V or current-voltage _____ is the current in a circuit as a function of the applied voltage
    - Receiver-Operator _____
- in fiction
    - in Dungeons ' Dragons, _____ is another name for ability score

a. Demand
b. Russian financial crisis
c. Technocracy
d. Characteristic

56. In economics, an _____ is any good or commodity, transported from one country to another country in a legitimate fashion, typically for use in trade. _____ goods or services are provided to foreign consumers by domestic producers. _____ is an important part of international trade.

a. Export
b. ACCRA Cost of Living Index
c. AD-IA Model
d. ACEA agreement

57. Manifesto of the Communist Party , often referred to as The _____, was first published on February 21, 1848, and is one of the world's most influential political manuscripts. Commissioned by the Communist League and written by communist theorists Karl Marx and Friedrich Engels, it laid out the League's purposes and program. It presents an analytical approach to the class struggle and the problems of capitalism, rather than a prediction of communism's potential future forms.

a. Differential and Absolute Ground Rent
b. Dialectical materialism
c. Labour power
d. Communist Manifesto

58. In economics, _____ is the transfer of income, wealth or property from some individuals to others.

One premise of _____ is that money should be distributed to benefit the poorer members of society, and that the rich have an obligation to assist the poor, thus creating a more financially egalitarian society. Another argument is that the rich exploit the poor or otherwise gain unfair benefits.

a. 1921 recession
b. Redistribution
c. 100-year flood
d. 130-30 fund

59.

_____ was a German philosopher, political economist, historian, political theorist, sociologist, communist and revolutionary credited as the founder of communism.

Chapter 12. The Challenge of Economic Development

Marx summarized his approach to history and politics in the opening line of the first chapter of The Communist Manifesto : e;The history of all hitherto existing society is the history of class struggles.e; Marx argued that capitalism, like previous socioeconomic systems, will produce internal tensions which will lead to its destruction. Just as capitalism replaced feudalism, socialism will in its turn replace capitalism and lead to a stateless, classless society which will emerge after a transitional period, the 'dictatorship of the proletariat'.

a. Marxism
b. Adam Smith
c. Neo-Gramscianism
d. Karl Heinrich Marx

60. There are two main interpretations of the idea of a _____:

- A model in which the state assumes primary responsibility for the welfare of its citizens. This responsibility in theory ought to be comprehensive, because all aspects of welfare are considered and universally applied to citizens as a 'right'. _____ can also mean the creation of a 'social safety net' of minimum standards of varying forms of welfare. Here is found some confusion between a '_____' and a 'welfare society' in common debate about the definition of the term.
- The provision of welfare in society. In many '_____s', especially in continental Europe, welfare is not actually provided by the state, but by a combination of independent, voluntary, mutualist and government services. The functional provider of benefits and services may be a central or state government, a state-sponsored company or agency, a private corporation, a charity or another form of non-profit organization. However, this phenomenon has been more appropriately termed a 'welfare society,' and the term 'welfare system' has been used to describe the range of _____ and welfare society mixes that are found.

The English term '_____' is believed by Asa Briggs to have been coined by Archbishop William Temple during the Second World War, contrasting wartime Britain with the 'warfare state' of Nazi Germany. Friedrich Hayek contends that the term derived from the older German word Wohlfahrtsstaat, which itself was used by nineteenth century historians to describe a variant of the ideal of Polizeistaat . It was fully developed by the German academic Sozialpolitiker--'socialists of the chair'--from 1870 and first implemented through Bismarck's 'state socialism'. Bismarck's policies have also been seen as the creation of a _____.

a. 130-30 fund
b. 1921 recession
c. Welfare state
d. 100-year flood

61. In financial accounting, a _____ or statement of financial position is a summary of a person's or organization's balances. Assets, liabilities and ownership equity are listed as of a specific date, such as the end of its financial year. A _____ is often described as a snapshot of a company's financial condition.

a. 100-year flood
b. 1921 recession
c. 130-30 fund
d. Balance sheet

62. _____ is a term that refers both to:

- a formal discipline used to help appraise, or assess, the case for a project or proposal, which itself is a process known as project appraisal; and
- an informal approach to making decisions of any kind.

Chapter 12. The Challenge of Economic Development

Under both definitions the process involves, whether explicitly or implicitly, weighing the total expected costs against the total expected benefits of one or more actions in order to choose the best or most profitable option. The formal process is often referred to as either CBA (_____) or BCost-benefit analysis

A hallmark of CBA is that all benefits and all costs are expressed in money terms, and are adjusted for the time value of money, so that all flows of benefits and flows of project costs over time (which tend to occur at different points in time) are expressed on a common basis in terms of their e;present value.e; Closely related, but slightly different, formal techniques include Cost-effectiveness analysis, Economic impact analysis, Fiscal impact analysis and Social Return on Investment(SROI) analysis. The latter builds upon the logic of _____, but differs in that it is explicitly designed to inform the practical decision-making of enterprise managers and investors focused on optimising their social and environmental impacts.

- a. Cost-benefit analysis
- b. 100-year flood
- c. Decision theory
- d. 130-30 fund

63. In finance, the _____ of a financial asset measures the sensitivity of the asset's price to interest rate movements. There are various definitions of _____ and derived quantities, discussed below. If not otherwise specified, '_____' generally means the Macaulay _____, as defined below.
- a. 100-year flood
- b. Time value of money
- c. Newtonian time
- d. Duration

64. To _____ is to impose a financial charge or other levy upon a taxpayer by a state or the functional equivalent of a state.

_____es are also imposed by many subnational entities. _____es consist of direct _____ or indirect _____, and may be paid in money or as its labour equivalent (often but not always unpaid.)

- a. Tax
- b. 100-year flood
- c. 1921 recession
- d. 130-30 fund

65. _____ is the a method of technical and economic research of the systems for purpose to optimize a parity between system's consumer functions or properties and expenses to achieve those functions or properties.

This methodology for continuous perfection of production, industrial technologies, organizational structures was developed by Juryj Sobolev in 1948 at the 'Perm telephone factory'

- 1948 Juryj Sobolev - the first success in application of a method analysis at the 'Perm telephone factory' .
- 1949 - the first application for the invention as result of use of the new method.

Chapter 12. The Challenge of Economic Development

Today in economically developed countries practically each enterprise or the company use methodology of the kind of functional-cost analysis as a practice of the quality management, most full satisfying to principles of standards of series ISO 9000.

- Interest of consumer not in products itself, but the advantage which it will receive from its usage.
- The consumer aspires to reduce his expenses
- Functions needed by consumer can be executed in the various ways, and, hence, with various efficiency and expenses. Among possible alternatives of realization of functions exist such in which the parity of quality and the price is the optimal for the consumer.

The goal of _____ is achievement of the highest consumer satisfaction of production at simultaneous decrease in all kinds of industrial expenses Classical _____ has three English synonyms - Value Engineering, Value Management, Value Analysis.

a. Monopoly wage
b. Willingness to pay
c. Staple financing
d. Function cost analysis

66. _____ was the General Secretary of the Communist Party of the Soviet Union's Central Committee from 1922 until his death in 1953. In the years following Lenin's death in 1924, he rose to become the leader of the Soviet Union.

Stalin launched a command economy, replacing the New Economic Policy of the 1920s with Five-Year Plans and launching a period of rapid industrialization and economic collectivization.

a. Adolph Fischer
b. Josef Stalin
c. Adam Smith
d. Adolf Hitler

67. In economics, the _____ is a historical inverse relation between the rate of unemployment and the rate of inflation in an economy. Stated simply, the lower the unemployment in an economy, the higher the rate of increase in nominal wages in the economy. Rate of Change of Wages against Unemployment, United Kingdom 1913-1948 from Phillips (1958)

William Phillips, a New Zealand born economist, wrote a paper in 1958 titled The Relationship between Unemployment and the Rate of Change of Money Wages in the United Kingdom 1861-1957, which was published in the quarterly journal Economica.

a. Cost curve
b. Lorenz curve
c. Demand curve
d. Phillips curve

68. In political science and economics, the _____ or agency dilemma treats the difficulties that arise under conditions of incomplete and asymmetric information when a principal hires an agent, such as the problem that the two may not have the same interests, while the principal is, presumably, hiring the agent to pursue the interests of the former.

Various mechanisms may be used to try to align the interests of the agent with those of the principal, such as piece rates/commissions, profit sharing, efficiency wages, performance measurement (including financial statements), the agent posting a bond, or fear of firing. The _____ is found in most employer/employee relationships, for example, when stockholders hire top executives of corporations.

a. Principal-agent problem
c. 100-year flood
b. 1921 recession
d. 130-30 fund

69. In economics, _____ is a rise in the general level of prices of goods and services in an economy over a period of time. When the general price level rises, each unit of currency buys fewer goods and services; consequently, _____ is also a decline in the real value of money--a loss of purchasing power in the medium of exchange which is also the monetary unit of account in the economy. A chief measure of general price-level _____ is the general _____ rate, which is the percentage change in a general price index (normally the Consumer Price Index) over time.

a. Inflation
c. Energy economics
b. Economic
d. Opportunity cost

70. A _____ represents the combinations of goods and services that a consumer can purchase given current prices and his income. Consumer theory uses the concepts of a _____ and a preference map to analyze consumer choices. Both concepts have a ready graphical representation in the two-good case.

a. Revealed preference
c. Joint demand
b. Quality bias
d. Budget constraint

71. _____ in economics and business is the result of an exchange and from that trade we assign a numerical monetary value to a good, service or asset. If Alice trades Bob 4 apples for an orange, the _____ of an orange is 4 apples. Inversely, the _____ of an apple is 1/4 oranges.

a. Price book
c. Price war
b. Premium pricing
d. Price

72. _____ is one of the four Ps of the marketing mix. The other three aspects are product, promotion, and place. It is also a key variable in microeconomic price allocation theory.

a. Guaranteed Maximum Price
c. Point of total assumption
b. Premium pricing
d. Pricing

73. _____ is the incidence or process of transferring ownership of a business, enterprise, agency or public service from the public sector (government) to the private sector (business.) In a broader sense, _____ refers to transfer of any government function to the private sector including governmental functions like revenue collection and law enforcement.

The term '_____' also has been used to describe two unrelated transactions.

a. Ricardian equivalence
c. Privatization
b. Performance reports
d. Compound empowerment

74. _____ is a social science concept used in business, economics, organizational behaviour, political science, public health and sociology that refers to connections within and between social networks. Though there are a variety of related definitions, which have been described as 'something of a cure-all' for the problems of modern society, they tend to share the core idea 'that social networks have value. Just as a screwdriver (physical capital) or a college education (human capital) can increase productivity (both individual and collective), so do social contacts affect the productivity of individuals and groups'.
 a. Social inequality
 b. Pre-industrial society
 c. Diversity training
 d. Social capital

Chapter 13. Exchange Rates and the International Financial System

1. _____s is the social science that studies the production, distribution, and consumption of goods and services. The term _____s comes from the Ancient Greek oá¼°κονομῖα from oá¼¶κος (oikos, 'house') + νῐ́Œμος (nomos, 'custom' or 'law'), hence 'rules of the house(hold)'. Current _____ models developed out of the broader field of political economy in the late 19th century, owing to a desire to use an empirical approach more akin to the physical sciences.
   a. Inflation
   b. Economic
   c. Energy economics
   d. Opportunity cost

2. _____ is a term used to describe how different aspects between economies are integrated. The basics of this theory were written by the Hungarian Economist Béla Balassa in the 1960s. As _____ increases, the barriers of trade between markets diminishes.
   a. Inward investment
   b. Economic integration
   c. Import license
   d. Import

3. _____ was an arrangement established in 1979 under the Jenkins European Commission where most nations of the European Economic Community (EEC) linked their currencies to prevent large fluctuations relative to one another.

   After the collapse of the Bretton Woods system in 1971, most of the EEC countries agreed in 1972 to maintain stable exchange rates by preventing exchange fluctuations of more than 2.25% (the European 'currency snake'.) In March 1979, this system was replaced by the _____, and the European Currency Unit (ECU) was defined.

   a. European Monetary System
   b. Euro Interbank Offered Rate
   c. Exchange rate mechanism
   d. European Monetary Union

4. The _____ is an economic and political union of 27 member states, located primarily in Europe. It was established by the Treaty of Maastricht on 1 November 1993, upon the foundations of the pre-existing European Economic Community. With a population of almost 500 million, the _____ generates an estimated 30% share (US$18.4 trillion in 2008) of the nominal gross world product.
   a. European Court of Justice
   b. ACCRA Cost of Living Index
   c. ACEA agreement
   d. European Union

5. The term financial crisis is applied broadly to a variety of situations in which some financial institutions or assets suddenly lose a large part of their value. In the 19th and early 20th centuries, many _____ were associated with banking panics, and many recessions coincided with these panics. Other situations that are often called _____ include stock market crashes and the bursting of other financial bubbles, currency crises, and sovereign defaults.
   a. Microeconomics
   b. Georgism
   c. General equilibrium
   d. Financial crises

6. The _____ or gross domestic income (GDI), a basic measure of an economy's economic performance, is the market value of all final goods and services produced within the borders of a nation in a year. _____ can be defined in three ways, all of which are conceptually identical. First, it is equal to the total expenditures for all final goods and services produced within the country in a stipulated period of time (usually a 365-day year.)
   a. Countercyclical
   b. Monopolistic competition
   c. Gross domestic product
   d. Market structure

7. A _____ secures the proper functioning of money by regulating economic agents, transaction types, and money supply.

Chapter 13. Exchange Rates and the International Financial System 163

_____s are traditionally formed by the policy decisions of individual governments and administrated as a domestic economic issue.

The current trend, however, is to use international trade and investment to alter the policy and legislation of individual governments.

a. Netting
c. Financial rand
b. Consumer basket
d. Monetary System

8. _____ is an economic system in which wealth, and the means of producing wealth, are privately owned. Through _____, the land, labor, and capital are owned, operated, and traded for the purpose of generating profits, without force or fraud, by private individuals either singly or jointly, and investments, distribution, income, production, pricing and supply of goods, commodities and services are determined by voluntary private decision in a market economy. A distinguishing feature of _____ is that each person owns his or her own labor and therefore is allowed to sell the use of it to employers.
a. Creative capitalism
c. Capitalism
b. Socialism for the rich and capitalism for the poor
d. Late capitalism

9. _____ is a term used in economics to describe how an economic quantity is related to economic fluctuations. It is the opposite of procyclical. However, it has more than one meaning.
a. Mathematical economics
c. Price revolution
b. Law of comparative advantage
d. Countercyclical

10. _____ is a negative term describing an claimed capitalist economy in which success in business depends on close relationships between businesspeople and government officials. It may be exhibited in the distribution of legal permits, government grants, special tax breaks, and so forth.

_____ is believed to arise when political cronyism spills over into the business world; self-serving friendships and family ties between businessmen and the government influence the economy and society to the extent that it corrupts public-serving economic and political ideals.

a. Good governance
c. 100-year flood
b. 130-30 fund
d. Crony capitalism

11. _____ is money accepted for exchange of goods in an economy. The prevalence of one money over another arises, usually, when a government designates through decrees that the government shall accept only particular notes and coins in payment for taxes. Typically, money of _____ consists of stamped coins and minted paper bills.
a. Totnes pound
c. Security thread
b. Local currency
d. Currency

12. A _____ is a monetary authority which is required to maintain a fixed exchange rate with a foreign currency. This policy objective requires the conventional objectives of a central bank to be subordinated to the exchange rate target.

The main qualities of an orthodox _____ are:

- A _____'s foreign currency reserves must be sufficient to ensure that all holders of its notes and coins (and all banks creditor of a Reserve Account at the _____) can convert them into the reserve currency (usually 110-115% of the monetary base M0.)
- A _____ maintains absolute, unlimited convertibility between its notes and coins and the currency against which they are pegged (the anchor currency), at a fixed rate of exchange, with no restrictions on current-account or capital-account transactions.
- A _____ only earns profit from interests on foreign reserves (less the expense of note-issuing), and does not engage in forward-exchange transactions. These foreign reserves exist (1) because local notes have been issued in exchange, or (2) because commercial banks must by regulation deposit a minimum reserve at the _____. (1) generates a seignorage revenue. (2) is the revenue on minimum reserves (revenue of investment activities less cost of minimum reserves remuneration)
- A _____ has no discretionary powers to effect monetary policy and does not lend to the government. Governments cannot print money, and can only tax or borrow to meet their spending commitments.
- A _____ does not act as a lender of last resort to commercial banks, and does not regulate reserve requirements.
- A _____ does not attempt to manipulate interest rates by establishing a discount rate like a central bank. The peg with the foreign currency tends to keep interest rates and inflation very closely aligned to those in the country against whose currency the peg is fixed.

The _____ in question will no longer issue fiat money but instead will only issue one unit of local currency for each unit (or decided amount) of foreign currency it has in its vault (often a hard currency such as the U.S. dollar or the euro.) The surplus on the balance of payments of that country is reflected by higher deposits local banks hold at the central bank as well as (initially) higher deposits of the (net) exporting firms at their local banks.

a. Currency board
c. Currency competition

b. Reserve currency
d. Petrodollar

13. A currency crisis, which is also called a balance-of-payments crisis, occurs when the value of a currency changes quickly, undermining its ability to serve as a medium of exchange or a store of value. It is a type of financial crisis and is often associated with a real economic crisis. _____ can be especially destructive to small open economies or bigger, but not sufficiently stable ones.

a. 1921 recession
c. 130-30 fund

b. 100-year flood
d. Currency crises

14. _____ is that which is owed; usually referencing assets owed, but the term can also cover moral obligations and other interactions not requiring money. In the case of assets, _____ is a means of using future purchasing power in the present before a summation has been earned. Some companies and corporations use _____ as a part of their overall corporate finance strategy.

a. Collateral Management
c. Debenture

b. Hard money loan
d. Debt

Chapter 13. Exchange Rates and the International Financial System

15. _____ is the increase in the amount of the goods and services produced by an economy over time. It is conventionally measured as the percent rate of increase in real gross domestic product, or real GDP. Growth is usually calculated in real terms, i.e. inflation-adjusted terms, in order to net out the effect of inflation on the price of the goods and services produced.

a. AD-IA Model
b. Economic growth
c. ACEA agreement
d. ACCRA Cost of Living Index

16. The term _____ is applied broadly to a variety of situations in which some financial institutions or assets suddenly lose a large part of their value. In the 19th and early 20th centuries, many financial crises were associated with banking panics, and many recessions coincided with these panics. Other situations that are often called financial crises include stock market crashes and the bursting of other financial bubbles, currency crises, and sovereign defaults.

a. Financial crisis
b. Market failure
c. Co-operative economics
d. Macroeconomics

17. In finance, the _____ is the system that allows the transfer of money between savers and borrowers.

Put another way: the _____ is a set of complex and closely interconnected financial institutions, markets, instruments, services, practices, and transactions.

a. Lean consumption
b. Foreign investment
c. Hedonimetry
d. Financial system

18. A _____ is the transfer of wealth from one party (such as a person or company) to another. A _____ is usually made in exchange for the provision of goods, services or both, or to fulfill a legal obligation.

The simplest and oldest form of _____ is barter, the exchange of one good or service for another.

a. Going concern
b. Soft count
c. Social gravity
d. Payment

19. An _____ is an economy in which people, including businesses, can trade in goods and services with other people and businesses in the international community at large. This contrasts with a closed economy in which international trade cannot take place.

The act of selling goods or services to a foreign country is called exporting.

a. Information economy
b. Attention work
c. Indicative planning
d. Open economy

20. _____ is a misspelled phrase from Latin 'pro capite' phrase meaning per head with pro meaning 'per' or 'for each' and capite meaning 'head.' Both words together equate to the phrase 'for each head.'

It is usually used in the field of statistics to indicate the average per person for any given concern, such as income, crime rate, etc.

It is also used in wills to indicate that each of the named beneficiaries should receive, by devise or bequest, equal shares of the estate. This is in contrast to a per stirpes division, in which each branch of the inheriting family inherits an equal share of the estate.

- a. Sargan test
- b. Per capita
- c. False positive rate
- d. Population statistics

21. An _____, in economics, is the amount by which the real Gross domestic product exceeds potential GDP. The real GDP is also known as GDP 'adjusted for inflation', 'constant prices' GDP or 'constant dollar' GDP, because it measures the aggregate output in a country's income accounts in a given year, expressed in base-year prices. On the other hand, the potential GDP is the quantity of real GDP when a country's economy is at full-employment.

- a. Inflationary gap
- b. ACEA agreement
- c. AD-IA Model
- d. ACCRA Cost of Living Index

22. In economics, the _____ measures the payments that flow between any individual country and all other countries. It is used to summarize all international economic transactions for that country during a specific time period, usually a year. The _____ is determined by the country's exports and imports of goods, services, and financial capital, as well as financial transfers.

- a. Gross world product
- b. Balance of payments
- c. Gross domestic product per barrel
- d. Skyscraper Index

23. _____ is the development of economic wealth of countries or regions for the well-being of their inhabitants. It is the process by which a nation improves the economic, political, and social well being of its people. From a policy perspective, _____ can be defined as efforts that seek to improve the economic well-being and quality of life for a community by creating and/or retaining jobs and supporting or growing incomes and the tax base.

- a. Economic development
- b. Experimental economics
- c. Inflation
- d. Economic methodology

24. The term '_____' refers to the concept of collecting information and attempting to spot a pattern in the information. In some fields of study, the term '_____' has more formally-defined meanings.

In project management _____ is a mathematical technique that uses historical results to predict future outcome.

- a. Coefficient of determination
- b. Quantile regression
- c. Probit model
- d. Trend analysis

25. The term _____ refers to economy-wide fluctuations in production or economic activity over several months or years. These fluctuations occur around a long-term growth trend, and typically involve shifts over time between periods of relatively rapid economic growth (expansion or boom), and periods of relative stagnation or decline (contraction or recession.)

These fluctuations are often measured using the growth rate of real gross domestic product.

a. Tobit model
b. Nominal value
c. Consumer theory
d. Business cycle

26. A _____ refers to any type debt instrument, such as a loan, bond, mortgage that does not have a fixed rate of interest over the life of the instrument. Such debt typically uses an index or other base rate for establishing the interest rate for each relevant period. One of the most common rates to use as the basis for applying interest rates is the London Inter-bank Offered Rate, or LIBOR

a. Money market
b. Moneylender
c. Floating interest rate
d. Disposal tax effect

27. In economics, the _____ is one of the two primary components of the balance of payments, the other being the capital account. It is the sum of the balance of trade (exports minus imports of goods and services), net factor income (such as interest and dividends) and net transfer payments (such as foreign aid.)

$$\text{Current account} = \text{Balance of trade} \\ + \text{ Net factor income from abroad} \\ + \text{ Net unilateral transfers from abroad}$$

The _____ balance is one of two major metrics of the nature of a country's foreign trade (the other being the net capital outflow.)

a. National Income and Product Accounts
b. Gross private domestic investment
c. Compensation of employees
d. Current account

28. In economics, an _____ is any good (e.g. a commodity) or service brought into one country from another country in a legitimate fashion, typically for use in trade. It is a good that is brought in from another country for sale. _____ goods or services are provided to domestic consumers by foreign producers. An _____ in the receiving country is an export to the sending country.

a. Economic integration
b. Incoterms
c. Import quota
d. Import

29. _____ is an economic theory that holds that the prosperity of a nation is dependent upon its supply of capital, and that the global volume of international trade is 'unchangeable.' Economic assets or capital, are represented by bullion (gold, silver, and trade value) held by the state, which is best increased through a positive balance of trade with other nations (exports minus imports.) _____ suggests that the ruling government should advance these goals by playing a protectionist role in the economy; by encouraging exports and discouraging imports, notably through the use of tariffs and subsidies.

_____ was the dominant school of thought throughout the early modern period (from the 16th to the 18th century.)

a. Consumer theory
b. Nominal value
c. General equilibrium theory
d. Mercantilism

30. The balance of trade (or net exports, sometimes symbolized as NX) is the difference between the monetary value of exports and imports in an economy over a certain period of time. It is the relationship between a nation's imports and exports. A favorable balance of trade is known as a trade surplus and consists of exporting more than is imported; an unfavorable balance of trade is known as a _____ or, informally, a trade gap.
   a. Trade deficit
   b. Complementary asset
   c. Computational economic
   d. Demographics of India

31. In economics, an _____ is any good or commodity, transported from one country to another country in a legitimate fashion, typically for use in trade. _____ goods or services are provided to foreign consumers by domestic producers. _____ is an important part of international trade.
   a. AD-IA Model
   b. ACCRA Cost of Living Index
   c. ACEA agreement
   d. Export

32. _____ is exchange of capital, goods, and services across international borders or territories. In most countries, it represents a significant share of gross domestic product (GDP.) While _____ has been present throughout much of history, its economic, social, and political importance has been on the rise in recent centuries.
   a. Import license
   b. International trade
   c. Intra-industry trade
   d. Incoterms

33. In economics a _____ is an entity that owes a debt to someone else. The entity may be an individual, a firm, a government, a company or other legal person. The counterparty is called a creditor.
   a. Duration gap
   b. Decision process tool
   c. Senior stretch loan
   d. Debtor

34. A _____, sometimes called a pegged exchange rate, is a type of exchange rate regime wherein a currency's value is matched to the value of another single currency or to a basket of other currencies such as gold.

    A _____ is usually used to stabilize the value of a currency, vis-a-vis the currency it is pegged to. This facilitates trade and investments between the two countries, and is especially useful for small economies where external trade forms a large part of their GDP.

   a. Law of supply
   b. Monetary economics
   c. Leading indicators
   d. Fixed exchange rate

35. In finance, the _____s between two currencies specifies how much one currency is worth in terms of the other. It is the value of a foreign natione;s currency in terms of the home natione;s currency. For example an _____ of 102 Japanese yen to the United States dollar means that JPY 102 is worth the same as USD 1.
   a. Interbank market
   b. ACEA agreement
   c. ACCRA Cost of Living Index
   d. Exchange rate

36. _____ is that part of the total debt in a country that is owed to creditors outside the country. The debtors can be the government, corporations or private households. The debt includes money owed to private commercial banks, other governments, or international financial institutions such as the IMF and World Bank.
   a. External debt
   b. Asset protection
   c. Internal debt
   d. International debt collection

Chapter 13. Exchange Rates and the International Financial System

37. In economics, _____ is the total demand for final goods and services in the economy (Y) at a given time and price level. It is the amount of goods and services in the economy that will be purchased at all possible price levels. This is the demand for the gross domestic product of a country when inventory levels are static.
   a. Aggregate demand
   b. Aggregation problem
   c. Aggregate supply
   d. Aggregate expenditure

38. In economics, _____ is the total supply of goods and services produced by a national economy during a specific time period. It is the total amount of goods and services in the economy available at all possible price levels.
   a. Aggregate demand
   b. Aggregate expenditure
   c. Aggregate supply
   d. Aggregation problem

39. The _____ is the official currency of 16 of the 27 member states of the European Union (EU.) The states, known collectively as the Eurozone, are Austria, Belgium, Cyprus, Finland, France, Germany, Greece, Ireland, Italy, Luxembourg, Malta, the Netherlands, Portugal, Slovakia, Slovenia, and Spain. The currency is also used in a further five European countries, with and without formal agreements and is consequently used daily by some 327 million Europeans.
   a. Import and Export Price Indices
   b. IRS Code 3401
   c. Equity capital market
   d. Euro

40. The _____ is where currency trading takes place. It is where banks and other official institutions facilitate the buying and selling of foreign currencies. FX transactions typically involve one party purchasing a quantity of one currency in exchange for paying a quantity of another.
   a. Currency swap
   b. Covered interest arbitrage
   c. Floating currency
   d. Foreign exchange market

41. _____ is an economic model based on price, utility and quantity in a market. It predicts that in a competitive market, price will function to equalize the quantity demanded by consumers, and the quantity supplied by producers, resulting in an economic equilibrium of price and quantity. The model incorporates other factors changing equilibrium as a shift of demand and/or supply.
   a. Rational addiction
   b. Joint demand
   c. Supply and demand
   d. Deferred gratification

42. Economics:

   - _____,the desire to own something and the ability to pay for it
   - _____ curve,a graphic representation of a _____ schedule
   - _____ deposit, the money in checking accounts
   - _____ pull theory,the theory that inflation occurs when _____ for goods and services exceeds existing supplies
   - _____ schedule,a table that lists the quantity of a good a person will buy it each different price
   - _____ side economics,the school of economics at believes government spending and tax cuts open economy by raising _____

   a. Variability
   b. McKesson ' Robbins scandal
   c. Production
   d. Demand

43. _____ is a term used in accounting relating to the increase in value of an asset. In this sense it is the reverse of depreciation, which measures the fall in value of assets over their normal life-time.

_____ is a rise of a currency in a floating exchange rate.

a. Appreciation
b. ACEA agreement
c. AD-IA Model
d. ACCRA Cost of Living Index

44. _____ is a term used in accounting, economics and finance to spread the cost of an asset over the span of several years.

In simple words we can say that _____ is the reduction in the value of an asset due to usage, passage of time, wear and tear, technological outdating or obsolescence, depletion, inadequacy, rot, rust, decay or other such factors.

In accounting, _____ is a term used to describe any method of attributing the historical or purchase cost of an asset across its useful life, roughly corresponding to normal wear and tear.

a. Net income per employee
b. Historical cost
c. Salvage value
d. Depreciation

45. _____ is a reduction in the value of a currency with respect to other monetary units. In common modern usage, it specifically implies an official lowering of the value of a country's currency within a fixed exchange rate system, by which the monetary authority formally sets a new fixed rate with respect to a foreign reference currency. In contrast, (currency) depreciation is used for the unofficial decrease in the exchange rate in a floating exchange rate system.

a. Devaluation
b. Reserve currency
c. Petrodollar recycling
d. Texas redbacks

46. A fixed exchange rate, sometimes called a _____, is a type of exchange rate regime wherein a currency's value is matched to the value of another single currency or to a basket of other currencies such as gold.

A fixed exchange rate is usually used to stabilize the value of a currency, vis-a-vis the currency it is pegged to. This facilitates trade and investments between the two countries, and is especially useful for small economies where external trade forms a large part of their GDP.

a. Pegged exchange rate
b. Mainstream economics
c. Leading indicators
d. Recession

47. _____ means a rise of a price of goods or products. This term is specially used as _____ of a currency, where it means a rise of currency to the relation with a foreign currency in a fixed exchange rate. In floating exchange rate correct term would be appreciation.

a. Revaluation
b. Legal monopoly
c. Death spiral financing
d. Deglobalization

48. _____ is a term used in economics to describe an economy where capital per worker is increasing. A process of increasing the amount of capital per worker. It is an increase in the capital intensity.

Chapter 13. Exchange Rates and the International Financial System

a. Firm-specific infrastructure
b. Capital formation
c. Capital expenditure
d. Capital deepening

49. In neoclassical economics and microeconomics, _____ describes the perfect being a market in which there are many small firms, all producing homogeneous goods. In the short term, such markets are productively inefficient as output will not occur where mc is equal to ac, but allocatively efficient, as output under _____ will always occur where mc is equal to mr, and therefore where mc equals ar. However, in the long term, such markets are both allocatively and productively efficient.
   a. Perfect competition
   b. Law of supply
   c. General equilibrium
   d. Co-operative economics

50. A _____, reserve bank, or monetary authority is the entity responsible for the monetary policy of a country or of a group of member states. It is a bank that can lend money to other banks in times of need. Its primary responsibility is to maintain the stability of the national currency and money supply, but more active duties include controlling subsidized-loan interest rates, and acting as a lender of last resort to the banking sector during times of financial crisis (private banks often being integral to the national financial system.)
   a. 100-year flood
   b. 130-30 fund
   c. 1921 recession
   d. Central bank

51. The _____ is the central banking system of the United States. Created in 1913 by the enactment of the Federal Reserve Act (signed by Woodrow Wilson), it is a quasi-public and quasi-private (government entity with private components) banking system that comprises (1) the presidentially appointed Board of Governors of the _____ in Washington, D.C.; (2) the Federal Open Market Committee; (3) twelve regional Federal Reserve Banks located in major cities throughout the nation acting as fiscal agents for the U.S. Treasury, each with its own nine-member board of directors; (4) numerous other private U.S. member banks, which subscribe to required amounts of non-transferable stock in their regional Federal Reserve Banks; and (5) various advisory councils. Since February 2006, Ben Bernanke has served as the Chairman of the Board of Governors of the _____.
   a. Federal Reserve System Open Market Account
   b. Monetary Policy Report to the Congress
   c. Federal Reserve System
   d. Term auction facility

52. The term _____ or commodity bundle refers to a fixed list of items used specifically to track the progress of inflation in an economy or specific market.

The most common type of _____ is the basket of consumer goods, used to define the Consumer Price Index (CPI.) Other types of baskets are used to define

- Producer Price Index (PPI), previously known as Wholesale Price Index (WPI)
- various commodity price indices

The term _____ analysis in the retail business refers to research that provides the retailer with information to understand the purchase behaviour of a buyer. This information will enable the retailer to understand the buyer's needs and rewrite the store's layout accordingly, develop cross-promotional programs, or even capture new buyers (much like the cross-selling concept.)

a. Robin Hood index
b. Category Development Index
c. Cost-weighted activity index
d. Market basket

53. _____ is an economic concept with commonplace familiarity. It is the price that a good or service is offered at, or will fetch, in the marketplace. It is of interest mainly in the study of microeconomics.
    a. Market anomaly
    b. Noisy market hypothesis
    c. Market price
    d. Paper trading

54. _____ refers to a business or organization attempting to acquire goods or services to accomplish the goals of the enterprise. Though there are several organizations that attempt to set standards in the _____ process, processes can vary greatly between organizations. Typically the word '_____' is not used interchangeably with the word 'procurement', since procurement typically includes Expediting, Supplier Quality, and Traffic and Logistics (T'L) in addition to _____.
    a. 130-30 fund
    b. Purchasing
    c. Free port
    d. 100-year flood

55. _____ is the number of goods/services that can be purchased with a unit of currency. For example, if you had taken one dollar to a store in the 1950s, you would have been able to buy a greater number of items than you would today, indicating that you would have had a greater _____ in the 1950s. Currency can be either a commodity money, like gold or silver, or fiat currency like US dollars.
    a. Genuine progress indicator
    b. Human Poverty Index
    c. Compliance cost
    d. Purchasing power

56. The _____ theory uses the long-term equilibrium exchange rate of two currencies to equalize their purchasing power. Developed by Gustav Cassel in 1920, it is based on the law of one price: the theory states that, in ideally efficient markets, identical goods should have only one price.

This purchasing power SEM rate equalizes the purchasing power of different currencies in their home countries for a given basket of goods.

    a. Measures of national income and output
    b. Bureau of Labor Statistics
    c. Purchasing power parity
    d. Gross national product

57. A _____ is an object whose consumption increases the utility of the consumer, for which the quantity demanded exceeds the quantity supplied at zero price. _____s are usually modeled as having diminishing marginal utility. The first individual purchase has high utility; the second has less.
    a. Pie method
    b. Good
    c. Merit good
    d. Composite good

58. _____ is the process by which the government, central bank (ii) availability of money, and (iii) cost of money or rate of interest, in order to attain a set of objectives oriented towards the growth and stability of the economy. Monetary theory provides insight into how to craft optimal _____.

_____ is referred to as either being an expansionary policy where an expansionary policy increases the total supply of money in the economy, and a contractionary policy decreases the total money supply.

Chapter 13. Exchange Rates and the International Financial System

a. 130-30 fund
b. 100-year flood
c. Monetary policy
d. 1921 recession

59. _____ in economics and business is the result of an exchange and from that trade we assign a numerical monetary value to a good, service or asset. If Alice trades Bob 4 apples for an orange, the _____ of an orange is 4 apples. Inversely, the _____ of an apple is 1/4 oranges.
   a. Price war
   b. Price book
   c. Premium pricing
   d. Price

60. In economics, _____ is a rise in the general level of prices of goods and services in an economy over a period of time. When the general price level rises, each unit of currency buys fewer goods and services; consequently, _____ is also a decline in the real value of money--a loss of purchasing power in the medium of exchange which is also the monetary unit of account in the economy. A chief measure of general price-level _____ is the general _____ rate, which is the percentage change in a general price index (normally the Consumer Price Index) over time.
   a. Economic
   b. Inflation
   c. Energy economics
   d. Opportunity cost

61. In economics, the _____ is a measure of inflation, the rate of increase of a price index (for example, a consumer price index.)It is the percentage rate of change in price level over time. The rate of decrease in the purchasing power of money is approximately equal.

It's used to calculate the real interest rate, as well as real increases in wages, and official measurements of this rate act as input variables to COLA adjustments and Inflation derivatives prices.

   a. Equity value
   b. Inflation rate
   c. Edgeworth paradox
   d. Interest rate option

62. The _____ is a monetary system in which a region's common medium of exchange are paper notes that are normally freely convertible into pre-set, fixed quantities of gold. The _____ is not currently used by any government, having been replaced completely by fiat currency. Gold certificates were used as paper currency in the United States from 1882 to 1933, these certificates were freely convertable into gold coins.

In the 1790s Britain suffered a massive shortage of silver coinage and ceased to mint larger silver coins.

   a. Gold standard
   b. 130-30 fund
   c. 1921 recession
   d. 100-year flood

63. _____, Jr. (January 29, 1843 - September 14, 1901) was the 25th President of the United States, and the last veteran of the American Civil War to be elected.

By the 1880s, McKinley was a national Republican leader; his signature issue was high tariffs on imports as a formula for prosperity, as typified by his McKinley Tariff of 1890.

   a. Adam Smith
   b. Adolf Hitler
   c. William McKinley
   d. Adolph Fischer

Chapter 13. Exchange Rates and the International Financial System

64. In economics, the _____ of money is a theory emphasizing the positive relationship of overall prices or the nominal value of expenditures to the quantity of money.

It is the mainstream economic theory of the price level. Alternative theories include the real bills doctrine and the more recent fiscal theory of the price level.

a. Quantity theory
c. Dishoarding

b. Real business cycle
d. Romer Model

65. _____ is the a method of technical and economic research of the systems for purpose to optimize a parity between system's consumer functions or properties and expenses to achieve those functions or properties.

This methodology for continuous perfection of production, industrial technologies, organizational structures was developed by Juryj Sobolev in 1948 at the 'Perm telephone factory'

- 1948 Juryj Sobolev - the first success in application of a method analysis at the 'Perm telephone factory'.
- 1949 - the first application for the invention as result of use of the new method.

Today in economically developed countries practically each enterprise or the company use methodology of the kind of functional-cost analysis as a practice of the quality management, most full satisfying to principles of standards of series ISO 9000.

- Interest of consumer not in products itself, but the advantage which it will receive from its usage.
- The consumer aspires to reduce his expenses
- Functions needed by consumer can be executed in the various ways, and, hence, with various efficiency and expenses. Among possible alternatives of realization of functions exist such in which the parity of quality and the price is the optimal for the consumer.

The goal of _____ is achievement of the highest consumer satisfaction of production at simultaneous decrease in all kinds of industrial expenses Classical _____ has three English synonyms - Value Engineering, Value Management, Value Analysis.

a. Staple financing
c. Willingness to pay

b. Monopoly wage
d. Function cost analysis

66. In economics, _____ is the total amount of money available in an economy at a particular point in time. There are several ways to define 'money', but standard measures usually include currency in circulation and demand deposits.

_____ data are recorded and published, usually by the government or the central bank of the country.

a. Velocity of money
c. Veil of money

b. Neutrality of money
d. Money supply

Chapter 13. Exchange Rates and the International Financial System

67. The _____ was the outcome of the failure of negotiating governments to create the International Trade Organization (ITO.) GATT was formed in 1947 and lasted until 1994, when it was replaced by the World Trade Organization. The Bretton Woods Conference had introduced the idea for an organization to regulate trade as part of a larger plan for economic recovery after World War II.
  a. General Agreement on Trade in Services
  b. Dutch-Scandinavian Economic Pact
  c. General Agreement on Tariffs and Trade
  d. GATT

68. The _____ is an international organization that oversees the global financial system by following the macroeconomic policies of its member countries, in particular those with an impact on exchange rates and the balance of payments. It is an organization formed to stabilize international exchange rates and facilitate development. It also offers financial and technical assistance to its members, making it an international lender of last resort.
  a. Office of Thrift Supervision
  b. ACCRA Cost of Living Index
  c. ACEA agreement
  d. International Monetary Fund

69. A _____ is a duty imposed on goods when they are moved across a political boundary. They are usually associated with protectionism, the economic policy of restraining trade between nations. For political reasons, _____s are usually imposed on imported goods, although they may also be imposed on exported goods.
  a. 100-year flood
  b. 1921 recession
  c. 130-30 fund
  d. Tariff

70. The _____ is an international financial institution that provides financial and technical assistance to developing countries for development programs (e.g. bridges, roads, schools, etc.) with the stated goal of reducing poverty.

The _____ differs from the _____ Group, in that the _____ comprises only two institutions:

- International Bank for Reconstruction and Development (IBRD)
- International Development Association (IDA)

Whereas the latter incorporates these two in addition to three more:

- International Finance Corporation (IFC)
- Multilateral Investment Guarantee Agency (MIGA)
- International Centre for Settlement of Investment Disputes (ICSID)

John Maynard Keynes (right) represented the UK at the conference, and Harry Dexter White represented the US.

The _____ is one of two major financial institutions created as a result of the Bretton Woods Conference in 1944. The International Monetary Fund, a related but separate institution, is the second.

  a. Flow to Equity-Approach
  b. Bank-State-Branch
  c. Financial costs of the 2003 Iraq War
  d. World Bank

71. The _____ is an important selective, mainly private, international organization designed by its founders to supervise and liberalize international trade. The organization officially commenced on 1 January 1995, under the Marrakesh Agreement, succeeding the 1947 General Agreement on Tariffs and Trade (GATT.)

The _____ deals with regulation of trade between participating countries; it provides a framework for negotiating and formalising trade agreements, and a dispute resolution process aimed at enforcing participants' adherence to _____ agreements which are signed by representatives of member governments and ratified by their parliaments.

a. Bio-energy village
b. 2009 G-20 London summit protests
c. World Trade Organization
d. Backus-Kehoe-Kydland consumption correlation puzzle

72. In economics, the concept of the _____ refers to the decision-making time frame of a firm in which at least one factor of production is fixed. Costs which are fixed in the _____ have no impact on a firms decisions. For example a firm can raise output by increasing the amount of labour through overtime.

a. Product Pipeline
b. Productivity model
c. Short-run
d. Hicks-neutral technical change

73. The _____ of monetary management established the rules for commercial and financial relations among the world's major industrial states in the mid 20th Century. The _____ was the first example of a fully negotiated monetary order intended to govern monetary relations among independent nation-states.

Preparing to rebuild the international economic system as World War II was still raging, 730 delegates from all 44 Allied nations gathered at the Mount Washington Hotel in Bretton Woods, New Hampshire, United States, for the United Nations Monetary and Financial Conference.

a. Bretton Woods system
b. 130-30 fund
c. 1921 recession
d. 100-year flood

74. _____ is sometimes referred to as _____, actually it means Economic Monetary Union.

First ideas of an economic and monetary union in Europe were raised well before establishing the European Communities. For example, already in the League of Nations, Gustav Stresemann asked in 1929 for a European currency (Link) against the background of an increased economic division due to a number of new nation states in Europe after WWI.

a. European Monetary Union
b. Euro Interbank Offered Rate
c. Exchange rate mechanism
d. European Monetary System

75. _____, 1st Baron Keynes was a renowned economist from Britain whose many ideas on economic and political theories as well as on many governments' monetary policies influenced America. He advocated a government that played an active role in the lives of people regarding business, economy, etc. In this role, the government would use fiscal measures to reduce the consequences of recessions, economic depressions and booms.

a. Adolf Hitler
b. Adam Smith
c. Adolph Fischer
d. John Maynard Keynes

76. An economic and _____ is a single market with a common currency. It is to be distinguished from a mere currency union, which does not involve a single market. This is the fifth stage of economic integration.

Chapter 13. Exchange Rates and the International Financial System

a. Free trade zone
c. Customs union
b. Commercial invoice
d. Monetary Union

77. A _____ is the massive selling of a country's currency assets by both domestic and foreign investors. Countries that utilize a fixed exchange rate are more susceptible to a _____ than countries utilizing a floating exchange rate. This is because of the large amount of reserves necessary to hold the fixed exchange rate in place at that fixed level.
   a. Currency crisis
   c. 130-30 fund
   b. 100-year flood
   d. Speculative attack

78. A _____ or a flexible exchange rate is a type of exchange rate regime wherein a currency's value is allowed to fluctuate according to the foreign exchange market. A currency that uses a _____ is known as a floating currency. The opposite of a _____ is a fixed exchange rate.
   a. Floating currency
   c. Foreign exchange market
   b. Trade Weighted US dollar Index
   d. Floating exchange rate

79. In economics, the term _____ of income or _____ refers to a simple economic model which describes the reciprocal circulation of income between producers and consumers. In the _____ model, the inter-dependent entities of producer and consumer are referred to as 'firms' and 'households' respectively and provide each other with factors in order to facilitate the flow of income. Firms provide consumers with goods and services in exchange for consumer expenditure and 'factors of production' from households.
   a. 100-year flood
   c. 130-30 fund
   b. 1921 recession
   d. Circular flow

Chapter 14. Open-Economy Macroeconomics

1. The term _____ refers to economy-wide fluctuations in production or economic activity over several months or years. These fluctuations occur around a long-term growth trend, and typically involve shifts over time between periods of relatively rapid economic growth (expansion or boom), and periods of relative stagnation or decline (contraction or recession.)

These fluctuations are often measured using the growth rate of real gross domestic product.

   a. Business cycle
   b. Nominal value
   c. Tobit model
   d. Consumer theory

2. In economics, an _____ is any good or commodity, transported from one country to another country in a legitimate fashion, typically for use in trade. _____ goods or services are provided to foreign consumers by domestic producers. _____ is an important part of international trade.
   a. ACCRA Cost of Living Index
   b. ACEA agreement
   c. AD-IA Model
   d. Export

3. In economics, an _____ is any good (e.g. a commodity) or service brought into one country from another country in a legitimate fashion, typically for use in trade. It is a good that is brought in from another country for sale. _____ goods or services are provided to domestic consumers by foreign producers. An _____ in the receiving country is an export to the sending country.
   a. Economic integration
   b. Import quota
   c. Incoterms
   d. Import

4. _____ is a term used to collectively describe topics relating to the operations of firms with interests in multiple countries. Such firms are sometimes called multinational corporations. Well known MNCs include fast food companies McDonald's and Yum Brands, vehicle manufacturers such as General Motors and Toyota, consumer electronics companies like Samsung, LG and Sony, and energy companies such as ExxonMobil and BP.
   a. AD-IA Model
   b. ACCRA Cost of Living Index
   c. ACEA agreement
   d. International business

5. An _____ is an economy in which people, including businesses, can trade in goods and services with other people and businesses in the international community at large. This contrasts with a closed economy in which international trade cannot take place.

The act of selling goods or services to a foreign country is called exporting.

   a. Information economy
   b. Attention work
   c. Indicative planning
   d. Open economy

6. _____ is a term used in economics to describe how an economic quantity is related to economic fluctuations. It is the opposite of procyclical. However, it has more than one meaning.
   a. Countercyclical
   b. Mathematical economics
   c. Price revolution
   d. Law of comparative advantage

7. In finance, _____ is investment originating from other countries. See Foreign direct investment.

a. Preclusive purchasing
b. Demand side economics
c. Horizontal merger
d. Foreign investment

8. _____ is a branch of economics that deals with the performance, structure, and behavior of a national or regional economy as a whole. Along with microeconomics, _____ is one of the two most general fields in economics. It is the study of the behavior and decision-making of entire economies.
   a. Nominal value
   b. Tobit model
   c. New Trade Theory
   d. Macroeconomics

9. A _____ is the transfer of wealth from one party (such as a person or company) to another. A _____ is usually made in exchange for the provision of goods, services or both, or to fulfill a legal obligation.

The simplest and oldest form of _____ is barter, the exchange of one good or service for another.

   a. Payment
   b. Social gravity
   c. Soft count
   d. Going concern

10. The _____ is a group of three respected economists who advise the President of the United States on economic policy. It is a part of the Executive Office of the President of the United States, and provides much of the economic policy of the White House. The council prepares the annual Economic Report of the President.
    a. Hybrid renewable energy systems
    b. Federal Reserve Bank Notes
    c. Council of Economic Advisers
    d. Constrained Pareto optimality

11. _____s is the social science that studies the production, distribution, and consumption of goods and services. The term _____s comes from the Ancient Greek οἰκονομία from οἶκος (oikos, 'house') + νόμος (nomos, 'custom' or 'law'), hence 'rules of the house(hold)'. Current _____ models developed out of the broader field of political economy in the late 19th century, owing to a desire to use an empirical approach more akin to the physical sciences.
    a. Energy economics
    b. Economic
    c. Inflation
    d. Opportunity cost

12. A _____ is an object whose consumption increases the utility of the consumer, for which the quantity demanded exceeds the quantity supplied at zero price. _____s are usually modeled as having diminishing marginal utility. The first individual purchase has high utility; the second has less.
    a. Pie method
    b. Composite good
    c. Good
    d. Merit good

13. In economics, economic output is divided into physical goods and intangible services. Consumption of _____ is assumed to produce utility. It is often used when referring to a _____ Tax.
    a. Manufactured goods
    b. Goods and services
    c. Private good
    d. Composite good

14. In microeconomics, _____ is quite simply the conversion of inputs into outputs. It is an economic process that uses resources to create a good or service that is suitable for exchange. This can include manufacturing, storing, shipping, and packaging.

Chapter 14. Open-Economy Macroeconomics

a. Solved
b. MET
c. Red Guards
d. Production

15. The balance of trade (or net exports, sometimes symbolized as NX) is the difference between the monetary value of exports and imports in an economy over a certain period of time. It is the relationship between a nation's imports and exports. A favorable balance of trade is known as a trade surplus and consists of exporting more than is imported; an unfavorable balance of trade is known as a _____ or, informally, a trade gap.

a. Complementary asset
b. Demographics of India
c. Computational economic
d. Trade deficit

16. In economics, the _____ measures the payments that flow between any individual country and all other countries. It is used to summarize all international economic transactions for that country during a specific time period, usually a year. The _____ is determined by the country's exports and imports of goods, services, and financial capital, as well as financial transfers.

a. Gross world product
b. Gross domestic product per barrel
c. Skyscraper Index
d. Balance of payments

17. Economics:

- _____, the desire to own something and the ability to pay for it
- _____ curve, a graphic representation of a _____ schedule
- _____ deposit, the money in checking accounts
- _____ pull theory, the theory that inflation occurs when _____ for goods and services exceeds existing supplies
- _____ schedule, a table that lists the quantity of a good a person will buy it each different price
- _____ side economics, the school of economics at believes government spending and tax cuts open economy by raising _____

a. Production
b. Variability
c. McKesson ' Robbins scandal
d. Demand

18. In algebra, a _____ is a function depending on n that associates a scalar, det(A), to an n×n square matrix A. The fundamental geometric meaning of a _____ is a scale factor for measure when A is regarded as a linear transformation. _____s are important both in calculus, where they enter the substitution rule for several variables, and in multilinear algebra.

For a fixed nonnegative integer n, there is a unique _____ function for the n×n matrices over any commutative ring R. In particular, this function exists when R is the field of real or complex numbers.

a. 1921 recession
b. 130-30 fund
c. 100-year flood
d. Determinant

19. _____ in economics refers to metrics and measures of output from production processes, per unit of input. Labor _____, for example, is typically measured as a ratio of output per labor-hour, an input. _____ may be conceived of as a metrics of the technical or engineering efficiency of production.

Chapter 14. Open-Economy Macroeconomics

a. Fordism
b. Productivity
c. Piece work
d. Production-possibility frontier

20. The _____ or gross domestic income (GDI), a basic measure of an economy's economic performance, is the market value of all final goods and services produced within the borders of a nation in a year. _____ can be defined in three ways, all of which are conceptually identical. First, it is equal to the total expenditures for all final goods and services produced within the country in a stipulated period of time (usually a 365-day year.)
   a. Countercyclical
   b. Monopolistic competition
   c. Market structure
   d. Gross domestic product

21. In economics, the concept of the _____ refers to the decision-making time frame of a firm in which at least one factor of production is fixed. Costs which are fixed in the _____ have no impact on a firms decisions. For example a firm can raise output by increasing the amount of labour through overtime.
   a. Productivity model
   b. Product Pipeline
   c. Hicks-neutral technical change
   d. Short-run

22. In economics, _____ is the total demand for final goods and services in the economy (Y) at a given time and price level. It is the amount of goods and services in the economy that will be purchased at all possible price levels. This is the demand for the gross domestic product of a country when inventory levels are static.
   a. Aggregate demand
   b. Aggregation problem
   c. Aggregate supply
   d. Aggregate expenditure

23. The _____ refers to the change in import expenditure that occurs with a change in disposable income (income after taxes and transfers.) For example, if a household earns one extra dollar of disposable income, and the _____ is 0.2, then of that dollar, the household will spend 20 cents of that dollar on imported goods and services.

Mathematically, the _____ (MPI) function is expressed as the derivative of the import (I) function with respect to disposable income (Y.)

   a. Minimum wage
   b. Complex multiplier
   c. Marginal propensity to import
   d. Hodrick-Prescott filter

24. The _____ refers to the increase in saving (non-purchase of current goods and services) that results from an increase in income. For example, if a household earns one extra dollar, and the _____ is 0.35, then of that dollar, the household will spend 65 cents and save 35 cents. It can also go the other way, referring to the decrease in saving that results from a decrease in income.
   a. Robertson lag
   b. Real business cycle
   c. Solow residual
   d. Marginal propensity to save

25. _____ is a common concept in economics, and gives rise to derived concepts such as consumer debt. Generally _____ is defined by opposition to production. But the precise definition can vary because different schools of economists define production quite differently.
   a. Federal Reserve Bank Notes
   b. Cash or share options
   c. Foreclosure data providers
   d. Consumption

Chapter 14. Open-Economy Macroeconomics

26. In economics, the _____ or marginal physical product is the extra output produced by one more unit of an input (for instance, the difference in output when a firm's labour is increased from five to six units.) Assuming that no other inputs to production change, the _____ of a given input (X) can be expressed as:

_____ = ΔY/ΔX = (the change of Y)/(the change of X.)

-
  -
    - Pending approval by Thomas Sowell***

In neoclassical economics, this is the mathematical derivative of the production function.... Note that the 'product' (Y) is typically defined ignoring external costs and benefits.

a. Factor prices
c. Productive capacity
b. Labor problem
d. Marginal product

27. In economics, the _____ also known as MPL or MPN is the change in output from hiring one additional unit of labor. It is the increase in output added by the last unit of labor. Assuming that no other inputs to production change, the marginal product of a given input (X) can be expressed as:

MP = ΔY/ΔX = (the change of Y)/(the change of X.)

a. Product Pipeline
c. Marginal product
b. Production function
d. Marginal product of labor

28. In economics, the _____ is an empirical metric that quantifies induced consumption, the concept that the increase in personal consumer spending (consumption) that occurs with an increase in disposable income (income after taxes and transfers.) For example, if a household earns one extra dollar of disposable income, and the _____ is 0.65, then of that dollar, the household will spend 65 cents and save 35 cents.

Mathematically, the _____ (MPC) function is expressed as the derivative of the consumption (C) function with respect to disposable income (Y.)

a. Supply shock
c. Marginal propensity to consume
b. Marginal propensity to import
d. Technology shock

29. _____ is a misspelled phrase from Latin 'pro capite' phrase meaning per head with pro meaning 'per' or 'for each' and capite meaning 'head.' Both words together equate to the phrase 'for each head.'

It is usually used in the field of statistics to indicate the average per person for any given concern, such as income, crime rate, etc.

It is also used in wills to indicate that each of the named beneficiaries should receive, by devise or bequest, equal shares of the estate. This is in contrast to a per stirpes division, in which each branch of the inheriting family inherits an equal share of the estate.

Chapter 14. Open-Economy Macroeconomics

a. Population statistics
b. Sargan test
c. False positive rate
d. Per capita

30. An _____, in economics, is the amount by which the real Gross domestic product exceeds potential GDP. The real GDP is also known as GDP 'adjusted for inflation', 'constant prices' GDP or 'constant dollar' GDP, because it measures the aggregate output in a country's income accounts in a given year, expressed in base-year prices. On the other hand, the potential GDP is the quantity of real GDP when a country's economy is at full-employment.
a. Inflationary gap
b. AD-IA Model
c. ACCRA Cost of Living Index
d. ACEA agreement

31. _____ is sometimes referred to as _____, actually it means Economic Monetary Union.

First ideas of an economic and monetary union in Europe were raised well before establishing the European Communities. For example, already in the League of Nations, Gustav Stresemann asked in 1929 for a European currency (Link) against the background of an increased economic division due to a number of new nation states in Europe after WWI.

a. Euro Interbank Offered Rate
b. Exchange rate mechanism
c. European Monetary System
d. European Monetary Union

32. A _____, sometimes called a pegged exchange rate, is a type of exchange rate regime wherein a currency's value is matched to the value of another single currency or to a basket of other currencies such as gold.

A _____ is usually used to stabilize the value of a currency, vis-a-vis the currency it is pegged to. This facilitates trade and investments between the two countries, and is especially useful for small economies where external trade forms a large part of their GDP.

a. Law of supply
b. Monetary economics
c. Leading indicators
d. Fixed exchange rate

33. _____ is a fee paid on borrowed assets. It is the price paid for the use of borrowed money, or, money earned by deposited funds. Assets that are sometimes lent with _____ include money, shares, consumer goods through hire purchase, major assets such as aircraft, and even entire factories in finance lease arrangements.
a. Interest
b. Insolvency
c. Internal debt
d. Asset protection

34. An _____ is the price a borrower pays for the use of money they do not own, for instance a small company might borrow from a bank to kick start their business, and the return a lender receives for deferring the use of funds, by lending it to the borrower. _____s are normally expressed as a percentage rate over the period of one year.

_____s targets are also a vital tool of monetary policy and are used to control variables like investment, inflation, and unemployment.

a. Interest rate
b. ACCRA Cost of Living Index
c. Enterprise value
d. Arrow-Debreu model

Chapter 14. Open-Economy Macroeconomics

35. An economic and _____ is a single market with a common currency. It is to be distinguished from a mere currency union, which does not involve a single market. This is the fifth stage of economic integration.
   a. Customs union
   b. Commercial invoice
   c. Free trade zone
   d. Monetary Union

36. In finance, the _____s between two currencies specifies how much one currency is worth in terms of the other. It is the value of a foreign natione;s currency in terms of the home natione;s currency. For example an _____ of 102 Japanese yen to the United States dollar means that JPY 102 is worth the same as USD 1.
   a. ACEA agreement
   b. ACCRA Cost of Living Index
   c. Interbank market
   d. Exchange rate

37. _____ is exchange of capital, goods, and services across international borders or territories. In most countries, it represents a significant share of gross domestic product (GDP.) While _____ has been present throughout much of history, its economic, social, and political importance has been on the rise in recent centuries.
   a. Intra-industry trade
   b. Import license
   c. International trade
   d. Incoterms

38. The _____ of monetary management established the rules for commercial and financial relations among the world's major industrial states in the mid 20th Century. The _____ was the first example of a fully negotiated monetary order intended to govern monetary relations among independent nation-states.

Preparing to rebuild the international economic system as World War II was still raging, 730 delegates from all 44 Allied nations gathered at the Mount Washington Hotel in Bretton Woods, New Hampshire, United States, for the United Nations Monetary and Financial Conference.

   a. 1921 recession
   b. Bretton Woods system
   c. 100-year flood
   d. 130-30 fund

39. _____ is money accepted for exchange of goods in an economy. The prevalence of one money over another arises, usually, when a government designates through decrees that the government shall accept only particular notes and coins in payment for taxes. Typically, money of _____ consists of stamped coins and minted paper bills.
   a. Totnes pound
   b. Currency
   c. Security thread
   d. Local currency

40. _____ is the a method of technical and economic research of the systems for purpose to optimize a parity between system's consumer functions or properties and expenses to achieve those functions or properties.

This methodology for continuous perfection of production, industrial technologies, organizational structures was developed by Juryj Sobolev in 1948 at the 'Perm telephone factory'

- 1948 Juryj Sobolev - the first success in application of a method analysis at the 'Perm telephone factory'.
- 1949 - the first application for the invention as result of use of the new method.

Chapter 14. Open-Economy Macroeconomics

Today in economically developed countries practically each enterprise or the company use methodology of the kind of functional-cost analysis as a practice of the quality management, most full satisfying to principles of standards of series ISO 9000.

- Interest of consumer not in products itself, but the advantage which it will receive from its usage.
- The consumer aspires to reduce his expenses
- Functions needed by consumer can be executed in the various ways, and, hence, with various efficiency and expenses. Among possible alternatives of realization of functions exist such in which the parity of quality and the price is the optimal for the consumer.

The goal of _____ is achievement of the highest consumer satisfaction of production at simultaneous decrease in all kinds of industrial expenses Classical _____ has three English synonyms - Value Engineering, Value Management, Value Analysis.

a. Monopoly wage
c. Willingness to pay
b. Staple financing
d. Function cost analysis

41. _____ is the increase in the amount of the goods and services produced by an economy over time. It is conventionally measured as the percent rate of increase in real gross domestic product, or real GDP. Growth is usually calculated in real terms, i.e. inflation-adjusted terms, in order to net out the effect of inflation on the price of the goods and services produced.

a. ACEA agreement
c. ACCRA Cost of Living Index
b. AD-IA Model
d. Economic growth

42. An autarky is an economy that is self-sufficient and does not take part in international trade, or severely limits trade with the outside world. Likewise the term refers to an ecosystem not affected by influences from the outside, which relies entirely on its own resources. In the economic meaning, it is also referred to as a _____.

a. Network Economy
c. Transition economy
b. Digital economy
d. Closed economy

43. In macroeconomics, _____ is a condition of the national economy, where all or nearly all persons willing and able to work at the prevailing wages and working conditions are able to do so. It is defined either as 0% unemployment, literally, no unemployment (the rate of unemployment is the fraction of the work force unable to find work), as by James Tobin, or as the level of employment rates when there is no cyclical unemployment. It is defined by the majority of mainstream economists as being an acceptable level of natural unemployment above 0%, the discrepancy from 0% being due to non-cyclical types of unemployment.

a. Marginal propensity to consume
c. Demand shock
b. Full employment
d. Harrod-Johnson diagram

44. A _____ occurs when an entity spends more money than it takes in. The opposite of a _____ is a budget surplus. Debt is essentially an accumulated flow of deficits.

a. Funding body
c. Public Financial Management
b. Lump-sum tax
d. Budget deficit

Chapter 14. Open-Economy Macroeconomics

45. _____, or a _____ is the concept of a resulting effect (cf. cause and effect, arising from another action. In general terms, it is used to indicate that all human actions, particularly crime and sin, have profound effects.
   a. Solved
   b. Rule
   c. Variability
   d. Consequence

46. In finance, the _____ is the system that allows the transfer of money between savers and borrowers.

Put another way: the _____ is a set of complex and closely interconnected financial institutions, markets, instruments, services, practices, and transactions.

   a. Foreign investment
   b. Financial system
   c. Lean consumption
   d. Hedonimetry

47. _____, in economics, occurs when assets and/or money rapidly flow out of a country, due to an economic event that disturbs investors and causes them to lower their valuation of the assets in that country, or otherwise to lose confidence in its economic strength. This leads to a disappearance of wealth and is usually accompanied by a sharp drop in the exchange rate of the affected country (depreciation in a variable exchange rate regime, or a forced devaluation in a fixed exchange rate regime.)

This fall is particularly damaging when the capital belongs to the people of the affected country, because not only are the citizens now burdened by the loss of faith in the economy and devaluation of their currency, but probably also their assets have lost much of their nominal value.

   a. Liquid capital
   b. Firm-specific infrastructure
   c. Capital formation
   d. Capital flight

48. _____ is the act of leaving one's native country or region to settle in another. It is the same as immigration but from the perspective of the country of origin. Human movement before the establishment of political boundaries or within one state, is termed migration.
   a. Emigration
   b. ACCRA Cost of Living Index
   c. AD-IA Model
   d. ACEA agreement

49. _____ according to Onuoha (2007) is the practice of starting new organizations or revitalizing mature organizations, particularly new businesses generally in response to identified opportunities. _____ is often a difficult undertaking, as a vast majority of new businesses fail. Entrepreneurial activities are substantially different depending on the type of organization that is being started.
   a. ACEA agreement
   b. ACCRA Cost of Living Index
   c. Intrapreneurship
   d. Entrepreneurship

50. _____ to the arrival of new individuals into a habitat or population. It is a biological concept and is important in population ecology, differentiated from emigration and migration.

_____ is a modern phenomenon.

Chapter 14. Open-Economy Macroeconomics

a. AD-IA Model
b. Immigration
c. ACCRA Cost of Living Index
d. ACEA agreement

51. _____ are legal property rights over creations of the mind, both artistic and commercial, and the corresponding fields of law. Under _____ law, owners are granted certain exclusive rights to a variety of intangible assets, such as musical, literary, and artistic works; ideas, discoveries and inventions; and words, phrases, symbols, and designs. Common types of _____ include copyrights, trademarks, patents, industrial design rights and trade secrets.
   a. Ease of Doing Business Index
   b. Intellectual property
   c. Expedited Funds Availability Act
   d. Independent contractor

52. An _____ is a financial institution that raises capital, trades in securities and manages corporate mergers and acquisitions. _____s profit from companies and governments by raising money through issuing and selling securities in the capital markets (both equity, bond) and insuring bonds (selling credit default swaps), as well as providing advice on transactions such as mergers and acquisitions. To perform these services in the United States, an adviser must be a licensed broker-dealer, and is subject to SEC (FINRA) regulation see SEC.
   a. Interbanca
   b. Anonymous internet banking
   c. Annual percentage rate
   d. Investment bank

53. In economics, the people in the _____ are the suppliers of labor. The _____ is all the nonmilitary people who are employed or unemployed. In 2005, the worldwide _____ was over 3 billion people.
   a. Departmentalization
   b. Grenelle agreements
   c. Distributed workforce
   d. Labor force

54. A _____ is the exclusive authority to determine how a resource is used, whether that resource is owned by government or by individuals. All economic goods have a _____s attribute. This attribute has three broad components

   1. The right to use the good
   2. The right to earn income from the good
   3. The right to transfer the good to others

   The concept of _____s as used by economists and legal scholars are related but distinct. The distinction is largely seen in the economists' focus on the ability of an individual or collective to control the use of the good.

   a. Post-sale restraint
   b. High-reeve
   c. Holder in due course
   d. Property right

55. In economics, a _____ is a function that specifies the output of a firm, an industry, or an entire economy for all combinations of inputs. A meta-_____ compares the practice of the existing entities converting inputs X into output y to determine the most efficient practice _____ of the existing entities, whether the most efficient feasible practice production or the most efficient actual practice production. In either case, the maximum output of a technologically-determined production process is a mathematical function of input factors of production.
   a. Post-Fordism
   b. Constant elasticity of substitution
   c. Short-run
   d. Production function

56. A _____ is the minimum difference a person requires to be willing to take an uncertain bet, between the expected value of the bet and the certain value that he is indifferent to.

The certainty equivalent is the guaranteed payoff at which a person is 'indifferent' between accepting the guaranteed payoff and a higher but uncertain payoff. (It is the amount of the higher payout minus the _____.)

a. Workers compensation
b. Ruin theory
c. Risk premium
d. Linear model

57. _____ is a comparative concept of the ability and performance of a firm, sub-sector or country to sell and supply goods and/or services in a given market. Although widely used in economics and business management, the usefulness of the concept, particularly in the context of national _____, is vigorously disputed by economists, such as Paul Krugman.

The term may also be applied to markets, where it is used to refer to the extent to which the market structure may be regarded as perfectly competitive.

a. Debt moratorium
b. Competitiveness
c. Countervailing duties
d. Quota share

58. _____ is an economic concept with commonplace familiarity. It is the price that a good or service is offered at, or will fetch, in the marketplace. It is of interest mainly in the study of microeconomics.

a. Market anomaly
b. Noisy market hypothesis
c. Paper trading
d. Market price

59. _____ is the income of individuals or nations after adjusting for inflation. It is calculated by subtracting inflation from the nominal income. Real variables, such as _____, real GDP, and real interest rate are variables that are measured in physical units, while nominal variables such as nominal income, nominal GDP, and nominal interest rate are measured in monetary units.

a. Windfall gain
b. Real income
c. Family income
d. Net national income

60. The balance of trade (or net exports, sometimes symbolized as NX) is the difference between the monetary value of exports and imports in an economy over a certain period of time. It is the relationship between a nation's imports and exports. A favorable balance of trade is known as a _____ and consists of exporting more than is imported; an unfavorable balance of trade is known as a trade deficit or, informally, a trade gap.

a. Black-Scholes
b. Business valuation standards
c. Dividend unit
d. Trade surplus

61. _____ in economics and business is the result of an exchange and from that trade we assign a numerical monetary value to a good, service or asset. If Alice trades Bob 4 apples for an orange, the _____ of an orange is 4 apples. Inversely, the _____ of an apple is 1/4 oranges.

a. Price war
b. Premium pricing
c. Price book
d. Price

62. The term '_____' refers to the concept of collecting information and attempting to spot a pattern in the information. In some fields of study, the term '_____' has more formally-defined meanings.

In project management _____ is a mathematical technique that uses historical results to predict future outcome.

a. Quantile regression
c. Coefficient of determination
b. Probit model
d. Trend analysis

63. _____ was an arrangement established in 1979 under the Jenkins European Commission where most nations of the European Economic Community (EEC) linked their currencies to prevent large fluctuations relative to one another.

After the collapse of the Bretton Woods system in 1971, most of the EEC countries agreed in 1972 to maintain stable exchange rates by preventing exchange fluctuations of more than 2.25% (the European 'currency snake'.) In March 1979, this system was replaced by the _____, and the European Currency Unit (ECU) was defined.

a. European Monetary Union
c. Exchange rate mechanism
b. Euro Interbank Offered Rate
d. European Monetary System

64. The _____ is an economic and political union of 27 member states, located primarily in Europe. It was established by the Treaty of Maastricht on 1 November 1993, upon the foundations of the pre-existing European Economic Community. With a population of almost 500 million, the _____ generates an estimated 30% share (US$18.4 trillion in 2008) of the nominal gross world product.
a. European Union
c. ACEA agreement
b. ACCRA Cost of Living Index
d. European Court of Justice

65. A _____ secures the proper functioning of money by regulating economic agents, transaction types, and money supply.

_____s are traditionally formed by the policy decisions of individual governments and administrated as a domestic economic issue.

The current trend, however, is to use international trade and investment to alter the policy and legislation of individual governments.

a. Consumer basket
c. Financial rand
b. Netting
d. Monetary System

66. A _____ is the massive selling of a country's currency assets by both domestic and foreign investors. Countries that utilize a fixed exchange rate are more susceptible to a _____ than countries utilizing a floating exchange rate. This is because of the large amount of reserves necessary to hold the fixed exchange rate in place at that fixed level.
a. 100-year flood
c. 130-30 fund
b. Currency crisis
d. Speculative attack

Chapter 14. Open-Economy Macroeconomics

67. A _____, reserve bank, or monetary authority is the entity responsible for the monetary policy of a country or of a group of member states. It is a bank that can lend money to other banks in times of need. Its primary responsibility is to maintain the stability of the national currency and money supply, but more active duties include controlling subsidized-loan interest rates, and acting as a lender of last resort to the banking sector during times of financial crisis (private banks often being integral to the national financial system.)

   a. Central bank
   b. 1921 recession
   c. 100-year flood
   d. 130-30 fund

68. _____ has several particular meanings:

   - in mathematics
     - _____ function
     - Euler _____
     - _____
     - _____ subgroup
     - method of _____s (partial differential equations)
   - in physics and engineering
     - any _____ curve that shows the relationship between certain input- and output parameters, e.g.
     - an I-V or current-voltage _____ is the current in a circuit as a function of the applied voltage
     - Receiver-Operator _____
   - in fiction
     - in Dungeons ' Dragons, _____ is another name for ability score

   a. Russian financial crisis
   b. Technocracy
   c. Demand
   d. Characteristic

69. _____ is a term used to describe how different aspects between economies are integrated. The basics of this theory were written by the Hungarian Economist Béla Balassa in the 1960s. As _____ increases, the barriers of trade between markets diminishes.

   a. Import license
   b. Import
   c. Inward investment
   d. Economic integration

70. The _____ is the official currency of 16 of the 27 member states of the European Union (EU.) The states, known collectively as the Eurozone, are Austria, Belgium, Cyprus, Finland, France, Germany, Greece, Ireland, Italy, Luxembourg, Malta, the Netherlands, Portugal, Slovakia, Slovenia, and Spain. The currency is also used in a further five European countries, with and without formal agreements and is consequently used daily by some 327 million Europeans.

   a. IRS Code 3401
   b. Equity capital market
   c. Import and Export Price Indices
   d. Euro

71. _____ is a term that refers both to:

   - a formal discipline used to help appraise, or assess, the case for a project or proposal, which itself is a process known as project appraisal; and
   - an informal approach to making decisions of any kind.

Chapter 14. Open-Economy Macroeconomics

Under both definitions the process involves, whether explicitly or implicitly, weighing the total expected costs against the total expected benefits of one or more actions in order to choose the best or most profitable option. The formal process is often referred to as either CBA (_____) or BCost-benefit analysis

A hallmark of CBA is that all benefits and all costs are expressed in money terms, and are adjusted for the time value of money, so that all flows of benefits and flows of project costs over time (which tend to occur at different points in time) are expressed on a common basis in terms of their e;present value.e; Closely related, but slightly different, formal techniques include Cost-effectiveness analysis, Economic impact analysis, Fiscal impact analysis and Social Return on Investment(SROI) analysis. The latter builds upon the logic of _____, but differs in that it is explicitly designed to inform the practical decision-making of enterprise managers and investors focused on optimising their social and environmental impacts.

a. Cost-benefit analysis
b. Decision theory
c. 100-year flood
d. 130-30 fund

72. The _____ is one of the world's most important central banks, responsible for monetary policy covering the 16 member States of the Eurozone. It was established by the European Union (EU) in 1998 with its headquarters in Frankfurt, Germany.

The predecessor to the _____ was the European Monetary Institute .

a. ACCRA Cost of Living Index
b. ACEA agreement
c. AD-IA Model
d. European Central Bank

73. In economics, _____ is the transfer of income, wealth or property from some individuals to others.

One premise of _____ is that money should be distributed to benefit the poorer members of society, and that the rich have an obligation to assist the poor, thus creating a more financially egalitarian society. Another argument is that the rich exploit the poor or otherwise gain unfair benefits.

a. 130-30 fund
b. 100-year flood
c. 1921 recession
d. Redistribution

74. A _____ is a theoretical term that economists use to describe a market which is free from government intervention (i.e. no regulation, no subsidization, no single monetary system and no governmental monopolies.) In a _____, property rights are voluntarily exchanged at a price arranged solely by the mutual consent of sellers and buyers. By definition, buyers and sellers do not coerce each other, in the sense that they obtain each other's property without the use of physical force, threat of physical force, or fraud, nor is the coerced by a third party (such as by government via transfer payments) and they engage in trade simply because they both consent and believe that it is a good enough choice.
a. Leninism
b. Delegation
c. Third camp
d. Free market

Chapter 15. Unemployment and the Foundations of Aggregate Supply

1. In economics, _____ is the total supply of goods and services produced by a national economy during a specific time period. It is the total amount of goods and services in the economy available at all possible price levels.
    a. Aggregation problem
    b. Aggregate demand
    c. Aggregate expenditure
    d. Aggregate supply

2. In economic models, the _____ time frame assumes no fixed factors of production. Firms can enter or leave the marketplace, and the cost (and availability) of land, labor, raw materials, and capital goods can be assumed to vary. In contrast, in the short-run time frame, certain factors are assumed to be fixed, because there is not sufficient time for them to change.
    a. Long-run
    b. Productivity world
    c. Price/performance ratio
    d. Diseconomies of scale

3. In economics, a _____ is a general slowdown in economic activity over a sustained period of time, or a business cycle contraction. During _____s, many macroeconomic indicators vary in a similar way. Production as measured by Gross Domestic Product (GDP), employment, investment spending, capacity utilization, household incomes and business profits all fall during _____s.
    a. Monetary economics
    b. Treasury View
    c. Leading indicators
    d. Recession

4. In economics, the concept of the _____ refers to the decision-making time frame of a firm in which at least one factor of production is fixed. Costs which are fixed in the _____ have no impact on a firms decisions. For example a firm can raise output by increasing the amount of labour through overtime.
    a. Short-run
    b. Hicks-neutral technical change
    c. Product Pipeline
    d. Productivity model

5. In economics, the _____ measures the payments that flow between any individual country and all other countries. It is used to summarize all international economic transactions for that country during a specific time period, usually a year. The _____ is determined by the country's exports and imports of goods, services, and financial capital, as well as financial transfers.
    a. Skyscraper Index
    b. Balance of payments
    c. Gross world product
    d. Gross domestic product per barrel

6. A _____ is the transfer of wealth from one party (such as a person or company) to another. A _____ is usually made in exchange for the provision of goods, services or both, or to fulfill a legal obligation.

    The simplest and oldest form of _____ is barter, the exchange of one good or service for another.

    a. Soft count
    b. Social gravity
    c. Going concern
    d. Payment

7. The _____ or gross domestic income (GDI), a basic measure of an economy's economic performance, is the market value of all final goods and services produced within the borders of a nation in a year. _____ can be defined in three ways, all of which are conceptually identical. First, it is equal to the total expenditures for all final goods and services produced within the country in a stipulated period of time (usually a 365-day year.)
    a. Gross domestic product
    b. Monopolistic competition
    c. Market structure
    d. Countercyclical

Chapter 15. Unemployment and the Foundations of Aggregate Supply

8. In economics, _____ refers to the highest level of real Gross Domestic Product output that can be sustained over the long term. The existence of a limit is due to natural and institutional constraints. If actual GDP rises and stays above _____, then (in the absence of wage and price controls) inflation tends to increase as demand exceeds supply.
   a. Monetary policy reaction function
   b. Potential output
   c. Monetary conditions index
   d. Fundamental psychological law

9. In algebra, a _____ is a function depending on n that associates a scalar, det(A), to an n×n square matrix A. The fundamental geometric meaning of a _____ is a scale factor for measure when A is regarded as a linear transformation. _____s are important both in calculus, where they enter the substitution rule for several variables, and in multilinear algebra.

   For a fixed nonnegative integer n, there is a unique _____ function for the n×n matrices over any commutative ring R. In particular, this function exists when R is the field of real or complex numbers.

   a. 130-30 fund
   b. 100-year flood
   c. Determinant
   d. 1921 recession

10. In economics, _____ is a rise in the general level of prices of goods and services in an economy over a period of time. When the general price level rises, each unit of currency buys fewer goods and services; consequently, _____ is also a decline in the real value of money--a loss of purchasing power in the medium of exchange which is also the monetary unit of account in the economy. A chief measure of general price-level _____ is the general _____ rate, which is the percentage change in a general price index (normally the Consumer Price Index) over time.
    a. Inflation
    b. Opportunity cost
    c. Economic
    d. Energy economics

11. In economics, the _____ is a measure of inflation, the rate of increase of a price index (for example, a consumer price index.)It is the percentage rate of change in price level over time. The rate of decrease in the purchasing power of money is approximately equal.

    It's used to calculate the real interest rate, as well as real increases in wages, and official measurements of this rate act as input variables to COLA adjustments and Inflation derivatives prices.

    a. Inflation rate
    b. Interest rate option
    c. Equity value
    d. Edgeworth paradox

12. _____ is the term denoting either an entrance or changes which are inserted into a system and which activate/modify a process. It is an abstract concept, used in the modeling, system(s) design and system(s) exploitation. It is usually connected with other terms, e.g., _____ field, _____ variable, _____ parameter, _____ value, _____ signal, _____ device and _____ file.
    a. Input
    b. AD-IA Model
    c. ACCRA Cost of Living Index
    d. ACEA agreement

13. In microeconomics, _____ is quite simply the conversion of inputs into outputs. It is an economic process that uses resources to create a good or service that is suitable for exchange. This can include manufacturing, storing, shipping, and packaging.

Chapter 15. Unemployment and the Foundations of Aggregate Supply

a. Solved
b. MET
c. Red Guards
d. Production

14. In economics, _____ is the total demand for final goods and services in the economy (Y) at a given time and price level. It is the amount of goods and services in the economy that will be purchased at all possible price levels. This is the demand for the gross domestic product of a country when inventory levels are static.

a. Aggregate expenditure
b. Aggregation problem
c. Aggregate supply
d. Aggregate demand

15. _____ is widely regarded as the first modern school of economic thought. It is the idea that free markets can regulate themselves. Its major developers include Adam Smith, David Ricardo, Thomas Malthus and John Stuart Mill. Sometimes the definition of _____ is expanded to include William Petty, Johann Heinrich von Thünen.

a. Schools of economic thought
b. Marginalism
c. Tendency of the rate of profit to fall
d. Classical economics

16. _____ and Keynesian Theory) is a macroeconomic theory based on the ideas of 20th-century British economist John Maynard Keynes. _____ argues that private sector decisions sometimes lead to inefficient macroeconomic outcomes and therefore advocates active policy responses by the public sector, including monetary policy actions by the central bank and fiscal policy actions by the government to stabilize output over the business cycle.

The theories forming the basis of _____ were first presented in The General Theory of Employment, Interest and Money, published in 1936.

a. Market failure
b. Rational choice theory
c. Keynesian economics
d. Deflation

17. Economics:

- _____, the desire to own something and the ability to pay for it
- _____ curve, a graphic representation of a _____ schedule
- _____ deposit, the money in checking accounts
- _____ pull theory, the theory that inflation occurs when _____ for goods and services exceeds existing supplies
- _____ schedule, a table that lists the quantity of a good a person will buy it each different price
- _____ side economics, the school of economics at believes government spending and tax cuts open economy by raising _____

a. Production
b. Variability
c. McKesson ' Robbins scandal
d. Demand

18. _____s is the social science that studies the production, distribution, and consumption of goods and services. The term _____s comes from the Ancient Greek οἰκονομία from οἶκος (oikos, 'house') + νόμος (nomos, 'custom' or 'law'), hence 'rules of the house(hold)'. Current _____ models developed out of the broader field of political economy in the late 19th century, owing to a desire to use an empirical approach more akin to the physical sciences.

Chapter 15. Unemployment and the Foundations of Aggregate Supply

a. Inflation
c. Energy economics
b. Economic
d. Opportunity cost

19. The _____ was a worldwide economic downturn starting in most places in 1929 and ending at different times in the 1930s or early 1940s for different countries. It was the largest and most important economic depression in the 20th century, and is used in the 21st century as an example of how far the world's economy can fall. The _____ originated in the United States; historians most often use as a starting date the stock market crash on October 29, 1929, known as Black Tuesday.
   a. Great Depression
   c. British Empire Economic Conference
   b. Wall Street Crash of 1929
   d. Jarrow March

20. Though there have been several definitions of voluntary and _____ in the economics literature, a simple distinction is often applied. Voluntary unemployment is attributed to the individual's decisions, whereas _____ exists because of the socio-economic environment (including the market structure, government intervention, and the level of aggregate demand) in which individuals operate. In these terms, much or most of frictional unemployment is voluntary, since it reflects individual search behavior.
   a. AD-IA Model
   c. ACEA agreement
   b. Involuntary unemployment
   d. ACCRA Cost of Living Index

21. A trade union or _____ is an organization of workers who have banded together to achieve common goals in key areas and working conditions. The trade union, through its leadership, bargains with the employer on behalf of union members (rank and file members) and negotiates labor contracts (Collective bargaining) with employers. This may include the negotiation of wages, work rules, complaint procedures, rules governing hiring, firing and promotion of workers, benefits, workplace safety and policies.
   a. Labor union
   c. Basis of futures
   b. Business valuation standards
   d. Demand-side technologies

22. In economics, the _____ is a historical inverse relation between the rate of unemployment and the rate of inflation in an economy. Stated simply, the lower the unemployment in an economy, the higher the rate of increase in nominal wages in the economy. Rate of Change of Wages against Unemployment, United Kingdom 1913-1948 from Phillips (1958)

William Phillips, a New Zealand born economist, wrote a paper in 1958 titled The Relationship between Unemployment and the Rate of Change of Money Wages in the United Kingdom 1861-1957, which was published in the quarterly journal Economica.

   a. Demand curve
   c. Cost curve
   b. Lorenz curve
   d. Phillips curve

23. _____ in economics and business is the result of an exchange and from that trade we assign a numerical monetary value to a good, service or asset. If Alice trades Bob 4 apples for an orange, the _____ of an orange is 4 apples. Inversely, the _____ of an apple is 1/4 oranges.
   a. Price war
   c. Price book
   b. Premium pricing
   d. Price

Chapter 15. Unemployment and the Foundations of Aggregate Supply

24. Unemployment occurs when a person is available to work and seeking work but currently without work. The prevalence of unemployment is usually measured using the _____, which is defined as the percentage of those in the labor force who are unemployed. The _____ is also used in economic studies and economic indexes such as the United States' Conference Board's Index of Leading Indicators as a measure of the state of the macroeconomics.
   a. ACCRA Cost of Living Index
   b. ACEA agreement
   c. AD-IA Model
   d. Unemployment rate

25. A _____ or labor union is an organization of workers who have banded together to achieve common goals in key areas and working conditions. The _____, through its leadership, bargains with the employer on behalf of union members (rank and file members) and negotiates labor contracts (Collective bargaining) with employers. This may include the negotiation of wages, work rules, complaint procedures, rules governing hiring, firing and promotion of workers, benefits, workplace safety and policies.
   a. Case-Shiller Home Price Indices
   b. Guaranteed investment contracts
   c. Trade union
   d. Consumer goods

26. In economics, the people in the _____ are the suppliers of labor. The _____ is all the nonmilitary people who are employed or unemployed. In 2005, the worldwide _____ was over 3 billion people.
   a. Grenelle agreements
   b. Labor force
   c. Departmentalization
   d. Distributed workforce

27. A _____ is an economy based on the division of labor in which the prices of goods and services are determined in a free price system set by supply and demand. This is often contrasted with a planned economy, in which a central government determines the price of goods and services using a fixed price system. Market economies are contrasted with mixed economy where the price system is not entirely free but under some government control that is not extensive enough to constitute a planned economy.
   a. Commons-based peer production
   b. Network Economy
   c. Nutritional Economics
   d. Market economy

28. _____ is a concept with somewhat disparate meanings in several fields. It also has a common meaning which has a loose connection with some of those more definite meanings.

Casually, it is typically used to denote a lack of order, or purpose, or cause.

   a. 100-year flood
   b. 1921 recession
   c. 130-30 fund
   d. Randomness

29. Economists distinguish between various types of unemployment, including cyclical unemployment, _____, structural unemployment and classical unemployment. Some additional types of unemployment that are occasionally mentioned are seasonal unemployment, hardcore unemployment, and hidden unemployment. Real-world unemployment may combine different types.
   a. Frictional unemployment
   b. Seasonal unemployment
   c. Structural unemployment
   d. Types of unemployment

Chapter 15. Unemployment and the Foundations of Aggregate Supply

30. _____ was an American economist, statistician and public intellectual, and a recipient of the Nobel Memorial Prize in Economic Sciences. He is best known among scholars for his theoretical and empirical research, especially consumption analysis, monetary history and theory, and for his demonstration of the complexity of stabilization policy. A global public followed his restatement of a political philosophy that insisted on minimizing the role of government in favor of the private sector.
   a. Adolph Fischer
   b. Adolf Hitler
   c. Adam Smith
   d. Milton Friedman

31. _____ is the view within monetary economics that variation in the money supply has major influences on national output in the short run and the price level over longer periods and that objectives of monetary policy are best met by targeting the growth rate of the money supply.

   _____ today is mainly associated with the work of Milton Friedman, who was among the generation of economists to accept Keynesian economics and then criticize it on his own terms. Friedman and Anna Schwartz wrote an influential book, Monetary History of the United States 1867-1960, and argued that 'inflation is always and everywhere a monetary phenomenon.' Friedman advocated a central bank policy aimed at keeping the supply and demand for money at equilibrium, as measured by growth in productivity and demand.

   a. Historical school of economics
   b. Complexity economics
   c. Marginal revenue productivity theory of wages
   d. Monetarism

32. Economists distinguish between various types of unemployment, including _____, frictional unemployment, structural unemployment and classical unemployment. Some additional types of unemployment that are occasionally mentioned are seasonal unemployment, hardcore unemployment, and hidden unemployment. Real-world unemployment may combine different types.
   a. Seasonal unemployment
   b. Structural unemployment
   c. Types of unemployment
   d. Cyclical unemployment

33. _____ is long-term and chronic unemployment arising from imbalances between the skills and other characteristics of workers in the market and the needs of employers. It involves a mismatch between workers looking for jobs and the vacancies available often despite the number of vacancies being similar to the number of unemployed people. In this case, the unemployed workers lack the specific skills required for the jobs, or are located in a different geographical region to the vacant jobs.
   a. Types of unemployment
   b. Frictional unemployment
   c. Seasonal unemployment
   d. Structural unemployment

34. _____ is a branch of economics that deals with the performance, structure, and behavior of a national or regional economy as a whole. Along with microeconomics, _____ is one of the two most general fields in economics. It is the study of the behavior and decision-making of entire economies.
   a. Tobit model
   b. Nominal value
   c. Macroeconomics
   d. New Trade Theory

35. _____, 1st Baron Keynes was a renowned economist from Britain whose many ideas on economic and political theories as well as on many governments' monetary policies influenced America. He advocated a government that played an active role in the lives of people regarding business, economy, etc. In this role, the government would use fiscal measures to reduce the consequences of recessions, economic depressions and booms.

a. Adam Smith
b. John Maynard Keynes
c. Adolph Fischer
d. Adolf Hitler

36. The _____ , established in 1848, is the world's oldest futures and options exchange. More than 50 different options and futures contracts are traded by over 3,600 _____ members through open outcry and eTrading. Volumes at the exchange in 2003 were a record breaking 454 million contracts.
   a. 130-30 fund
   b. 100-year flood
   c. New York Mercantile Exchange
   d. Chicago Board of Trade

37. A _____ is a group of people who share or are motivated by at least one common issue or interest, or work together on a specific project(s) to achieve a common objective. _____s are also characterised by attempts to share and exercise political and social power and to make decisions on a consensus-driven and egalitarian basis. _____s differ from cooperatives in that they are not necessarily focused upon an economic benefit or saving (but can be that as well.)
   a. 1921 recession
   b. 130-30 fund
   c. 100-year flood
   d. Collective

38. In organized labor, _____ is the method whereby workers organize together (usually in unions) to meet, converse, and negotiate upon the work conditions with their employers normally resulting in a written contract setting forth the wages, hours, and other conditions to be observed for a stipulated period.It is the practice in which union and company representatives meet to negotiate a new labor contract. In various national labor and employment law contexts, _____ takes on a more specific legal meaning and so, in a broad sense, however, it is the coming together of workers to negotiate their employment.

A collective agreement is a labor contract between an employer and one or more unions.

   a. Demarcation dispute
   b. Designated Suppliers Program
   c. Strikebreaker
   d. Collective bargaining

39. _____ data refers to selected population characteristics as used in government, marketing or opinion research, or the _____ profiles used in such research. Note the distinction from the term 'demography' Commonly-used _____s include race, age, income, disabilities, mobility (in terms of travel time to work or number of vehicles available), educational attainment, home ownership, employment status, and even location.
   a. Demographic warfare
   b. NEET
   c. Demographic
   d. Generation Z

40. In finance, the _____ of a financial asset measures the sensitivity of the asset's price to interest rate movements. There are various definitions of _____ and derived quantities, discussed below. If not otherwise specified, '_____' generally means the Macaulay _____, as defined below.
   a. 100-year flood
   b. Time value of money
   c. Newtonian time
   d. Duration

41. The term _____ refers to economy-wide fluctuations in production or economic activity over several months or years. These fluctuations occur around a long-term growth trend, and typically involve shifts over time between periods of relatively rapid economic growth (expansion or boom), and periods of relative stagnation or decline (contraction or recession.)

These fluctuations are often measured using the growth rate of real gross domestic product.

a. Nominal value
b. Business cycle
c. Tobit model
d. Consumer theory

42. The _____ is the central banking system of the United States. Created in 1913 by the enactment of the Federal Reserve Act (signed by Woodrow Wilson), it is a quasi-public and quasi-private (government entity with private components) banking system that comprises (1) the presidentially appointed Board of Governors of the _____ in Washington, D.C.; (2) the Federal Open Market Committee; (3) twelve regional Federal Reserve Banks located in major cities throughout the nation acting as fiscal agents for the U.S. Treasury, each with its own nine-member board of directors; (4) numerous other private U.S. member banks, which subscribe to required amounts of non-transferable stock in their regional Federal Reserve Banks; and (5) various advisory councils. Since February 2006, Ben Bernanke has served as the Chairman of the Board of Governors of the _____.

a. Federal Reserve System Open Market Account
b. Monetary Policy Report to the Congress
c. Term auction facility
d. Federal Reserve System

43. A _____ is the lowest hourly, daily or monthly wage that employers may legally pay to employees or workers. Equivalently, it is the lowest wage at which workers may sell their labor. Although _____ laws are in effect in a great many jurisdictions, there are differences of opinion about the benefits and drawbacks of a _____.

a. Marginal propensity to consume
b. Permanent war economy
c. Microfoundations
d. Minimum wage

44. _____ to the arrival of new individuals into a habitat or population. It is a biological concept and is important in population ecology, differentiated from emigration and migration.

_____ is a modern phenomenon.

a. ACCRA Cost of Living Index
b. ACEA agreement
c. AD-IA Model
d. Immigration

45. A _____, reserve bank, or monetary authority is the entity responsible for the monetary policy of a country or of a group of member states. It is a bank that can lend money to other banks in times of need. Its primary responsibility is to maintain the stability of the national currency and money supply, but more active duties include controlling subsidized-loan interest rates, and acting as a lender of last resort to the banking sector during times of financial crisis (private banks often being integral to the national financial system.)

a. 130-30 fund
b. 100-year flood
c. 1921 recession
d. Central Bank

46. In economics, _____ is the art or science of controlling economic demand to avoid a recession. In natural resources management and environmental policy more generally, it refers to policies to control consumer demand for environmentally sensitive or harmful goods such as water and energy. Within manufacturing firms the term is used to describe the activities of demand forecasting, planning and order fulfillment.

a. Peak-load pricing
b. Cobra effect
c. Fiscal imbalance
d. Demand management

Chapter 15. Unemployment and the Foundations of Aggregate Supply

47. The _____ is one of the world's most important central banks, responsible for monetary policy covering the 16 member States of the Eurozone. It was established by the European Union (EU) in 1998 with its headquarters in Frankfurt, Germany.

The predecessor to the _____ was the European Monetary Institute .

   a. ACCRA Cost of Living Index
   c. AD-IA Model
   b. ACEA agreement
   d. European Central Bank

48. The _____ is an economic and political union of 27 member states, located primarily in Europe. It was established by the Treaty of Maastricht on 1 November 1993, upon the foundations of the pre-existing European Economic Community. With a population of almost 500 million, the _____ generates an estimated 30% share (US$18.4 trillion in 2008) of the nominal gross world product.

   a. ACEA agreement
   c. European Court of Justice
   b. European Union
   d. ACCRA Cost of Living Index

49. There are two main interpretations of the idea of a _____:

   - A model in which the state assumes primary responsibility for the welfare of its citizens. This responsibility in theory ought to be comprehensive, because all aspects of welfare are considered and universally applied to citizens as a 'right'. _____ can also mean the creation of a 'social safety net' of minimum standards of varying forms of welfare. Here is found some confusion between a '_____' and a 'welfare society' in common debate about the definition of the term.
   - The provision of welfare in society. In many '_____s', especially in continental Europe, welfare is not actually provided by the state, but by a combination of independent, voluntary, mutualist and government services. The functional provider of benefits and services may be a central or state government, a state-sponsored company or agency, a private corporation, a charity or another form of non-profit organization. However, this phenomenon has been more appropriately termed a 'welfare society,' and the term 'welfare system' has been used to describe the range of _____ and welfare society mixes that are found.

The English term '_____' is believed by Asa Briggs to have been coined by Archbishop William Temple during the Second World War, contrasting wartime Britain with the 'warfare state' of Nazi Germany. Friedrich Hayek contends that the term derived from the older German word Wohlfahrtsstaat, which itself was used by nineteenth century historians to describe a variant of the ideal of Polizeistaat . It was fully developed by the German academic Sozialpolitiker--'socialists of the chair'--from 1870 and first implemented through Bismarck's 'state socialism'. Bismarck's policies have also been seen as the creation of a _____.

   a. 1921 recession
   c. 130-30 fund
   b. 100-year flood
   d. Welfare state

50. An economic and _____ is a single market with a common currency. It is to be distinguished from a mere currency union , which does not involve a single market. This is the fifth stage of economic integration.

   a. Commercial invoice
   c. Customs union
   b. Free trade zone
   d. Monetary union

Chapter 16. Ensuring Price Stability

1. _____ is a broad label that refers to any individuals or households that use goods and services generated within the economy. The concept of a _____ is used in different contexts, so that the usage and significance of the term may vary.

Typically when business people and economists talk of _____s they are talking about person as _____, an aggregated commodity item with little individuality other than that expressed in the buy/not-buy decision.

- a. Consumer
- b. 1921 recession
- c. 100-year flood
- d. 130-30 fund

2. A _____ is a measure of the average price of consumer goods and services purchased by households. A _____ measures a price change for a constant market basket of goods and services from one period to the next within the same area (city, region, or nation.) It is a price index determined by measuring the price of a standard group of goods meant to represent the typical market basket of a typical urban consumer.
- a. CPI
- b. Consumer price index
- c. Cost-of-living index
- d. Lipstick index

3. The _____ or gross domestic income (GDI), a basic measure of an economy's economic performance, is the market value of all final goods and services produced within the borders of a nation in a year. _____ can be defined in three ways, all of which are conceptually identical. First, it is equal to the total expenditures for all final goods and services produced within the country in a stipulated period of time (usually a 365-day year.)
- a. Countercyclical
- b. Gross domestic product
- c. Monopolistic competition
- d. Market structure

4. _____ in its literal sense is the process of transformation of local or regional phenomena into global ones. It can be described as a process by which the people of the world are unified into a single society and function together.

This process is a combination of economic, technological, sociocultural and political forces.

- a. Globalization
- b. Helsinki Process on Globalisation and Democracy
- c. Globally Integrated Enterprise
- d. Global Cosmopolitanism

5. In economics, the _____ is a historical inverse relation between the rate of unemployment and the rate of inflation in an economy. Stated simply, the lower the unemployment in an economy, the higher the rate of increase in nominal wages in the economy. Rate of Change of Wages against Unemployment, United Kingdom 1913-1948 from Phillips (1958)

William Phillips, a New Zealand born economist, wrote a paper in 1958 titled The Relationship between Unemployment and the Rate of Change of Money Wages in the United Kingdom 1861-1957, which was published in the quarterly journal Economica.

- a. Demand curve
- b. Cost curve
- c. Phillips curve
- d. Lorenz curve

6. In microeconomics, _____ is quite simply the conversion of inputs into outputs. It is an economic process that uses resources to create a good or service that is suitable for exchange. This can include manufacturing, storing, shipping, and packaging.

a. MET
b. Solved
c. Red Guards
d. Production

7. In statistics, a _____ is a value that allows data to be measured over time in terms of some base period ussually through a price index in order to distinguish between changes in the money value of GNP which result from a change in prices and those which result from a change in physical output. It is the measure of the price level for some quantity. A _____ serves as a price index in which the effects of inflation are nulled.

   a. Market microstructure
   b. Blanket order
   c. Contingent employment
   d. Deflator

8. In economics, _____ is a rise in the general level of prices of goods and services in an economy over a period of time. When the general price level rises, each unit of currency buys fewer goods and services; consequently, _____ is also a decline in the real value of money--a loss of purchasing power in the medium of exchange which is also the monetary unit of account in the economy. A chief measure of general price-level _____ is the general _____ rate, which is the percentage change in a general price index (normally the Consumer Price Index) over time.

   a. Economic
   b. Opportunity cost
   c. Energy economics
   d. Inflation

9. _____ in economics and business is the result of an exchange and from that trade we assign a numerical monetary value to a good, service or asset. If Alice trades Bob 4 apples for an orange, the _____ of an orange is 4 apples. Inversely, the _____ of an apple is 1/4 oranges.

   a. Premium pricing
   b. Price war
   c. Price book
   d. Price

10. A _____ is a normalized average (typically a weighted average) of prices for a given class of goods or services in a given region, during a given interval of time. It is a statistic designed to help to compare how these prices, taken as a whole, differ between time periods or geographical locations.

Price indices have several potential uses.

   a. Transactional Net Margin Method
   b. Product sabotage
   c. Two-part tariff
   d. Price index

11. In economics, the _____ is a measure of inflation, the rate of increase of a price index (for example, a consumer price index.)It is the percentage rate of change in price level over time. The rate of decrease in the purchasing power of money is approximately equal.

It's used to calculate the real interest rate, as well as real increases in wages, and official measurements of this rate act as input variables to COLA adjustments and Inflation derivatives prices.

   a. Edgeworth paradox
   b. Equity value
   c. Interest rate option
   d. Inflation rate

Chapter 16. Ensuring Price Stability

12. _____, 1st Baron Keynes was a renowned economist from Britain whose many ideas on economic and political theories as well as on many governments' monetary policies influenced America. He advocated a government that played an active role in the lives of people regarding business, economy, etc. In this role, the government would use fiscal measures to reduce the consequences of recessions, economic depressions and booms.
   a. Adam Smith
   b. Adolf Hitler
   c. Adolph Fischer
   d. John Maynard Keynes

13. _____s is the social science that studies the production, distribution, and consumption of goods and services. The term _____s comes from the Ancient Greek οá¼°κονομῖα from οá¼¶κος (oikos, 'house') + vÏŒμος (nomos, 'custom' or 'law'), hence 'rules of the house(hold)'. Current _____ models developed out of the broader field of political economy in the late 19th century, owing to a desire to use an empirical approach more akin to the physical sciences.
   a. Opportunity cost
   b. Economic
   c. Inflation
   d. Energy economics

14. _____ refers to the actions that governments take in the economic field. It covers the systems for setting interest rates and government deficit as well as the labour market, national ownership, and many other areas of government.

Such policies are often influenced by international institutions like the International Monetary Fund or World Bank as well as political beliefs and the consequent policies of parties.

   a. ACEA agreement
   b. AD-IA Model
   c. Economic policy
   d. ACCRA Cost of Living Index

15. A _____ is a hypothetical measure of overall prices for some set of goods and services, in a given region during a given interval, normalized relative to some base set. Typically, a _____ is approximated with a price index.

The classical dichotomy is the assumption that there is a relatively clean distinction between overall increases or decreases in prices and underlying, e;reale; economic variables.

   a. Discouraged worker
   b. Price level
   c. Discretionary spending
   d. Price elasticity of supply

16. _____ is an economic concept with commonplace familiarity. It is the price that a good or service is offered at, or will fetch, in the marketplace. It is of interest mainly in the study of microeconomics.
   a. Noisy market hypothesis
   b. Paper trading
   c. Market anomaly
   d. Market price

17. In economics, the _____ measures the payments that flow between any individual country and all other countries. It is used to summarize all international economic transactions for that country during a specific time period, usually a year. The _____ is determined by the country's exports and imports of goods, services, and financial capital, as well as financial transfers.
   a. Skyscraper Index
   b. Gross domestic product per barrel
   c. Gross world product
   d. Balance of payments

18. A _____, reserve bank, or monetary authority is the entity responsible for the monetary policy of a country or of a group of member states. It is a bank that can lend money to other banks in times of need. Its primary responsibility is to maintain the stability of the national currency and money supply, but more active duties include controlling subsidized-loan interest rates, and acting as a lender of last resort to the banking sector during times of financial crisis (private banks often being integral to the national financial system.)
   a. 130-30 fund
   b. 100-year flood
   c. 1921 recession
   d. Central bank

19. In economics, _____ is inflation that is very high or 'out of control', a condition in which prices increase rapidly as a currency loses its value. Definitions used by the media vary from a cumulative inflation rate over three years approaching 100% to 'inflation exceeding 50% a month.' In informal usage the term is often applied to much lower rates. As a rule of thumb, normal inflation is reported per year, but _____ is often reported for much shorter intervals, often per month.
   a. 100-year flood
   b. 1921 recession
   c. 130-30 fund
   d. Hyperinflation

20. A _____ is the transfer of wealth from one party (such as a person or company) to another. A _____ is usually made in exchange for the provision of goods, services or both, or to fulfill a legal obligation.

The simplest and oldest form of _____ is barter, the exchange of one good or service for another.

   a. Soft count
   b. Social gravity
   c. Going concern
   d. Payment

21. In business and accounting, _____ are everything of value that is owned by a person or company. It is a claim on the property your income of a borrower. The balance sheet of a firm records the monetary value of the _____ owned by the firm.
   a. Amortization schedule
   b. ACEA agreement
   c. Assets
   d. ACCRA Cost of Living Index

22. In economics, _____ is a sustained decrease in the general price level of goods and services. _____ occurs when the annual inflation rate falls below zero percent, resulting in an increase in the real value of money -- a negative inflation rate. This should not be confused with disinflation, a slow-down in the inflation rate (i.e. when the inflation decreases, but still remains positive.)
   a. Price revolution
   b. Deflation
   c. Tobit model
   d. Literacy rate

23. _____ is a fee paid on borrowed assets. It is the price paid for the use of borrowed money , or, money earned by deposited funds . Assets that are sometimes lent with _____ include money, shares, consumer goods through hire purchase, major assets such as aircraft, and even entire factories in finance lease arrangements.
   a. Asset protection
   b. Interest
   c. Internal debt
   d. Insolvency

24. An _____ is the price a borrower pays for the use of money they do not own, for instance a small company might borrow from a bank to kick start their business, and the return a lender receives for deferring the use of funds, by lending it to the borrower. _____s are normally expressed as a percentage rate over the period of one year.

_____s targets are also a vital tool of monetary policy and are used to control variables like investment, inflation, and unemployment.

a. Arrow-Debreu model
c. Enterprise value
b. ACCRA Cost of Living Index
d. Interest rate

25. Market _____ is a business, economics or investment term that refers to an asset's ability to be easily converted through an act of buying or selling without causing a significant movement in the price and with minimum loss of value. Money, or cash on hand, is the most liquid asset. An act of exchange of a less liquid asset with a more liquid asset is called liquidation.

a. 1921 recession
c. 100-year flood
b. 130-30 fund
d. Liquidity

26. The term _____ is used in macroeconomics to refer to a situation where a country's nominal interest rate has been lowered nearly to or equal to zero to avoid a recession, but the liquidity in the market created by these low interest rates does not stimulate the economy to full employment. In this situation, any further increase in the money supply will not stimulate the economy any further. This is because any further injection of liquidity will no longer lower the nominal interest rate, as the nominal interest rate cannot drop below zero.

a. Macroeconomic models
c. Robertson lag
b. Minimum wage
d. Liquidity trap

27. In finance and economics _____ or nominal rate of interest refers to the rate of interest before adjustment for inflation (in contrast with the real interest rate); or, for interest rates 'as stated' without adjustment for the full effect of compounding (also referred to as the nominal annual rate.) An interest rate is called nominal if the frequency of compounding (e.g. a month) is not identical to the basic time unit (normally a year.)

The real interest rate includes compensation for the lender's lost value due to inflation, whereas the _____ excludes inflation.

a. London Interbank Offered Rate
c. Risk-free interest rate
b. Fixed interest
d. Nominal interest rate

28. The '_____' is approximately the nominal interest rate minus the inflation rate Since the inflation rate over the course of a loan is not known initially, volatility in inflation represents a risk to both the lender and the borrower.

In economics and finance, an individual who lends money for repayment at a later point in time expects to be compensated for the time value of money, or not having the use of that money while it is lent.

a. Core inflation
c. Cost-push inflation
b. Reflation
d. Real interest rate

29. The term _____ refers to government debt, expenditures and revenues, or to finance (particularly financial revenue) in general.

- _____ deficit is the budget deficit of federal or local government
- _____ policy is the discretionary spending of governments. Contrasts with monetary policy.
- _____ year and _____ quarter are reporting periods for firms and other agencies.

a. Drawdown
c. Bucket shop
b. Procter ' Gamble
d. Fiscal

30. In economics, _____ is the use of government spending and revenue collection to influence the economy.

_____ can be contrasted with the other main type of economic policy, monetary policy, which attempts to stabilize the economy by controlling interest rates and the supply of money. The two main instruments of _____ are government spending and taxation.

a. Fiscal policy
c. Sustainable investment rule
b. 100-year flood
d. Fiscalism

31. In economics, _____ is how a natione;s total economy is distributed among its population. ._____ has always been a central concern of economic theory and economic policy. Classical economists such as Adam Smith, Thomas Malthus and David Ricardo were mainly concerned with factor _____, that is, the distribution of income between the main factors of production, land, labour and capital.

a. Eco commerce
c. Equipment trust certificate
b. Authorised capital
d. Income distribution

32. In economics, _____ is the transfer of income, wealth or property from some individuals to others.

One premise of _____ is that money should be distributed to benefit the poorer members of society, and that the rich have an obligation to assist the poor, thus creating a more financially egalitarian society. Another argument is that the rich exploit the poor or otherwise gain unfair benefits.

a. 1921 recession
c. 100-year flood
b. 130-30 fund
d. Redistribution

33. _____ is a common concept in economics, and gives rise to derived concepts such as consumer debt. Generally _____ is defined by opposition to production. But the precise definition can vary because different schools of economists define production quite differently.

a. Federal Reserve Bank Notes
c. Consumption
b. Foreclosure data providers
d. Cash or share options

Chapter 16. Ensuring Price Stability

34. _____ is a term that refers both to:

- a formal discipline used to help appraise, or assess, the case for a project or proposal, which itself is a process known as project appraisal; and
- an informal approach to making decisions of any kind.

Under both definitions the process involves, whether explicitly or implicitly, weighing the total expected costs against the total expected benefits of one or more actions in order to choose the best or most profitable option. The formal process is often referred to as either CBA (_____) or BCost-benefit analysis

A hallmark of CBA is that all benefits and all costs are expressed in money terms, and are adjusted for the time value of money, so that all flows of benefits and flows of project costs over time (which tend to occur at different points in time) are expressed on a common basis in terms of their e;present value.e; Closely related, but slightly different, formal techniques include Cost-effectiveness analysis, Economic impact analysis, Fiscal impact analysis and Social Return on Investment(SROI) analysis. The latter builds upon the logic of _____, but differs in that it is explicitly designed to inform the practical decision-making of enterprise managers and investors focused on optimising their social and environmental impacts.

a. Decision theory
b. Cost-benefit analysis
c. 130-30 fund
d. 100-year flood

35. In algebra, a _____ is a function depending on n that associates a scalar, det(A), to an n×n square matrix A. The fundamental geometric meaning of a _____ is a scale factor for measure when A is regarded as a linear transformation. _____s are important both in calculus, where they enter the substitution rule for several variables, and in multilinear algebra.

For a fixed nonnegative integer n, there is a unique _____ function for the n×n matrices over any commutative ring R. In particular, this function exists when R is the field of real or complex numbers.

a. 130-30 fund
b. 100-year flood
c. 1921 recession
d. Determinant

36. A _____ is message sent to consumers and producers in the form of a price charged for a commodity; this is seen as indicating a signal for producers to increase supplies and/or consumers to reduce demand.

For example, in a free price system, rising prices may indicate a shortage of supply, increase in demand, or a rise in input costs. Regardless of the underlying reason--and without the consumer needing to know the cause--the price increase communicates the notion that consumer demand (at this new, higher price) should recede or that supplies should increase.

a. Mohring effect
b. Price signal
c. Market demand schedule
d. Threshold population

37. To _____ is to impose a financial charge or other levy upon a taxpayer by a state or the functional equivalent of a state.

_____es are also imposed by many subnational entities. _____es consist of direct _____ or indirect _____, and may be paid in money or as its labour equivalent (often but not always unpaid.)

   a. Tax
   c. 1921 recession
   b. 100-year flood
   d. 130-30 fund

38. _____ are the divisions at which tax rates change in a progressive tax system (or an explicitly regressive tax system, although this is much rarer.) Essentially, they are the cutoff values for taxable income -- income past a certain point will be taxed at a higher rate.
   a. Disposable income
   c. Tax farming
   b. Popiwek
   d. Tax brackets

39. In economics, _____ is the total demand for final goods and services in the economy (Y) at a given time and price level. It is the amount of goods and services in the economy that will be purchased at all possible price levels. This is the demand for the gross domestic product of a country when inventory levels are static.
   a. Aggregation problem
   c. Aggregate demand
   b. Aggregate supply
   d. Aggregate expenditure

40. _____ arises when aggregate demand in an economy outpaces aggregate supply. It involves inflation rising as real gross domestic product rises and unemployment falls, as the economy moves along the Phillips curve. This is commonly described as 'too much money chasing too few goods'.
   a. Marshallian demand function
   c. Demand-pull inflation
   b. Kinked demand curve
   d. Kinked demand

41. _____ is widely regarded as the first modern school of economic thought. It is the idea that free markets can regulate themselves. Its major developers include Adam Smith, David Ricardo, Thomas Malthus and John Stuart Mill. Sometimes the definition of _____ is expanded to include William Petty, Johann Heinrich von Thünen.
   a. Classical economics
   c. Marginalism
   b. Schools of economic thought
   d. Tendency of the rate of profit to fall

42. Economics:

- _____, the desire to own something and the ability to pay for it
- _____ curve, a graphic representation of a _____ schedule
- _____ deposit, the money in checking accounts
- _____ pull theory, the theory that inflation occurs when _____ for goods and services exceeds existing supplies
- _____ schedule, a table that lists the quantity of a good a person will buy it each different price
- _____ side economics, the school of economics at believes government spending and tax cuts open economy by raising _____

   a. McKesson ' Robbins scandal
   c. Production
   b. Demand
   d. Variability

43. _____ is a concept coined by structuralist inflation theorists. It refers to a situation where all prices in an economy are continuously adjusted with relation to a price index by force of contracts.

Changes in price indices trigger changes in prices of goods.

a. Incomes policies
b. Employment Cost Index
c. Inflationary Spikes
d. Inertial Inflation

44. _____ is a type of inflation caused by substantial increases in the cost of important goods or services where no suitable alternative is available. A situation that has been often cited of this was the oil crisis of the 1970s, which some economists see as a major cause of the inflation experienced in the Western world in that decade. It is argued that this inflation resulted from increases in the cost of petroleum imposed by the member states of OPEC.

a. Cost-push inflation
b. Headline inflation
c. Chronic inflation
d. Mundell-Tobin effect

45. _____ is an assumption used in many contemporary macroeconomic models, and also in other areas of contemporary economics and game theory and in other applications of rational choice theory.

Since most macroeconomic models today study decisions over many periods, the expectations of workers, consumers, and firms about future economic conditions are an essential part of the model. How to model these expectations has long been controversial, and it is well known that the macroeconomic predictions of the model may differ depending on the assumptions made about expectations

a. Potential output
b. Balanced-growth equilibrium
c. Minimum wage
d. Rational expectations

46. In economics, _____ is the total supply of goods and services produced by a national economy during a specific time period. It is the total amount of goods and services in the economy available at all possible price levels.

a. Aggregate supply
b. Aggregate expenditure
c. Aggregation problem
d. Aggregate demand

47. In economics, a _____ is a sudden event that increases or decreases demand for goods or services temporarily. A positive _____ increases demand and a negative _____ decreases demand. Prices of goods and services are affected in both cases.

a. Lucas-Islands model
b. War economy
c. Robertson lag
d. Demand shock

48. A _____ is an event that suddenly changes the price of a commodity or service. It may be caused by a sudden increase or decrease in the supply of a particular good. This sudden change affects the equilibrium price.

a. SIMIC
b. Friedman rule
c. Supply shock
d. Demand shock

49. _____ in economics refers to metrics and measures of output from production processes, per unit of input. Labor _____, for example, is typically measured as a ratio of output per labor-hour, an input. _____ may be conceived of as a metrics of the technical or engineering efficiency of production.

a. Fordism
b. Production-possibility frontier
c. Piece work
d. Productivity

50. In economics, the concept of the _____ refers to the decision-making time frame of a firm in which at least one factor of production is fixed. Costs which are fixed in the _____ have no impact on a firms decisions. For example a firm can raise output by increasing the amount of labour through overtime.
    a. Product Pipeline
    b. Productivity model
    c. Hicks-neutral technical change
    d. Short-run

51. The term _____ refers to economy-wide fluctuations in production or economic activity over several months or years. These fluctuations occur around a long-term growth trend, and typically involve shifts over time between periods of relatively rapid economic growth (expansion or boom), and periods of relative stagnation or decline (contraction or recession.)

These fluctuations are often measured using the growth rate of real gross domestic product.

    a. Consumer theory
    b. Nominal value
    c. Tobit model
    d. Business cycle

52. In economics, _____ is when quantity demanded is more than quantity supplied.See Economic shortage.
    a. ACEA agreement
    b. AD-IA Model
    c. Excess demand
    d. ACCRA Cost of Living Index

53. In economics, _____ is when quantity supplied is more than quantity demanded. .
    a. Effective unemployment rate
    b. Illicit financial flows
    c. Excess supply
    d. Economic Value Creation

54. _____ was an American economist, statistician and public intellectual, and a recipient of the Nobel Memorial Prize in Economic Sciences. He is best known among scholars for his theoretical and empirical research, especially consumption analysis, monetary history and theory, and for his demonstration of the complexity of stabilization policy. A global public followed his restatement of a political philosophy that insisted on minimizing the role of government in favor of the private sector.
    a. Milton Friedman
    b. Adam Smith
    c. Adolph Fischer
    d. Adolf Hitler

55. In economic models, the _____ time frame assumes no fixed factors of production. Firms can enter or leave the marketplace, and the cost (and availability) of land, labor, raw materials, and capital goods can be assumed to vary. In contrast, in the short-run time frame, certain factors are assumed to be fixed, because there is not sufficient time for them to change.
    a. Price/performance ratio
    b. Productivity world
    c. Diseconomies of scale
    d. Long-run

56. The term _____ is an acronym for Non-Accelerating Inflation Rate of Unemployment. It is a concept in economic theory significant in the interplay of macroeconomics and microeconomics. This 'full employment' unemployment rate is sometimes termed the 'inflation-threshold unemployment rate': Actual unemployment cannot fall below the _____, and the inflation rate is likely to rise quickly (accelerate) in times of strong labor demands during periods of growth.

Chapter 16. Ensuring Price Stability

a. NAIRU
c. Social Credit
b. Coal depletion
d. Cobweb model

57. In economics, a _____ is a general slowdown in economic activity over a sustained period of time, or a business cycle contraction. During _____s, many macroeconomic indicators vary in a similar way. Production as measured by Gross Domestic Product (GDP), employment, investment spending, capacity utilization, household incomes and business profits all fall during _____s.

a. Monetary economics
c. Leading indicators
b. Treasury View
d. Recession

58. _____ is an American economist and was the Chairman of the Federal Reserve of the United States from 1987 to 2006. He currently works as a private advisor and providing consulting for firms through his company, Greenspan Associates LLC.

First appointed Federal Reserve chairman by President Ronald Reagan in August 1987, he was reappointed at successive four-year intervals until retiring on January 31, 2006 after the second-longest tenure in the position.

a. Adolph Fischer
c. Adam Smith
b. Adolf Hitler
d. Alan Greenspan

59. _____ is a school of macroeconomic thought that argues that economic growth can be most effectively created using incentives for people to produce (supply) goods and services, such as adjusting income tax and capital gains tax rates, and by allowing greater flexibility by reducing regulation. Consumers will then benefit from a greater supply of goods and services at lower prices.

The term _____ was coined by journalist Jude Wanniski in 1975, and popularized the ideas of economists Robert Mundell and Arthur Laffer.

a. Fiscal stimulus plans
c. Clap note
b. Supply-side economics
d. Commodity trading advisors

60. _____ is a decrease in the rate of inflation. This phase of the business cycle, in which retailers can no longer pass on higher prices to their customers, often occurs during a recession. In contrast, deflation occurs when prices are actually dropping.

a. Reflation
c. Mundell-Tobin effect
b. Stealth inflation
d. Disinflation

61. A _____ occurs when an entity spends more money than it takes in. The opposite of a _____ is a budget surplus. Debt is essentially an accumulated flow of deficits.

a. Funding body
c. Budget deficit
b. Public Financial Management
d. Lump-sum tax

62. In finance, the _____ of a financial asset measures the sensitivity of the asset's price to interest rate movements. There are various definitions of _____ and derived quantities, discussed below. If not otherwise specified, '_____' generally means the Macaulay _____, as defined below.

a. Time value of money
b. Newtonian time
c. 100-year flood
d. Duration

63. _____ to the arrival of new individuals into a habitat or population. It is a biological concept and is important in population ecology, differentiated from emigration and migration.

_____ is a modern phenomenon.

a. ACEA agreement
b. Immigration
c. ACCRA Cost of Living Index
d. AD-IA Model

64. _____ refers to the objective and subjective components of the believability of a source or message.

Traditionally, _____ has two key components: trustworthiness and expertise, which both have objective and subjective components. Trustworthiness is a based more on subjective factors, but can include objective measurements such as established reliability.

a. 1921 recession
b. 100-year flood
c. Credibility
d. 130-30 fund

65. The _____ is the central banking system of the United States. Created in 1913 by the enactment of the Federal Reserve Act (signed by Woodrow Wilson), it is a quasi-public and quasi-private (government entity with private components) banking system that comprises (1) the presidentially appointed Board of Governors of the _____ in Washington, D.C.; (2) the Federal Open Market Committee; (3) twelve regional Federal Reserve Banks located in major cities throughout the nation acting as fiscal agents for the U.S. Treasury, each with its own nine-member board of directors; (4) numerous other private U.S. member banks, which subscribe to required amounts of non-transferable stock in their regional Federal Reserve Banks; and (5) various advisory councils. Since February 2006, Ben Bernanke has served as the Chairman of the Board of Governors of the _____.

a. Term auction facility
b. Federal Reserve System
c. Federal Reserve System Open Market Account
d. Monetary Policy Report to the Congress

Chapter 17. The Warring Schools of Macroeconomics

1. _____ originally was the term for studying production, buying and selling, and their relations with law, custom, and government. _____ originated in moral philosophy. It developed in the 18th century as the study of the economies of states -- polities, hence _____.
   a. Dirigisme
   b. Productive and unproductive labour
   c. Geoeconomics
   d. Political Economy

2. _____ by John Stuart Mill was the most important economics or political economy textbook of the mid nineteenth century. It was revised until its seventh edition in 1871, shortly before Mill's death in 1873, and republished in numerous other editions.

   Mill's Principles were written in a style of prose far flung from the introductory texts of today.

   a. Principles of Political Economy and Taxation
   b. Limits to Growth
   c. The Rise and Fall of the Great Powers
   d. Principles of Political Economy

3. _____ is widely regarded as the first modern school of economic thought. It is the idea that free markets can regulate themselves. Its major developers include Adam Smith, David Ricardo, Thomas Malthus and John Stuart Mill. Sometimes the definition of _____ is expanded to include William Petty, Johann Heinrich von Thünen.
   a. Marginalism
   b. Classical economics
   c. Tendency of the rate of profit to fall
   d. Schools of economic thought

4. _____s is the social science that studies the production, distribution, and consumption of goods and services. The term _____s comes from the Ancient Greek οἰκονομῐ́α from οἶκος (oikos, 'house') + νόμος (nomos, 'custom' or 'law'), hence 'rules of the house(hold)'. Current _____ models developed out of the broader field of political economy in the late 19th century, owing to a desire to use an empirical approach more akin to the physical sciences.
   a. Inflation
   b. Opportunity cost
   c. Energy economics
   d. Economic

5. In macroeconomics, _____ is a condition of the national economy, where all or nearly all persons willing and able to work at the prevailing wages and working conditions are able to do so. It is defined either as 0% unemployment, literally, no unemployment (the rate of unemployment is the fraction of the work force unable to find work), as by James Tobin, or as the level of employment rates when there is no cyclical unemployment. It is defined by the majority of mainstream economists as being an acceptable level of natural unemployment above 0%, the discrepancy from 0% being due to non-cyclical types of unemployment.
   a. Marginal propensity to consume
   b. Full employment
   c. Demand shock
   d. Harrod-Johnson diagram

6. _____, 1st Baron Keynes was a renowned economist from Britain whose many ideas on economic and political theories as well as on many governments' monetary policies influenced America. He advocated a government that played an active role in the lives of people regarding business, economy, etc. In this role, the government would use fiscal measures to reduce the consequences of recessions, economic depressions and booms.
   a. Adolph Fischer
   b. Adam Smith
   c. Adolf Hitler
   d. John Maynard Keynes

7. A _____ is an economy based on the division of labor in which the prices of goods and services are determined in a free price system set by supply and demand. This is often contrasted with a planned economy, in which a central government determines the price of goods and services using a fixed price system. Market economies are contrasted with mixed economy where the price system is not entirely free but under some government control that is not extensive enough to constitute a planned economy.
   a. Network Economy
   b. Market economy
   c. Nutritional Economics
   d. Commons-based peer production

8. _____ is an economic concept with commonplace familiarity. It is the price that a good or service is offered at, or will fetch, in the marketplace. It is of interest mainly in the study of microeconomics.
   a. Paper trading
   b. Noisy market hypothesis
   c. Market anomaly
   d. Market price

9. The term _____s refers to wages that have been adjusted for inflation. This term is used in contrast to nominal wages or unadjusted wages.

The use of adjusted figures is in undertaking some form of economic analysis.

   a. Real wage
   b. Federal Wage System
   c. Profit sharing
   d. Living wage

10. _____ in economics and business is the result of an exchange and from that trade we assign a numerical monetary value to a good, service or asset. If Alice trades Bob 4 apples for an orange, the _____ of an orange is 4 apples. Inversely, the _____ of an apple is 1/4 oranges.
    a. Price war
    b. Premium pricing
    c. Price book
    d. Price

11. A _____, reserve bank, or monetary authority is the entity responsible for the monetary policy of a country or of a group of member states. It is a bank that can lend money to other banks in times of need. Its primary responsibility is to maintain the stability of the national currency and money supply, but more active duties include controlling subsidized-loan interest rates, and acting as a lender of last resort to the banking sector during times of financial crisis (private banks often being integral to the national financial system.)
    a. 1921 recession
    b. 100-year flood
    c. Central bank
    d. 130-30 fund

12. The _____ is the central banking system of the United States. Created in 1913 by the enactment of the Federal Reserve Act (signed by Woodrow Wilson), it is a quasi-public and quasi-private (government entity with private components) banking system that comprises (1) the presidentially appointed Board of Governors of the _____ in Washington, D.C.; (2) the Federal Open Market Committee; (3) twelve regional Federal Reserve Banks located in major cities throughout the nation acting as fiscal agents for the U.S. Treasury, each with its own nine-member board of directors; (4) numerous other private U.S. member banks, which subscribe to required amounts of non-transferable stock in their regional Federal Reserve Banks; and (5) various advisory councils. Since February 2006, Ben Bernanke has served as the Chairman of the Board of Governors of the _____.
    a. Federal Reserve System Open Market Account
    b. Term auction facility
    c. Monetary Policy Report to the Congress
    d. Federal Reserve System

13. The term _____ refers to government debt, expenditures and revenues, or to finance (particularly financial revenue) in general.

- _____ deficit is the budget deficit of federal or local government
- _____ policy is the discretionary spending of governments. Contrasts with monetary policy.
- _____ year and _____ quarter are reporting periods for firms and other agencies.

a. Bucket shop
b. Procter ' Gamble
c. Drawdown
d. Fiscal

14. In economics, _____ is the use of government spending and revenue collection to influence the economy.

_____ can be contrasted with the other main type of economic policy, monetary policy, which attempts to stabilize the economy by controlling interest rates and the supply of money. The two main instruments of _____ are government spending and taxation.

a. Fiscalism
b. Fiscal policy
c. Sustainable investment rule
d. 100-year flood

15. The _____ was written by the English economist John Maynard Keynes. The book, generally considered to be his magnum opus, is largely credited with creating the terminology and shape of modern macroeconomics. Published in February 1936 it sought to bring about a revolution, commonly referred to as the 'Keynesian Revolution', in the way economists thought - especially in relation to the proposition that a market economy tends naturally to restore itself to full employment after temporary shocks.

a. General Theory of Employment, Interest and Money
b. The General Theory of Employment, Interest and Money
c. Black Book of Communism
d. Human Action

16. _____ is a fee paid on borrowed assets. It is the price paid for the use of borrowed money , or, money earned by deposited funds . Assets that are sometimes lent with _____ include money, shares, consumer goods through hire purchase, major assets such as aircraft, and even entire factories in finance lease arrangements.

a. Internal debt
b. Insolvency
c. Asset protection
d. Interest

17. _____ and Keynesian Theory) is a macroeconomic theory based on the ideas of 20th-century British economist John Maynard Keynes. _____ argues that private sector decisions sometimes lead to inefficient macroeconomic outcomes and therefore advocates active policy responses by the public sector, including monetary policy actions by the central bank and fiscal policy actions by the government to stabilize output over the business cycle.

The theories forming the basis of _____ were first presented in The General Theory of Employment, Interest and Money, published in 1936.

Chapter 17. The Warring Schools of Macroeconomics

   a. Rational choice theory
   b. Deflation
   c. Market failure
   d. Keynesian economics

18. The _____ was a fundamental reworking of economic theory concerning the factors determining employment levels in the overall economy. The revolution was set against the orthodox classical economic framework, which based on Say's Law argued that unless special conditions prevailed the free market would naturally establish full employment equilibrium with no need for government intervention. Employers will be able to make a profit by employing all available workers as long as workers drop their wages below the value of the total output they are able to produce - and classical economics assumed that in a free market workers would be willing to lower their wage demands accordingly , because they are rational agents who would rather work for less than face unemployment.
   a. Keynesian revolution
   b. Speculative demand
   c. Neo-Keynesian economics
   d. Military Keynesianism

19. _____ emerged as a school in macroeconomics during the 1970s. As opposed to Keynesian macroeconomics, it builds its analysis on an entirely neoclassical framework. Specifically, _____ emphasises the importance of rigorous foundations, in which the macroeconomic model is built in analogy to the actions of individual agents, whose behaviour is modelled by microeconomics.
   a. Henry George Theorem
   b. Dominant Design
   c. Developmentalism
   d. New classical macroeconomics

20. In economics, _____ is the total demand for final goods and services in the economy (Y) at a given time and price level. It is the amount of goods and services in the economy that will be purchased at all possible price levels. This is the demand for the gross domestic product of a country when inventory levels are static.
   a. Aggregate demand
   b. Aggregation problem
   c. Aggregate expenditure
   d. Aggregate supply

21. _____, or a _____ is the concept of a resulting effect (cf. cause and effect, arising from another action. In general terms, it is used to indicate that all human actions, particularly crime and sin, have profound effects.
   a. Rule
   b. Consequence
   c. Solved
   d. Variability

22. Economics:

   - _____,the desire to own something and the ability to pay for it
   - _____ curve,a graphic representation of a _____ schedule
   - _____ deposit, the money in checking accounts
   - _____ pull theory,the theory that inflation occurs when _____ for goods and services exceeds existing supplies
   - _____ schedule,a table that lists the quantity of a good a person will buy it each different price
   - _____ side economics,the school of economics at believes government spending and tax cuts open economy by raising _____

   a. Production
   b. McKesson ' Robbins scandal
   c. Demand
   d. Variability

Chapter 17. The Warring Schools of Macroeconomics

23. _____ is a branch of economics that deals with the performance, structure, and behavior of a national or regional economy as a whole. Along with microeconomics, _____ is one of the two most general fields in economics. It is the study of the behavior and decision-making of entire economies.
    a. Nominal value
    b. New Trade Theory
    c. Tobit model
    d. Macroeconomics

24. The _____ was a worldwide economic downturn starting in most places in 1929 and ending at different times in the 1930s or early 1940s for different countries. It was the largest and most important economic depression in the 20th century, and is used in the 21st century as an example of how far the world's economy can fall. The _____ originated in the United States; historians most often use as a starting date the stock market crash on October 29, 1929, known as Black Tuesday.
    a. Great Depression
    b. British Empire Economic Conference
    c. Jarrow March
    d. Wall Street Crash of 1929

25. In economics, the term _____ has three different distinct meanings and applications. While it is related to unemployment, a situation in which a person who is searching for work cannot find a job, in the case of _____, a person is working. All three of the definitions of '_____' involve underutilization of labor that critics say is missed by most official (governmental agency) definitions and measurements of unemployment.
    a. Employability
    b. Encore career
    c. Informational interview
    d. Underemployment

26. In Keynesian economics, _____ refers to a situation with a persistent shortfall relative to full employment and potential output so that unemployment is higher than at the NAIRU or the 'natural' rate of unemployment. This situation is not seen as solvable via laissez-faire polices of 'letting nature take its course' (price adjustment.) Instead, fiscal policy (i.e., deficit spending) or monetary policy is needed to 'prime the pump' or 'jump-start the economy' to abolish cyclical unemployment and the 'GDP gap.' .
    a. ACEA agreement
    b. AD-IA Model
    c. ACCRA Cost of Living Index
    d. Underemployment equilibrium

27. The _____ says that it is naïve to try to predict the effects of a change in economic policy entirely on the basis of relationships observed in historical data, especially highly aggregated historical data.

The basic idea pre-dates Lucas's contribution, but in a 1976 paper he drove home the point that this simple notion invalidated policy advice based on conclusions drawn from estimated system of equation models. Because the parameters of those models were not structural - that is, not policy-invariant - they would necessarily change whenever policy - the rules of the game - was changed.

    a. Lucas critique
    b. Dahrendorf hypothesis
    c. Peak-load pricing
    d. Demand management

28. _____ is the view within monetary economics that variation in the money supply has major influences on national output in the short run and the price level over longer periods and that objectives of monetary policy are best met by targeting the growth rate of the money supply.

Chapter 17. The Warring Schools of Macroeconomics

_____ today is mainly associated with the work of Milton Friedman, who was among the generation of economists to accept Keynesian economics and then criticize it on his own terms. Friedman and Anna Schwartz wrote an influential book, Monetary History of the United States 1867-1960, and argued that 'inflation is always and everywhere a monetary phenomenon.' Friedman advocated a central bank policy aimed at keeping the supply and demand for money at equilibrium, as measured by growth in productivity and demand.

a. Complexity economics
b. Monetarism
c. Historical school of economics
d. Marginal revenue productivity theory of wages

29. In economics, _____ is the total amount of money available in an economy at a particular point in time. There are several ways to define 'money', but standard measures usually include currency in circulation and demand deposits.

_____ data are recorded and published, usually by the government or the central bank of the country.

a. Veil of money
b. Neutrality of money
c. Velocity of money
d. Money supply

30. In economics, the _____ is the relation:

$$M \cdot V = P \cdot Q$$

where, for a given period,

M is the total amount of money in circulation on average in an economy.
V is the velocity of money, that is the average frequency with which a unit of money is spent.
P is the price level.

a. Equation of exchange
b. ACCRA Cost of Living Index
c. Open market
d. Outside money

31. The _____ is the average frequency with which a unit of money is spent in a specific period of time. Velocity associates the amount of economic activity associated with a given money supply. When the period is understood, the velocity may be present as a pure number; otherwise it should be given as a pure number over time.

a. Velocity of Money
b. Chartalism
c. Neutrality of money
d. Money supply

32. In economics, the _____ of money is a theory emphasizing the positive relationship of overall prices or the nominal value of expenditures to the quantity of money.

It is the mainstream economic theory of the price level. Alternative theories include the real bills doctrine and the more recent fiscal theory of the price level.

a. Real business cycle
b. Romer Model
c. Dishoarding
d. Quantity theory

33. In economics, the _____ is a theory emphasizing the positive relationship of overall prices or the nominal value of expenditures to the quantity of money.

It is the mainstream economic theory of the price level. Alternative theories include the real bills doctrine and the more recent fiscal theory of the price level.

a. Consumer spending
b. Microsimulation
c. Fundamental psychological law
d. Quantity theory of money

34. _____ is an economic system in which wealth, and the means of producing wealth, are privately owned. Through _____, the land, labor, and capital are owned, operated, and traded for the purpose of generating profits, without force or fraud, by private individuals either singly or jointly, and investments, distribution, income, production, pricing and supply of goods, commodities and services are determined by voluntary private decision in a market economy. A distinguishing feature of _____ is that each person owns his or her own labor and therefore is allowed to sell the use of it to employers.

a. Capitalism
b. Late capitalism
c. Socialism for the rich and capitalism for the poor
d. Creative capitalism

35. _____ was an American economist, statistician and public intellectual, and a recipient of the Nobel Memorial Prize in Economic Sciences. He is best known among scholars for his theoretical and empirical research, especially consumption analysis, monetary history and theory, and for his demonstration of the complexity of stabilization policy. A global public followed his restatement of a political philosophy that insisted on minimizing the role of government in favor of the private sector.

a. Milton Friedman
b. Adolf Hitler
c. Adam Smith
d. Adolph Fischer

36. A _____ is an object whose consumption increases the utility of the consumer, for which the quantity demanded exceeds the quantity supplied at zero price. _____s are usually modeled as having diminishing marginal utility. The first individual purchase has high utility; the second has less.

a. Good
b. Pie method
c. Merit good
d. Composite good

37. In economics, economic output is divided into physical goods and intangible services. Consumption of _____ is assumed to produce utility. It is often used when referring to a _____ Tax.

a. Private good
b. Goods and services
c. Manufactured goods
d. Composite good

38. In economics, _____ is inflation that is very high or 'out of control', a condition in which prices increase rapidly as a currency loses its value. Definitions used by the media vary from a cumulative inflation rate over three years approaching 100% to 'inflation exceeding 50% a month.' In informal usage the term is often applied to much lower rates. As a rule of thumb, normal inflation is reported per year, but _____ is often reported for much shorter intervals, often per month.

a. Hyperinflation
b. 100-year flood
c. 1921 recession
d. 130-30 fund

Chapter 17. The Warring Schools of Macroeconomics

39. _____ in economics refers to metrics and measures of output from production processes, per unit of input. Labor _____, for example, is typically measured as a ratio of output per labor-hour, an input. _____ may be conceived of as a metrics of the technical or engineering efficiency of production.

a. Productivity
b. Fordism
c. Piece work
d. Production-possibility frontier

40. In economics, the _____ is a historical inverse relation between the rate of unemployment and the rate of inflation in an economy. Stated simply, the lower the unemployment in an economy, the higher the rate of increase in nominal wages in the economy. Rate of Change of Wages against Unemployment, United Kingdom 1913-1948 from Phillips (1958)

William Phillips, a New Zealand born economist, wrote a paper in 1958 titled The Relationship between Unemployment and the Rate of Change of Money Wages in the United Kingdom 1861-1957, which was published in the quarterly journal Economica.

a. Lorenz curve
b. Cost curve
c. Phillips curve
d. Demand curve

41. In economics, _____ is the total supply of goods and services produced by a national economy during a specific time period. It is the total amount of goods and services in the economy available at all possible price levels.

a. Aggregate expenditure
b. Aggregate demand
c. Aggregation problem
d. Aggregate supply

42. The _____ or gross domestic income (GDI), a basic measure of an economy's economic performance, is the market value of all final goods and services produced within the borders of a nation in a year. _____ can be defined in three ways, all of which are conceptually identical. First, it is equal to the total expenditures for all final goods and services produced within the country in a stipulated period of time (usually a 365-day year.)

a. Market structure
b. Gross domestic product
c. Countercyclical
d. Monopolistic competition

43. _____ is a misspelled phrase from Latin 'pro capite' phrase meaning per head with pro meaning 'per' or 'for each' and capite meaning 'head.' Both words together equate to the phrase 'for each head.'

It is usually used in the field of statistics to indicate the average per person for any given concern, such as income, crime rate, etc.

It is also used in wills to indicate that each of the named beneficiaries should receive, by devise or bequest, equal shares of the estate. This is in contrast to a per stirpes division, in which each branch of the inheriting family inherits an equal share of the estate.

a. Population statistics
b. False positive rate
c. Sargan test
d. Per capita

44. An _____, in economics, is the amount by which the real Gross domestic product exceeds potential GDP. The real GDP is also known as GDP 'adjusted for inflation', 'constant prices' GDP or 'constant dollar' GDP, because it measures the aggregate output in a country's income accounts in a given year, expressed in base-year prices. On the other hand, the potential GDP is the quantity of real GDP when a country's economy is at full-employment.

a. AD-IA Model
b. ACEA agreement
c. ACCRA Cost of Living Index
d. Inflationary gap

45. A _____ is:

- Rewrite _____, in generative grammar and computer science
- Standardization, a formal and widely-accepted statement, fact, definition, or qualification
- Operation, a determinate _____ for performing a mathematical operation and obtaining a certain result (Mathematics, Logic)
    - Unary operation
    - Binary operation
- _____ of inference, a function from sets of formulae to formulae (Mathematics, Logic)
- _____ of thumb, principle with broad application that is not intended to be strictly accurate or reliable for every situation. Also often simply referred to as a _____
- Moral, an atomic element of a moral code for guiding choices in human behavior
- Heuristic, a quantized '_____' which shows a tendency or probability for successful function
- A regulation, as in sports
- A Production _____, as in computer science
- Procedural law, a _____ set governing the application of laws to cases
    - A law, which may informally be called a '_____'
    - A court ruling, a decision by a court
- In the U.S. Government, a regulation mandated by Congress, but written or expanded upon by the Executive Branch.
- Norm (sociology), an informal but widely accepted _____, concept, truth, definition, or qualification (social norms, legal norms, coding norms)
- Norm (philosophy), a kind of sentence or a reason to act, feel or believe
- 'Rulership' is the concept of governance by a government:
    - Military _____, governance by a military body
    - Monastic _____, a collection of precepts that guides the life of monks or nuns in a religious order where the superior holds the place of Christ
- Slide _____

- '_____,' a song by Ayumi Hamasaki
- '_____,' a song by rapper Nas
- '_____s,' an album by the band The Whitest Boy Alive
- _____s: Pyaar Ka Superhit Formula, a 2003 Bollywood film
- ruler, an instrument for measuring lengths
- _____, a component of an astrolabe, circumferator or similar instrument
- The _____s, a bestselling self-help book
- _____ Project (Run Up-to-date Linux Everywhere), a project that aims to use up-to-date Linux software on old PCs
- _____ engine, a software system that helps managing business _____s
- Ja _____, a hip hop artist
    - R.U.L.E., a 2005 greatest hits album by rapper Ja _____
- '_____s,' a KMFDM song

Chapter 17. The Warring Schools of Macroeconomics

   a. Rule
   b. Procter ' Gamble
   c. Demand
   d. Technocracy

46. The _____ , a component of the Federal Reserve System, is charged under United States law with overseeing the nation's open market operations. It is the Federal Reserve Committee that makes key decisions about interest rates and the growth jam of the United States money supply. It is the principal organ of United States national monetary policy.
   a. Primary Dealer Credit Facility
   b. Federal Reserve Transparency Act
   c. Federal Open Market Committee
   d. Fed Funds Probability

47. In economics, the _____ is the term used to refer to the environment in which bonds are bought and sold between a central bank ' its regulated banks. It is not a free market process.

- To intervene in the 'business cycle', a central bank may choose to go into the _____ and buy or sell government bonds, which is known as _____ operations to increase reserves.

   a. ACCRA Cost of Living Index
   b. Inside money
   c. Outside money
   d. Open Market

48. _____ is the process of estimation in unknown situations. Prediction is a similar, but more general term. Both can refer to estimation of time series, cross-sectional or longitudinal data.
   a. Forecasting
   b. 1921 recession
   c. 100-year flood
   d. 130-30 fund

49. _____ is an assumption used in many contemporary macroeconomic models, and also in other areas of contemporary economics and game theory and in other applications of rational choice theory.

Since most macroeconomic models today study decisions over many periods, the expectations of workers, consumers, and firms about future economic conditions are an essential part of the model. How to model these expectations has long been controversial, and it is well known that the macroeconomic predictions of the model may differ depending on the assumptions made about expectations

   a. Minimum wage
   b. Balanced-growth equilibrium
   c. Potential output
   d. Rational expectations

50. _____ is a term used to described a tendency or preference towards a particular perspective, ideology or result, especially when the tendency interferes with the ability to be impartial, unprejudiced, or objective. The term _____ed is used to describe an action, judgment, or other outcome influenced by a prejudged perspective. It is also used to refer to a person or body of people whose actions or judgments exhibit _____.
   a. 100-year flood
   b. Bias
   c. 1921 recession
   d. 130-30 fund

51. The term _____ refers to economy-wide fluctuations in production or economic activity over several months or years. These fluctuations occur around a long-term growth trend, and typically involve shifts over time between periods of relatively rapid economic growth (expansion or boom), and periods of relative stagnation or decline (contraction or recession.)

These fluctuations are often measured using the growth rate of real gross domestic product.

- a. Business cycle
- b. Tobit model
- c. Consumer theory
- d. Nominal value

52. _____s is concerned with the tasks of developing and applying quantitative or statistical methods to the study and elucidation of economic principles. _____s combines economic theory with statistics to analyze and test economic relationships. Theoretical _____s considers questions about the statistical properties of estimators and tests, while applied _____s is concerned with the application of _____ methods to assess economic theories.
- a. Econometric
- b. Evolutionary economics
- c. Experimental economics
- d. Economic

53. _____s are statistical models used in econometrics. An _____ specifies the statistical relationship that is believed to hold between the various economic quantities pertaining a particular economic phenomena under study. An _____ can be derived from a deterministic economic model by allowing for uncertainty or from an economic model which itself is stochastic.
- a. Econometric model
- b. Economic statistics
- c. Event study
- d. ACCRA Cost of Living Index

54. A _____ is an event that suddenly changes the price of a commodity or service. It may be caused by a sudden increase or decrease in the supply of a particular good. This sudden change affects the equilibrium price.
- a. Demand shock
- b. Friedman rule
- c. SIMIC
- d. Supply shock

55. In labor economics, the _____ hypothesis argues that wages, at least in some markets, are determined by more than simply supply and demand. Specifically, it points to the incentive for managers to pay their employees more than the market-clearing wage in order to increase their productivity or efficiency. This increased labor productivity pays for the relatively higher wages.
- a. Efficiency wage
- b. Exogenous growth model
- c. Inflatable rats
- d. Earnings calls

56. In economics, _____ is a rise in the general level of prices of goods and services in an economy over a period of time. When the general price level rises, each unit of currency buys fewer goods and services; consequently, _____ is also a decline in the real value of money--a loss of purchasing power in the medium of exchange which is also the monetary unit of account in the economy. A chief measure of general price-level _____ is the general _____ rate, which is the percentage change in a general price index (normally the Consumer Price Index) over time.
- a. Energy economics
- b. Opportunity cost
- c. Economic
- d. Inflation

57. In economics, the _____ is a measure of inflation, the rate of increase of a price index (for example, a consumer price index.)It is the percentage rate of change in price level over time. The rate of decrease in the purchasing power of money is approximately equal.

It's used to calculate the real interest rate, as well as real increases in wages, and official measurements of this rate act as input variables to COLA adjustments and Inflation derivatives prices.

a. Edgeworth paradox
b. Equity value
c. Interest rate option
d. Inflation rate

58. In microeconomics, _____ is quite simply the conversion of inputs into outputs. It is an economic process that uses resources to create a good or service that is suitable for exchange. This can include manufacturing, storing, shipping, and packaging.

a. Red Guards
b. MET
c. Solved
d. Production

59. In economics, a _____ is a function that specifies the output of a firm, an industry, or an entire economy for all combinations of inputs. A meta-_____ compares the practice of the existing entities converting inputs X into output y to determine the most efficient practice _____ of the existing entities, whether the most efficient feasible practice production or the most efficient actual practice production. In either case, the maximum output of a technologically-determined production process is a mathematical function of input factors of production.

a. Short-run
b. Constant elasticity of substitution
c. Post-Fordism
d. Production function

60. Though there have been several definitions of voluntary and _____ in the economics literature, a simple distinction is often applied. Voluntary unemployment is attributed to the individual's decisions, whereas _____ exists because of the socio-economic environment (including the market structure, government intervention, and the level of aggregate demand) in which individuals operate. In these terms, much or most of frictional unemployment is voluntary, since it reflects individual search behavior.

a. ACCRA Cost of Living Index
b. AD-IA Model
c. ACEA agreement
d. Involuntary unemployment

61. In economics, the _____ is used to illustrate the idea that increases in the rate of taxation do not necessarily increase tax revenue. (For instance, whereas a 0% income tax rate will generate no revenue, neither will a 100% rate, as citizens will have no incentive to make money.) Increasing taxes beyond the peak of the curve point will decrease tax revenue.

a. Laffer curve
b. 100-year flood
c. 130-30 fund
d. 1921 recession

62. _____ is a school of macroeconomic thought that argues that economic growth can be most effectively created using incentives for people to produce (supply) goods and services, such as adjusting income tax and capital gains tax rates, and by allowing greater flexibility by reducing regulation. Consumers will then benefit from a greater supply of goods and services at lower prices.

The term _____ was coined by journalist Jude Wanniski in 1975, and popularized the ideas of economists Robert Mundell and Arthur Laffer.

a. Fiscal stimulus plans
b. Clap note
c. Supply-side economics
d. Commodity trading advisors

63. To _____ is to impose a financial charge or other levy upon a taxpayer by a state or the functional equivalent of a state.

_____es are also imposed by many subnational entities. _____es consist of direct _____ or indirect _____, and may be paid in money or as its labour equivalent (often but not always unpaid.)

a. 100-year flood
c. Tax

b. 1921 recession
d. 130-30 fund

64. In economics, _____ is a measure of the relative satisfaction from consumption of various goods and services. Given this measure, one may speak meaningfully of increasing or decreasing _____, and thereby explain economic behavior in terms of attempts to increase one's _____. For illustrative purposes, changes in _____ are sometimes expressed in units called utils.

a. Ordinal utility
c. Expected utility hypothesis

b. Utility function
d. Utility

65. In economics, _____ means that people form their expectations about what will happen in the future based on what has happened in the past. For example, if inflation has been higher than expected in the past, people would revise expectations for the future.

One simple version of _____ is stated in the following equation, where p^e is the next year's rate of inflation that is currently expected; p^e_{-1} is this year's rate of inflation that was expected last year; and p is this year's actual rate of inflation:

$$p^e = p^e_{-1} + \lambda(p_{-1} - p^e_{-1})$$

With λ is between 0 and 1, this says that current expectations of future inflation reflect past expectations and an 'error-adjustment' term, in which current expectations are raised (or lowered) according to the gap between actual inflation and previous expectations.

a. AD-IA Model
c. Economic interdependence

b. Adaptive expectations
d. Investment-specific technological progress

66. A model in macroeconomics is a logical, mathematical, and/or computational framework designed to describe the operation of a national or regional economy, and especially the dynamics of aggregate quantities such as the total amount of goods and services produced, total income earned, the level of employment of productive resources, and the level of prices.

There are different types of _____ that serve different purposes and have different advantages and disadvantages. Models are used to clarify and illustrate basic theoretical principles in macroeconomics; they are used to test, compare, and quantify different theories of the macroeconomy; they are used to produce 'what if' scenarios, and especially to evaluate the possible effects of changes in monetary, fiscal, or other macroeconomic policies; and they are used for generating economic forecasts.

a. Factor shares
c. Natural rate of unemployment

b. High-powered money
d. Macroeconomic models

67. In economic models, the _____ time frame assumes no fixed factors of production. Firms can enter or leave the marketplace, and the cost (and availability) of land, labor, raw materials, and capital goods can be assumed to vary. In contrast, in the short-run time frame, certain factors are assumed to be fixed, because there is not sufficient time for them to change.
   a. Price/performance ratio
   b. Productivity world
   c. Diseconomies of scale
   d. Long-run

68. A _____ occurs when an entity spends more money than it takes in. The opposite of a _____ is a budget surplus. Debt is essentially an accumulated flow of deficits.
   a. Funding body
   b. Public Financial Management
   c. Lump-sum tax
   d. Budget deficit

69. _____ is the increase in the amount of the goods and services produced by an economy over time. It is conventionally measured as the percent rate of increase in real gross domestic product, or real GDP. Growth is usually calculated in real terms, i.e. inflation-adjusted terms, in order to net out the effect of inflation on the price of the goods and services produced.
   a. ACCRA Cost of Living Index
   b. ACEA agreement
   c. AD-IA Model
   d. Economic growth

70. _____ refers to a business or organization attempting to acquire goods or services to accomplish the goals of the enterprise. Though there are several organizations that attempt to set standards in the _____ process, processes can vary greatly between organizations. Typically the word '_____' is not used interchangeably with the word 'procurement', since procurement typically includes Expediting, Supplier Quality, and Traffic and Logistics (T'L) in addition to _____.
   a. 100-year flood
   b. Purchasing
   c. Free port
   d. 130-30 fund

71. In economics, the concept of the _____ refers to the decision-making time frame of a firm in which at least one factor of production is fixed. Costs which are fixed in the _____ have no impact on a firms decisions. For example a firm can raise output by increasing the amount of labour through overtime.
   a. Product Pipeline
   b. Hicks-neutral technical change
   c. Short-run
   d. Productivity model

72. A _____ is a situation that involves losing one quality or aspect of something in return for gaining another quality or aspect. It implies a decision to be made with full comprehension of both the upside and downside of a particular choice.

In economics the term is expressed as opportunity cost, referring the most preferred alternative given up.

   a. Friedman-Savage utility function
   b. Whitemail
   c. Nonmarket
   d. Trade-off

Chapter 18. Policies for Growth and Stability

1. A _____ occurs when an entity spends more money than it takes in. The opposite of a _____ is a budget surplus. Debt is essentially an accumulated flow of deficits.
   - a. Funding body
   - b. Budget deficit
   - c. Lump-sum tax
   - d. Public Financial Management

2. _____ and Keynesian Theory) is a macroeconomic theory based on the ideas of 20th-century British economist John Maynard Keynes. _____ argues that private sector decisions sometimes lead to inefficient macroeconomic outcomes and therefore advocates active policy responses by the public sector, including monetary policy actions by the central bank and fiscal policy actions by the government to stabilize output over the business cycle.

   The theories forming the basis of _____ were first presented in The General Theory of Employment, Interest and Money, published in 1936.
   - a. Rational choice theory
   - b. Deflation
   - c. Market failure
   - d. Keynesian economics

3. In economics, the _____ measures the payments that flow between any individual country and all other countries. It is used to summarize all international economic transactions for that country during a specific time period, usually a year. The _____ is determined by the country's exports and imports of goods, services, and financial capital, as well as financial transfers.
   - a. Skyscraper Index
   - b. Gross domestic product per barrel
   - c. Gross world product
   - d. Balance of payments

4. _____, or a _____ is the concept of a resulting effect (cf. cause and effect, arising from another action. In general terms, it is used to indicate that all human actions, particularly crime and sin, have profound effects.
   - a. Rule
   - b. Consequence
   - c. Variability
   - d. Solved

5. _____s is the social science that studies the production, distribution, and consumption of goods and services. The term _____s comes from the Ancient Greek oá¼°κονομῖα from oá¼¶κος (oikos, 'house') + vÏŒμος (nomos, 'custom' or 'law'), hence 'rules of the house(hold)'. Current _____ models developed out of the broader field of political economy in the late 19th century, owing to a desire to use an empirical approach more akin to the physical sciences.
   - a. Energy economics
   - b. Inflation
   - c. Opportunity cost
   - d. Economic

6. A _____ is the transfer of wealth from one party (such as a person or company) to another. A _____ is usually made in exchange for the provision of goods, services or both, or to fulfill a legal obligation.

   The simplest and oldest form of _____ is barter, the exchange of one good or service for another.

   - a. Payment
   - b. Soft count
   - c. Going concern
   - d. Social gravity

7. From a Keynesian point of view, a _____ in the public sector is achieved when the government equates the revenues with expenditure over the business cycles. In other words, a government's budget is balanced if its income is equal to its expenditure. It is a budget in which revenues are equal to spending.

a. Budget support
b. Budget theory
c. Balanced budget
d. Budget crisis

8. A _____ is a situation in which the government takes in more than it spends.
   a. Budget surplus
   b. 130-30 fund
   c. Budget set
   d. 100-year flood

9. _____ is a school of macroeconomic thought that argues that economic growth can be most effectively created using incentives for people to produce (supply) goods and services, such as adjusting income tax and capital gains tax rates, and by allowing greater flexibility by reducing regulation. Consumers will then benefit from a greater supply of goods and services at lower prices.

The term _____ was coined by journalist Jude Wanniski in 1975, and popularized the ideas of economists Robert Mundell and Arthur Laffer.

   a. Commodity trading advisors
   b. Fiscal stimulus plans
   c. Clap note
   d. Supply-side economics

10. _____ is that which is owed; usually referencing assets owed, but the term can also cover moral obligations and other interactions not requiring money. In the case of assets, _____ is a means of using future purchasing power in the present before a summation has been earned. Some companies and corporations use _____ as a part of their overall corporate finance strategy.
   a. Debenture
   b. Collateral Management
   c. Debt
   d. Hard money loan

11. The term _____ refers to government debt, expenditures and revenues, or to finance (particularly financial revenue) in general.

   - _____ deficit is the budget deficit of federal or local government
   - _____ policy is the discretionary spending of governments. Contrasts with monetary policy.
   - _____ year and _____ quarter are reporting periods for firms and other agencies.

   a. Procter ' Gamble
   b. Drawdown
   c. Bucket shop
   d. Fiscal

12. To _____ is to impose a financial charge or other levy upon a taxpayer by a state or the functional equivalent of a state.

_____es are also imposed by many subnational entities. _____es consist of direct _____ or indirect _____, and may be paid in money or as its labour equivalent (often but not always unpaid.)

   a. 1921 recession
   b. 130-30 fund
   c. 100-year flood
   d. Tax

Chapter 18. Policies for Growth and Stability

13. A _____ is a reduction in taxes. Economic stimulus via _____s, along with interest rate intervention and deficit spending, are one of the central tenets of Keynesian economics.

The immediate effects of a _____ are, generally, a decrease in the real income of the government and an increase in the real income of those whose tax rate has been lowered.

- a. Tax cut
- b. Direct taxes
- c. Withholding tax
- d. Popiwek

14. In economics, _____ is the total demand for final goods and services in the economy (Y) at a given time and price level. It is the amount of goods and services in the economy that will be purchased at all possible price levels. This is the demand for the gross domestic product of a country when inventory levels are static.
- a. Aggregate supply
- b. Aggregation problem
- c. Aggregate demand
- d. Aggregate expenditure

15. In economics, _____ is the use of government spending and revenue collection to influence the economy.

_____ can be contrasted with the other main type of economic policy, monetary policy, which attempts to stabilize the economy by controlling interest rates and the supply of money. The two main instruments of _____ are government spending and taxation.

- a. 100-year flood
- b. Fiscalism
- c. Fiscal policy
- d. Sustainable investment rule

16. The _____ or gross domestic income (GDI), a basic measure of an economy's economic performance, is the market value of all final goods and services produced within the borders of a nation in a year. _____ can be defined in three ways, all of which are conceptually identical. First, it is equal to the total expenditures for all final goods and services produced within the country in a stipulated period of time (usually a 365-day year.)
- a. Monopolistic competition
- b. Market structure
- c. Countercyclical
- d. Gross domestic product

17. _____, 1st Baron Keynes was a renowned economist from Britain whose many ideas on economic and political theories as well as on many governments' monetary policies influenced America. He advocated a government that played an active role in the lives of people regarding business, economy, etc. In this role, the government would use fiscal measures to reduce the consequences of recessions, economic depressions and booms.
- a. Adolf Hitler
- b. Adolph Fischer
- c. Adam Smith
- d. John Maynard Keynes

18. _____ is a misspelled phrase from Latin 'pro capite' phrase meaning per head with pro meaning 'per' or 'for each' and capite meaning 'head.' Both words together equate to the phrase 'for each head.'

It is usually used in the field of statistics to indicate the average per person for any given concern, such as income, crime rate, etc.

It is also used in wills to indicate that each of the named beneficiaries should receive, by devise or bequest, equal shares of the estate. This is in contrast to a per stirpes division, in which each branch of the inheriting family inherits an equal share of the estate.

a. Per capita
b. False positive rate
c. Sargan test
d. Population statistics

19. An _____, in economics, is the amount by which the real Gross domestic product exceeds potential GDP. The real GDP is also known as GDP 'adjusted for inflation', 'constant prices' GDP or 'constant dollar' GDP, because it measures the aggregate output in a country's income accounts in a given year, expressed in base-year prices. On the other hand, the potential GDP is the quantity of real GDP when a country's economy is at full-employment.

a. ACEA agreement
b. AD-IA Model
c. Inflationary gap
d. ACCRA Cost of Living Index

20. The term _____ refers to economy-wide fluctuations in production or economic activity over several months or years. These fluctuations occur around a long-term growth trend, and typically involve shifts over time between periods of relatively rapid economic growth (expansion or boom), and periods of relative stagnation or decline (contraction or recession.)

These fluctuations are often measured using the growth rate of real gross domestic product.

a. Consumer theory
b. Business cycle
c. Nominal value
d. Tobit model

21. Economics:

- _____, the desire to own something and the ability to pay for it
- _____ curve, a graphic representation of a _____ schedule
- _____ deposit, the money in checking accounts
- _____ pull theory, the theory that inflation occurs when _____ for goods and services exceeds existing supplies
- _____ schedule, a table that lists the quantity of a good a person will buy it each different price
- _____ side economics, the school of economics at believes government spending and tax cuts open economy by raising _____

a. Production
b. Variability
c. Demand
d. McKesson ' Robbins scandal

22. The term '_____' refers to the concept of collecting information and attempting to spot a pattern in the information. In some fields of study, the term '_____' has more formally-defined meanings.

In project management _____ is a mathematical technique that uses historical results to predict future outcome.

Chapter 18. Policies for Growth and Stability

a. Quantile regression
c. Probit model
b. Coefficient of determination
d. Trend analysis

23. In economic models, the _____ time frame assumes no fixed factors of production. Firms can enter or leave the marketplace, and the cost (and availability) of land, labor, raw materials, and capital goods can be assumed to vary. In contrast, in the short-run time frame, certain factors are assumed to be fixed, because there is not sufficient time for them to change.
a. Diseconomies of scale
c. Productivity world
b. Price/performance ratio
d. Long-run

24. In economics, the concept of the _____ refers to the decision-making time frame of a firm in which at least one factor of production is fixed. Costs which are fixed in the _____ have no impact on a firms decisions. For example a firm can raise output by increasing the amount of labour through overtime.
a. Productivity model
c. Short-run
b. Product Pipeline
d. Hicks-neutral technical change

25. In economics and sociology, an _____ is any factor (financial or non-financial) that enables or motivates a particular course of action, or counts as a reason for preferring one choice to the alternatives. It is an expectation that encourages people to behave in a certain way. Since human beings are purposeful creatures, the study of _____ structures is central to the study of all economic activity (both in terms of individual decision-making and in terms of co-operation and competition within a larger institutional structure.)
a. Economic reform
c. Isocost
b. Incentive
d. Epstein-Zin preferences

26. _____ is the part of a country's debts that is owed to creditors who are citizens of that country.

It is a form of fiat creation of money, in which the government obtains cash not by printing it, but by borrowing it. The money created is in the form of treasury securities or securities borrowed from the central bank.

a. External debt
c. Interest
b. Internal debt
d. International debt collection

27. A _____ is an expression that compares quantities relative to each other. The most common examples involve two quantities, but any number of quantities can be compared. _____s are represented mathematically by separating each quantity with a colon, for example the _____ 2:3, which is read as the _____ 'two to three'.
a. 130-30 fund
c. Ratio
b. 100-year flood
d. Y-intercept

28. To tax is to impose a financial charge or other levy upon a taxpayer by a state or the functional equivalent of a state. _____ are also imposed by many subnational entities. _____ consist of direct tax or indirect tax, and may be paid in money or as its labour equivalent (often but not always unpaid.)

a. 1921 recession
c. 130-30 fund
b. 100-year flood
d. Taxes

Chapter 18. Policies for Growth and Stability

29. In business and accounting, _____ are everything of value that is owned by a person or company. It is a claim on the property your income of a borrower. The balance sheet of a firm records the monetary value of the _____ owned by the firm.
    a. Amortization schedule
    b. ACCRA Cost of Living Index
    c. Assets
    d. ACEA agreement

30. _____ is an economic model based on price, utility and quantity in a market. It predicts that in a competitive market, price will function to equalize the quantity demanded by consumers, and the quantity supplied by producers, resulting in an economic equilibrium of price and quantity. The model incorporates other factors changing equilibrium as a shift of demand and/or supply.
    a. Deferred gratification
    b. Supply and demand
    c. Joint demand
    d. Rational addiction

31. _____ is the capital that a business raises by taking out a loan. It is a loan made to a company that is normally repaid at some future date. _____ differs from equity or share capital because subscribers to _____ do not become part owners of the business, but are merely creditors, and the suppliers of _____ usually receive a contractually fixed annual percentage return on their loan, and this is known as the coupon rate.
    a. Debt cash flow
    b. Financial rand
    c. Blank endorsement
    d. Debt Capital

32. _____ is the increase in the amount of the goods and services produced by an economy over time. It is conventionally measured as the percent rate of increase in real gross domestic product, or real GDP. Growth is usually calculated in real terms, i.e. inflation-adjusted terms, in order to net out the effect of inflation on the price of the goods and services produced.
    a. ACEA agreement
    b. Economic growth
    c. ACCRA Cost of Living Index
    d. AD-IA Model

33. _____ is a type of private equity investment, most often a minority investment, in relatively mature companies that are looking for capital to expand or restructure operations, enter new markets or finance a significant acquisition without a change of control of the business.

    Companies that seek _____, will often do so in order to finance a transformational event in their lifecycle. These companies are likely to be more mature than venture capital funded companies, able to generate revenue and operating profits but unable to generate sufficient cash to fund major expansions, acquisitions or other investments.

    a. Club deal
    b. Growth capital
    c. Startup company
    d. Seed money

34. In economics, _____ is a rise in the general level of prices of goods and services in an economy over a period of time. When the general price level rises, each unit of currency buys fewer goods and services; consequently, _____ is also a decline in the real value of money--a loss of purchasing power in the medium of exchange which is also the monetary unit of account in the economy. A chief measure of general price-level _____ is the general _____ rate, which is the percentage change in a general price index (normally the Consumer Price Index) over time.

a. Energy economics
b. Inflation
c. Economic
d. Opportunity cost

35. In economics, the _____ is a measure of inflation, the rate of increase of a price index (for example, a consumer price index.)It is the percentage rate of change in price level over time. The rate of decrease in the purchasing power of money is approximately equal.

It's used to calculate the real interest rate, as well as real increases in wages, and official measurements of this rate act as input variables to COLA adjustments and Inflation derivatives prices.

a. Interest rate option
b. Inflation rate
c. Equity value
d. Edgeworth paradox

36. In economics, _____ is the art or science of controlling economic demand to avoid a recession. In natural resources management and environmental policy more generally, it refers to policies to control consumer demand for environmentally sensitive or harmful goods such as water and energy. Within manufacturing firms the term is used to describe the activities of demand forecasting, planning and order fulfillment.
a. Peak-load pricing
b. Demand management
c. Fiscal imbalance
d. Cobra effect

37. The _____ was a fundamental reworking of economic theory concerning the factors determining employment levels in the overall economy. The revolution was set against the orthodox classical economic framework, which based on Say's Law argued that unless special conditions prevailed the free market would naturally establish full employment equilibrium with no need for government intervention. Employers will be able to make a profit by employing all available workers as long as workers drop their wages below the value of the total output they are able to produce - and classical economics assumed that in a free market workers would be willing to lower their wage demands accordingly , because they are rational agents who would rather work for less than face unemployment.
a. Speculative demand
b. Neo-Keynesian economics
c. Keynesian revolution
d. Military Keynesianism

38. _____ is an economic system in which wealth, and the means of producing wealth, are privately owned. Through _____, the land, labor, and capital are owned, operated, and traded for the purpose of generating profits, without force or fraud, by private individuals either singly or jointly, and investments, distribution, income, production, pricing and supply of goods, commodities and services are determined by voluntary private decision in a market economy. A distinguishing feature of _____ is that each person owns his or her own labor and therefore is allowed to sell the use of it to employers.
a. Creative capitalism
b. Late capitalism
c. Socialism for the rich and capitalism for the poor
d. Capitalism

39. _____ is widely regarded as the first modern school of economic thought. It is the idea that free markets can regulate themselves.Its major developers include Adam Smith, David Ricardo, Thomas Malthus and John Stuart Mill. Sometimes the definition of _____ is expanded to include William Petty, Johann Heinrich von Thünen.
a. Marginalism
b. Classical economics
c. Tendency of the rate of profit to fall
d. Schools of economic thought

40. _____ is a negative term describing an claimed capitalist economy in which success in business depends on close relationships between businesspeople and government officials. It may be exhibited in the distribution of legal permits, government grants, special tax breaks, and so forth.

_____ is believed to arise when political cronyism spills over into the business world; self-serving friendships and family ties between businessmen and the government influence the economy and society to the extent that it corrupts public-serving economic and political ideals.

- a. 100-year flood
- b. 130-30 fund
- c. Good governance
- d. Crony capitalism

41. In finance, the _____ of a financial asset measures the sensitivity of the asset's price to interest rate movements. There are various definitions of _____ and derived quantities, discussed below. If not otherwise specified, '_____' generally means the Macaulay _____, as defined below.

- a. 100-year flood
- b. Newtonian time
- c. Time value of money
- d. Duration

42. The term _____ is applied broadly to a variety of situations in which some financial institutions or assets suddenly lose a large part of their value. In the 19th and early 20th centuries, many financial crises were associated with banking panics, and many recessions coincided with these panics. Other situations that are often called financial crises include stock market crashes and the bursting of other financial bubbles, currency crises, and sovereign defaults.

- a. Financial crisis
- b. Macroeconomics
- c. Co-operative economics
- d. Market failure

43. _____ refers to the state of not requiring any outside aid, support for survival; it is therefore a type of personal or collective autonomy. On a large scale, a totally self-sufficient economy that does not trade with the outside world is called an autarky.

The term _____ is usually applied to varieties of sustainable living in which nothing is consumed outside of what is produced by the self-sufficient individuals.

- a. Sustainable forest management
- b. Global Reporting Initiative
- c. Sustainability science
- d. Self-sufficiency

44. _____ is the process by which the government, central bank (ii) availability of money, and (iii) cost of money or rate of interest, in order to attain a set of objectives oriented towards the growth and stability of the economy. Monetary theory provides insight into how to craft optimal _____.

_____ is referred to as either being an expansionary policy where an expansionary policy increases the total supply of money in the economy, and a contractionary policy decreases the total money supply.

- a. 130-30 fund
- b. Monetary policy
- c. 1921 recession
- d. 100-year flood

45. A _____, reserve bank, or monetary authority is the entity responsible for the monetary policy of a country or of a group of member states. It is a bank that can lend money to other banks in times of need. Its primary responsibility is to maintain the stability of the national currency and money supply, but more active duties include controlling subsidized-loan interest rates, and acting as a lender of last resort to the banking sector during times of financial crisis (private banks often being integral to the national financial system.)

    a. 1921 recession
    b. 130-30 fund
    c. Central bank
    d. 100-year flood

46. The _____ is the central banking system of the United States. Created in 1913 by the enactment of the Federal Reserve Act (signed by Woodrow Wilson), it is a quasi-public and quasi-private (government entity with private components) banking system that comprises (1) the presidentially appointed Board of Governors of the _____ in Washington, D.C.; (2) the Federal Open Market Committee; (3) twelve regional Federal Reserve Banks located in major cities throughout the nation acting as fiscal agents for the U.S. Treasury, each with its own nine-member board of directors; (4) numerous other private U.S. member banks, which subscribe to required amounts of non-transferable stock in their regional Federal Reserve Banks; and (5) various advisory councils. Since February 2006, Ben Bernanke has served as the Chairman of the Board of Governors of the _____.

    a. Monetary Policy Report to the Congress
    b. Term auction facility
    c. Federal Reserve System Open Market Account
    d. Federal Reserve System

47. _____ is an economic concept with commonplace familiarity. It is the price that a good or service is offered at, or will fetch, in the marketplace. It is of interest mainly in the study of microeconomics.

    a. Noisy market hypothesis
    b. Market anomaly
    c. Market price
    d. Paper trading

48. In economics, _____ is the total amount of money available in an economy at a particular point in time. There are several ways to define 'money', but standard measures usually include currency in circulation and demand deposits.

_____ data are recorded and published, usually by the government or the central bank of the country.

    a. Veil of money
    b. Neutrality of money
    c. Velocity of money
    d. Money supply

49. _____ in economics and business is the result of an exchange and from that trade we assign a numerical monetary value to a good, service or asset. If Alice trades Bob 4 apples for an orange, the _____ of an orange is 4 apples. Inversely, the _____ of an apple is 1/4 oranges.

    a. Price book
    b. Premium pricing
    c. Price
    d. Price war

50. _____s is concerned with the tasks of developing and applying quantitative or statistical methods to the study and elucidation of economic principles. _____s combines economic theory with statistics to analyze and test economic relationships. Theoretical _____s considers questions about the statistical properties of estimators and tests, while applied _____s is concerned with the application of _____ methods to assess economic theories.

    a. Econometric
    b. Economic
    c. Experimental economics
    d. Evolutionary economics

51. _____s are statistical models used in econometrics. An _____ specifies the statistical relationship that is believed to hold between the various economic quantities pertaining a particular economic phenomena under study. An _____ can be derived from a deterministic economic model by allowing for uncertainty or from an economic model which itself is stochastic.
   a. Economic statistics
   b. ACCRA Cost of Living Index
   c. Event study
   d. Econometric model

52. In economics, an _____ is any good or commodity, transported from one country to another country in a legitimate fashion, typically for use in trade. _____ goods or services are provided to foreign consumers by domestic producers. _____ is an important part of international trade.
   a. ACEA agreement
   b. AD-IA Model
   c. ACCRA Cost of Living Index
   d. Export

53. A _____ represents the combinations of goods and services that a consumer can purchase given current prices and his income. Consumer theory uses the concepts of a _____ and a preference map to analyze consumer choices. Both concepts have a ready graphical representation in the two-good case.
   a. Joint demand
   b. Quality bias
   c. Revealed preference
   d. Budget constraint

54. A _____ is:

- Rewrite _____, in generative grammar and computer science
- Standardization, a formal and widely-accepted statement, fact, definition, or qualification
- Operation, a determinate _____ for performing a mathematical operation and obtaining a certain result (Mathematics, Logic)
    - Unary operation
    - Binary operation
- _____ of inference, a function from sets of formulae to formulae (Mathematics, Logic)
- _____ of thumb, principle with broad application that is not intended to be strictly accurate or reliable for every situation. Also often simply referred to as a _____
- Moral, an atomic element of a moral code for guiding choices in human behavior
- Heuristic, a quantized '_____' which shows a tendency or probability for successful function
- A regulation, as in sports
- A Production _____, as in computer science
- Procedural law, a _____ set governing the application of laws to cases
    - A law, which may informally be called a '_____'
    - A court ruling, a decision by a court
- In the U.S. Government, a regulation mandated by Congress, but written or expanded upon by the Executive Branch.
- Norm (sociology), an informal but widely accepted _____, concept, truth, definition, or qualification (social norms, legal norms, coding norms)
- Norm (philosophy), a kind of sentence or a reason to act, feel or believe
- 'Rulership' is the concept of governance by a government:
    - Military _____, governance by a military body
    - Monastic _____, a collection of precepts that guides the life of monks or nuns in a religious order where the superior holds the place of Christ
- Slide _____

- '_____,' a song by Ayumi Hamasaki
- '_____,' a song by rapper Nas
- '_____s,' an album by the band The Whitest Boy Alive
- _____s: Pyaar Ka Superhit Formula, a 2003 Bollywood film
- ruler, an instrument for measuring lengths
- _____, a component of an astrolabe, circumferator or similar instrument
- The _____s, a bestselling self-help book
- _____ Project (Run Up-to-date Linux Everywhere), a project that aims to use up-to-date Linux software on old PCs
- _____ engine, a software system that helps managing business _____s
- Ja _____, a hip hop artist
    - R.U.L.E., a 2005 greatest hits album by rapper Ja _____
- '_____s,' a KMFDM song

a. Procter ' Gamble
b. Demand
c. Technocracy
d. Rule

Chapter 18. Policies for Growth and Stability

55. _____ is a common concept in economics, and gives rise to derived concepts such as consumer debt. Generally _____ is defined by opposition to production. But the precise definition can vary because different schools of economists define production quite differently.

   a. Cash or share options
   b. Federal Reserve Bank Notes
   c. Foreclosure data providers
   d. Consumption

56. The _____ is one of the world's most important central banks, responsible for monetary policy covering the 16 member States of the Eurozone. It was established by the European Union (EU) in 1998 with its headquarters in Frankfurt, Germany.

The predecessor to the _____ was the European Monetary Institute .

   a. ACCRA Cost of Living Index
   b. ACEA agreement
   c. AD-IA Model
   d. European Central Bank

57. _____ is an economic policy in which a central bank estimates and makes public a projected, or 'target,' inflation rate and then attempts to steer actual inflation towards the target through the use of interest rate changes and other monetary tools.

Because interest rates and the inflation rate tend to be inversely related, the likely moves of the central bank to raise or lower interest rates become more transparent under the policy of _____. Examples:

- if inflation appears to be above the target, the bank is likely to raise interest rates. This usually (but not always) has the effect over time of cooling the economy and bringing down inflation.

- if inflation appears to be below the target, the bank is likely to lower interest rates. This usually (again, not always) has the effect over time of accelerating the economy and raising inflation.

   a. Incomes policies
   b. Inflation swap
   c. Employment Cost Index
   d. Inflation targeting

58. _____ is an American economist and was the Chairman of the Federal Reserve of the United States from 1987 to 2006. He currently works as a private advisor and providing consulting for firms through his company, Greenspan Associates LLC.

First appointed Federal Reserve chairman by President Ronald Reagan in August 1987, he was reappointed at successive four-year intervals until retiring on January 31, 2006 after the second-longest tenure in the position.

   a. Alan Greenspan
   b. Adolph Fischer
   c. Adolf Hitler
   d. Adam Smith

59. _____ refers to a business or organization attempting to acquire goods or services to accomplish the goals of the enterprise. Though there are several organizations that attempt to set standards in the _____ process, processes can vary greatly between organizations. Typically the word '_____' is not used interchangeably with the word 'procurement', since procurement typically includes Expediting, Supplier Quality, and Traffic and Logistics (T'L) in addition to _____.

Chapter 18. Policies for Growth and Stability

a. 130-30 fund
b. 100-year flood
c. Free port
d. Purchasing

60. _____ is the number of goods/services that can be purchased with a unit of currency. For example, if you had taken one dollar to a store in the 1950s, you would have been able to buy a greater number of items than you would today, indicating that you would have had a greater _____ in the 1950s. Currency can be either a commodity money, like gold or silver, or fiat currency like US dollars.
a. Compliance cost
b. Purchasing power
c. Human Poverty Index
d. Genuine progress indicator

61. The _____ theory uses the long-term equilibrium exchange rate of two currencies to equalize their purchasing power. Developed by Gustav Cassel in 1920, it is based on the law of one price: the theory states that, in ideally efficient markets, identical goods should have only one price.

This purchasing power SEM rate equalizes the purchasing power of different currencies in their home countries for a given basket of goods.

a. Measures of national income and output
b. Bureau of Labor Statistics
c. Gross national product
d. Purchasing power parity

62. A _____ or directed economy is an economic system in which the government or workers' councils manages the economy. It is an economic system in which the central government makes all decisions on the production and consumption of goods and services. Its most extensive form is referred to as a _____, centrally planned economy, or command and control economy.
a. Transition economy
b. Nutritional Economics
c. Subsistence economy
d. Command economy

63. A _____ is a theoretical term that economists use to describe a market which is free from government intervention (i.e. no regulation, no subsidization, no single monetary system and no governmental monopolies.) In a _____, property rights are voluntarily exchanged at a price arranged solely by the mutual consent of sellers and buyers. By definition, buyers and sellers do not coerce each other, in the sense that they obtain each other's property without the use of physical force, threat of physical force, or fraud, nor is the coerced by a third party (such as by government via transfer payments) and they engage in trade simply because they both consent and believe that it is a good enough choice.
a. Leninism
b. Delegation
c. Third camp
d. Free market

64. _____ means how much each individual receives, in monetary terms, of the yearly income generated in the country. This is what each citizen is to receive if the yearly national income is divided equally among everyone. _____ is usually reported in units of currency per year.
a. Real income
b. Lerman ratio
c. Family income
d. Per capita income

65. _____ in political thought refers to economic theories of social organization advocating collective ownership and administration of the means of production and distribution of goods, and a society characterized by equality for all individuals, with an egalitarian method of compensation. Modern _____ originated in the late 19th-century intellectual and working class political movement that criticized the effects of industrialization and private ownership on society. Karl Marx posited that _____ would be achieved via class struggle and a proletarian revolution after a transitional stage from capitalism called the dictatorship of the proletariat.
   a. Adam Smith
   b. Adolf Hitler
   c. Adolph Fischer
   d. Socialism

66. _____ is a term that is used to describe the overall process of invention, innovation and diffusion of technology or processes. The term is redundant with technological development, technological achievement, and technological progress. In essence _____ is the invention of a technology (or a process), the continuous process of improving a technology (in which it often becomes cheaper) and its diffusion throughout industry or society.
   a. 130-30 fund
   b. 1921 recession
   c. 100-year flood
   d. Technological change

67. _____ is the development of economic wealth of countries or regions for the well-being of their inhabitants. It is the process by which a nation improves the economic, political, and social well being of its people. From a policy perspective, _____ can be defined as efforts that seek to improve the economic well-being and quality of life for a community by creating and/or retaining jobs and supporting or growing incomes and the tax base.
   a. Inflation
   b. Experimental economics
   c. Economic methodology
   d. Economic development

68. In economics, _____ is the total supply of goods and services produced by a national economy during a specific time period. It is the total amount of goods and services in the economy available at all possible price levels.
   a. Aggregation problem
   b. Aggregate expenditure
   c. Aggregate demand
   d. Aggregate supply

69. In finance, _____ is investment originating from other countries. See Foreign direct investment.
   a. Horizontal merger
   b. Demand side economics
   c. Preclusive purchasing
   d. Foreign investment

70. A _____ is an economy based on the division of labor in which the prices of goods and services are determined in a free price system set by supply and demand. This is often contrasted with a planned economy, in which a central government determines the price of goods and services using a fixed price system. Market economies are contrasted with mixed economy where the price system is not entirely free but under some government control that is not extensive enough to constitute a planned economy.
   a. Commons-based peer production
   b. Nutritional Economics
   c. Network Economy
   d. Market economy

71. In economics, _____ is the active redirecting resources from being consumed today so that they may create benefits in the future; the use of assets to earn income or profit. _____ is the process of making an investment in order to earn a profit, for example equity investment either through a fund, a 401k plan, or individually. People often invest in order to build up their estate or to accumulate funds for retirement.

To try to predict good stocks to invest in, two main schools of thought exist: technical analysis and fundamentals analysis.

a. ACEA agreement
c. AD-IA Model
b. ACCRA Cost of Living Index
d. Investing

Chapter 1
1. a	2. d	3. c	4. b	5. a	6. d	7. d	8. c	9. a	10. b
11. c	12. b	13. c	14. d	15. d	16. a	17. a	18. d	19. b	20. d
21. b	22. a	23. b	24. d	25. d	26. d	27. c	28. b	29. c	30. d
31. d	32. a	33. b	34. d	35. b	36. c	37. d	38. b	39. a	40. a
41. a	42. a	43. b	44. d	45. d	46. d	47. a	48. d	49. d	50. a
51. d	52. d	53. c	54. b	55. a					

Chapter 2
1. c	2. b	3. a	4. a	5. c	6. d	7. b	8. b	9. d	10. d
11. b	12. d	13. c	14. b	15. d	16. b	17. a	18. d	19. c	20. c
21. d	22. d	23. b	24. b	25. b	26. d	27. d	28. c	29. c	30. d
31. b	32. a	33. a	34. d	35. d	36. d	37. b	38. c	39. b	40. d
41. d	42. d	43. d	44. d	45. d	46. b	47. c	48. d	49. d	50. d
51. b	52. a	53. c	54. a	55. d	56. d	57. b	58. c	59. a	60. c
61. d	62. d	63. a	64. a	65. d	66. d	67. b	68. a	69. a	70. c
71. d	72. a	73. c	74. a	75. b	76. a	77. c	78. d	79. d	80. d
81. d	82. a	83. d	84. d	85. d	86. d	87. c	88. d	89. d	90. d
91. a	92. a	93. c	94. c	95. d	96. a	97. a	98. b	99. d	100. d
101. d	102. a								

Chapter 3
1. d	2. d	3. c	4. a	5. a	6. d	7. a	8. a	9. d	10. d
11. d	12. d	13. d	14. c	15. d	16. d	17. d	18. d	19. a	20. d
21. b	22. d	23. d	24. d	25. d	26. c	27. d	28. c	29. d	30. b
31. a	32. a	33. a	34. d						

Chapter 4
1. c	2. a	3. d	4. d	5. d	6. b	7. d	8. a	9. d	10. b
11. b	12. d	13. c	14. d	15. c	16. c	17. a	18. a	19. c	20. d
21. c	22. d	23. c	24. a	25. c	26. d	27. d	28. d	29. a	30. d
31. a	32. a	33. d	34. d	35. d	36. d	37. c	38. a	39. d	40. c
41. a	42. b	43. c	44. d	45. d	46. c	47. c	48. d	49. b	50. b
51. d	52. d	53. d	54. d	55. a	56. d	57. a	58. a	59. a	60. c
61. d	62. b	63. d	64. c	65. c	66. d	67. d	68. d	69. d	70. c
71. a									

Chapter 5
1. d	2. d	3. b	4. d	5. d	6. d	7. b	8. b	9. d	10. d
11. a	12. d	13. d	14. a	15. b	16. c	17. d	18. d	19. d	20. c
21. d	22. c	23. c	24. d	25. b	26. c	27. a	28. b	29. a	30. b
31. b	32. c	33. b	34. d	35. d	36. d	37. d	38. a	39. d	40. c
41. d	42. b	43. d	44. a	45. d	46. b	47. d	48. d	49. c	50. d
51. c	52. d	53. d	54. b	55. d	56. a	57. d	58. d	59. d	60. d
61. c	62. a	63. c	64. b						

ANSWER KEY

Chapter 6

1. d	2. d	3. d	4. d	5. a	6. d	7. c	8. d	9. d	10. d
11. d	12. d	13. a	14. b	15. c	16. b	17. d	18. d	19. a	20. d
21. a	22. c	23. b	24. d	25. c	26. a	27. d	28. d	29. c	30. c
31. b	32. a	33. d	34. c	35. b	36. c	37. b	38. b	39. d	40. d
41. d	42. b	43. b	44. d	45. d	46. c	47. a	48. d	49. d	50. a
51. d	52. d	53. c	54. c						

Chapter 7

1. a	2. c	3. d	4. d	5. d	6. d	7. d	8. d	9. a	10. c
11. a	12. d	13. b	14. b	15. d	16. d	17. d	18. d	19. d	20. d
21. a	22. d	23. d	24. a	25. a	26. a	27. a	28. d	29. d	30. a
31. d	32. d	33. b	34. d	35. d	36. d	37. b	38. d	39. b	40. d
41. d	42. b	43. d	44. d	45. d	46. a	47. d	48. a	49. a	50. a
51. d									

Chapter 8

1. a	2. d	3. b	4. a	5. d	6. d	7. d	8. d	9. c	10. d
11. d	12. d	13. d	14. d	15. b	16. b	17. b	18. c	19. d	20. d
21. d	22. b	23. d	24. b	25. c	26. b	27. a	28. a	29. a	30. c
31. b	32. c	33. d	34. b	35. d	36. d	37. d	38. b	39. b	40. a
41. d	42. c	43. a	44. d	45. d	46. b				

Chapter 9

1. c	2. d	3. d	4. c	5. a	6. c	7. d	8. d	9. d	10. d
11. c	12. d	13. d	14. c	15. d	16. d	17. b	18. d	19. d	20. a
21. c	22. d	23. b	24. c	25. b	26. c	27. d	28. a	29. a	30. d
31. d	32. a	33. d	34. c	35. b	36. c	37. c	38. c	39. d	40. d
41. b	42. b	43. d	44. d	45. c	46. d	47. d	48. b	49. d	50. d
51. d	52. d	53. b	54. a	55. b	56. d	57. d	58. d	59. b	60. d
61. a	62. d	63. d	64. a	65. d	66. b	67. d	68. b	69. d	70. d
71. b	72. d	73. d	74. b	75. d	76. c	77. a	78. b	79. b	80. d
81. d	82. b								

Chapter 10

1. d	2. d	3. d	4. d	5. a	6. c	7. d	8. d	9. d	10. b
11. d	12. d	13. b	14. a	15. a	16. a	17. b	18. d	19. c	20. c
21. c	22. d	23. d	24. d	25. a	26. d	27. d	28. d	29. b	30. c
31. d	32. d	33. d	34. d	35. d	36. c	37. c	38. d	39. d	40. d
41. d	42. d	43. a	44. c	45. b	46. b	47. c	48. d	49. d	50. b
51. d	52. d	53. a	54. c	55. d	56. d	57. d	58. b	59. a	60. b
61. b	62. c	63. c	64. d	65. c	66. d	67. a	68. c	69. a	70. d
71. d	72. a	73. a	74. a	75. a					

Chapter 11

1. d	2. a	3. a	4. d	5. a	6. c	7. a	8. b	9. a	10. a
11. d	12. b	13. b	14. c	15. a	16. d	17. a	18. c	19. b	20. d
21. a	22. c	23. d	24. d	25. a	26. c	27. d	28. b	29. a	30. d
31. d	32. a	33. d	34. d	35. d	36. d	37. d	38. d	39. d	40. d
41. d	42. b	43. c	44. d	45. d	46. c	47. b	48. d	49. d	50. a
51. b	52. d	53. a	54. a	55. b	56. b	57. d	58. d	59. d	

Chapter 12

1. d	2. a	3. d	4. d	5. d	6. d	7. c	8. a	9. c	10. d
11. c	12. a	13. d	14. b	15. d	16. d	17. d	18. d	19. d	20. a
21. d	22. d	23. d	24. d	25. d	26. b	27. b	28. d	29. b	30. d
31. a	32. d	33. d	34. d	35. d	36. b	37. b	38. d	39. c	40. d
41. c	42. a	43. b	44. d	45. d	46. d	47. d	48. d	49. d	50. d
51. a	52. a	53. a	54. d	55. d	56. a	57. d	58. b	59. d	60. c
61. d	62. a	63. d	64. a	65. d	66. b	67. d	68. a	69. a	70. d
71. d	72. d	73. c	74. d						

Chapter 13

1. b	2. b	3. a	4. d	5. d	6. c	7. d	8. c	9. d	10. d
11. d	12. a	13. d	14. d	15. b	16. a	17. d	18. d	19. d	20. b
21. a	22. b	23. a	24. d	25. d	26. c	27. d	28. d	29. d	30. a
31. d	32. b	33. d	34. d	35. d	36. a	37. a	38. c	39. d	40. d
41. c	42. d	43. a	44. d	45. a	46. a	47. a	48. d	49. a	50. d
51. c	52. d	53. c	54. b	55. d	56. c	57. b	58. c	59. d	60. b
61. b	62. a	63. c	64. a	65. d	66. d	67. c	68. d	69. d	70. d
71. c	72. c	73. a	74. a	75. d	76. d	77. d	78. d	79. d	

Chapter 14

1. a	2. d	3. d	4. d	5. d	6. a	7. d	8. d	9. a	10. c
11. b	12. c	13. b	14. d	15. d	16. d	17. d	18. d	19. b	20. d
21. d	22. a	23. c	24. d	25. d	26. d	27. d	28. c	29. d	30. a
31. d	32. d	33. a	34. a	35. d	36. d	37. c	38. b	39. b	40. d
41. d	42. d	43. b	44. d	45. d	46. b	47. d	48. a	49. d	50. b
51. b	52. d	53. d	54. d	55. d	56. c	57. b	58. d	59. b	60. d
61. d	62. d	63. d	64. a	65. d	66. d	67. a	68. d	69. d	70. d
71. a	72. d	73. d	74. d						

Chapter 15

1. d	2. a	3. d	4. a	5. b	6. d	7. a	8. b	9. c	10. a
11. a	12. a	13. d	14. d	15. d	16. c	17. d	18. b	19. a	20. b
21. a	22. d	23. d	24. d	25. c	26. b	27. d	28. d	29. a	30. d
31. d	32. d	33. d	34. c	35. b	36. d	37. d	38. d	39. c	40. d
41. b	42. d	43. d	44. d	45. d	46. d	47. d	48. b	49. d	50. d

ANSWER KEY

Chapter 16

1. a	2. b	3. b	4. a	5. c	6. d	7. d	8. d	9. d	10. d
11. d	12. d	13. b	14. c	15. b	16. d	17. d	18. d	19. d	20. d
21. c	22. b	23. b	24. d	25. d	26. d	27. d	28. d	29. d	30. a
31. d	32. d	33. c	34. b	35. d	36. b	37. a	38. d	39. c	40. c
41. a	42. b	43. d	44. a	45. d	46. a	47. d	48. c	49. d	50. d
51. d	52. c	53. c	54. a	55. d	56. a	57. d	58. d	59. b	60. d
61. c	62. d	63. b	64. c	65. b					

Chapter 17

1. d	2. d	3. b	4. d	5. b	6. d	7. b	8. d	9. a	10. d
11. c	12. d	13. d	14. b	15. a	16. d	17. d	18. a	19. d	20. a
21. b	22. c	23. d	24. a	25. d	26. d	27. a	28. b	29. d	30. a
31. a	32. d	33. d	34. a	35. a	36. a	37. b	38. a	39. a	40. c
41. d	42. b	43. d	44. d	45. a	46. c	47. d	48. a	49. d	50. b
51. a	52. a	53. a	54. d	55. a	56. d	57. d	58. d	59. d	60. d
61. a	62. c	63. c	64. d	65. b	66. d	67. d	68. d	69. d	70. b
71. c	72. d								

Chapter 18

1. b	2. d	3. d	4. b	5. d	6. a	7. c	8. a	9. d	10. c
11. d	12. d	13. a	14. c	15. c	16. d	17. d	18. a	19. c	20. b
21. c	22. d	23. d	24. c	25. b	26. b	27. c	28. d	29. c	30. b
31. d	32. b	33. b	34. b	35. b	36. b	37. c	38. d	39. b	40. d
41. d	42. a	43. d	44. b	45. c	46. d	47. c	48. d	49. c	50. a
51. d	52. d	53. d	54. d	55. d	56. d	57. d	58. a	59. d	60. b
61. d	62. d	63. d	64. d	65. d	66. d	67. d	68. d	69. d	70. d
71. d									

www.ingramcontent.com/pod-product-compliance
Lightning Source LLC
Chambersburg PA
CBHW080729230426
43665CB00020B/2675